D0041157

SIERRA CROSSING

THOMAS FREDERICK HOWARD

SIERRA CROSSING

FIRST ROADS TO CALIFORNIA

University of California Press
Berkeley · Los Angeles · London

University of California Press
Berkeley and Los Angeles, California

University of California Press, Ltd.
London, England

© 1998 by
The Regents of the University of California

Howard, Thomas Frederick
    Sierra crossing: first roads to California /
Thomas Frederick Howard.
        p.   cm.
    Includes bibliographical references (p.   ) and
index.
    ISBN 0-520-20670-3 (cloth : alk. paper)
    1. Roads—Sierra Nevada (Calif. and Nev.)—
History—19th century.   2. Sierra Nevada
(Calif. and Nev.)—Description and travel.
3. Overland journeys to the Pacific. I. Title.
HE356.C2H68 1998
388.1'09794'4—dc21   97-28012
                                                 CIP

Printed in the United States of America
9 8 7 6 5 4 3 2 1

CONTENTS

PREFACE

This book has its origins in my surprised discovery that no one had written it before. While working on another project I became curious about the way California was linked with the rest of the country in its early years. I particularly wanted to know how regular transportation was established over the formidable barrier posed by the Sierra Nevada. Information on this subject proved to be very hard to find.

Much has been written about the first transcontinental railroad, but that great project was not completed until the summer of 1869, almost two decades after the gold rush had propelled California into the Union. There is also a considerable body of work on the California Trail, but it tends to focus on the heroic period before statehood: early explorations by mountain men like Jedediah Smith and Joseph Walker, the Bidwell party of 1841, the peregrinations of John C. Frémont, the near-disaster but final triumph of the Stevens party of 1844, and of course the sensationalized sufferings of the Donner party in 1846. But for the years between the gold rush and the completion of the railroad, there was just enough information to hint at an untold story of great interest.

From the beginning Californians looked forward to railroad connections with the eastern United States, where track was already being laid at a rapid rate, but these connections took much longer than the optimists thought. In the meantime the well heeled could travel by ship, with a land transit of the Isthmus of Panama. Most others came overland. The wagon trains of the "emigrants" (people who moved from the eastern states to California or Oregon with the intention of settling down were known as emigrants, not only at the point of departure, which would be logical enough, but also at the western end of the journey) continued to wend their way across the interior west and cross the Sierra by a variety of routes, the choice depending on trail lore and rumor and the blandishments of promoters from the various end-of-trail towns. Slowly and haltingly, roads were improved. Mail and express services were launched. Eventually it became possible to travel all the way to California by stagecoach.

This has been very much a University of California at Berkeley project, even though the final text was written on the other side of the country. It began as a Ph.D. dissertation in the U.C. Berkeley Geography Department. Though I discussed my work with numerous faculty members and fellow graduate students, my greatest debts are to Professor (Emeritus) James E. Vance, Jr., and the late Professor James J. Parsons. Professor Vance is perhaps best known as a scholar of the historical geography of cities, but he has also delved deeply into the development of transportation in America and thus was a most valuable resource. Professor Parsons was well known for his enthusiastic interest in practically all topics students wished to discuss with him, an interest that continued unabated for many years after his ostensible retirement. I would also like to express my appreciation for the efforts of Professor Richard Hutson, my outside reader from the U.C. Berkeley English Department, whom I recruited rather late in the dissertation project but who graciously read the manuscript and offered useful suggestions for improving its readability. I hasten to add that I have thoroughly revised and rewritten what these scholars signed off on some years ago, and they are not responsible for the present text.

Most of the documentary raw material for this book came from the Bancroft Library or the Government Documents Collection at U.C. Berkeley, and I would like to express my appreciation for the help I received from many librarians over the years. I am especially indebted to the Bancroft for providing me with a carrel for a year where I could leave books from one day to the next. I also received valuable assistance on the illustrations from the California State Library in Sacramento and from Wells Fargo Historical Services and the Society of California Pioneers, both in San Francisco.

One of the great attractions of geography as a field of study is the chance to get out of the library and into the field, and I would like to acknowledge the help and advice I received from a wide range of people I met on my trips to the mountains. Much of this came in brief and chance encounters, on trails and at roadside turnouts, with people whose names I never learned. With others I had more substantial contact. If I had not, on the trail one day, run into Jeanne and Bill Watson, members of the Oregon-California Trails Association and annual caretakers of the stretch of the Carson Trail between Caples Lake and West Pass, I would have been much longer in figuring out just where West Pass and its approaches were. On another occasion a chance remark by Denis Witcher, director of the El Dorado County Historical Society and keeper of lore about what is now U.S. 50 from Placerville over the western summit to Lake Tahoe, introduced me to the photography of Thomas Houseworth, some of which is reproduced here.

Perhaps my greatest debts are to people I never met, never could have met, because they died long before I was born, people who toiled and struggled in the mountains but still found time and energy to write their impressions in diaries, letters, newspaper stories, and official reports to the state and federal governments, little thinking perhaps that their words would be read with such interest almost a century and a half later. The immediacy of personal experience in some of these documents can make a day in the library as rewarding as a day on the trail.

Finally, there are those to whom I was sometimes lost, against my will, in the demands of finishing this project. Barbara was especially patient in this regard.

INTRODUCTION

On May 12, 1841, the first group of overland emigrants seeking a new home in California, known to history as the Bidwell party, left the Missouri settlements and headed west. By the middle of September they had abandoned their cumbersome wagons in what is now northeastern Nevada and struggled on across the Great Basin and the Sierra Nevada using the mules and oxen as pack animals. Ascending the eastern slope of the Sierra along the valley of the West Walker River, they reached the crest somewhere in the vicinity of Sonora Pass on October 18, 1841. According to Bidwell's own account this climb was not terribly difficult, but then it took them twelve long days to find their way down through the canyons of the Stanislaus River to the Central Valley.[1]

Nothing about the experiences of the Bidwell party's 2,000-mile journey brightened the prospects for taking wagon trains to California on a regular basis.[2] There would have been no reason for a contemporary observer to see in them the advance guard of an overland migration from the United States that was to bring more than 165,000 people across the Sierra by 1857, swamp the Mexican and remaining Indian societies, and irrevocably alter the social and political geography of North America.[3] Yet that is what they were.

The adventures and misadventures of the Bidwell party show how meager geographic knowledge of the Sierra Nevada barrier was in the early 1840s. Then, in a remarkably short time, the Sierra Nevada was reduced in public perception from a mysterious and impenetrable moun-

1

tain wall blocking off California to a challenging yet manageable stage of the overland journey. By the middle of the 1860s the mountains had been transformed into scenery, to be enjoyed from a good coach road. When Samuel Bowles, the nationally known editor of the Springfield, Massachusetts, *Republican,* made a tour "out west" in 1865, he described his stagecoach trip over the Sierra in glowing terms:

> Thus munificently prepared, and amid the finest mountain scenery in the world, we swept up the hills at a round trot, and rolled down again at the sharpest gallop, turning abrupt corners without a pull-up, twisting among and past the loaded teams of freight toiling over into Nevada, and running along the edge of high precipices, all as deftly as the skater flies or the steam car runs; though for many a moment we held our fainting breath at what seemed great risks or dare-devil performances. A full day's ride was made at a rate exceeding ten miles an hour; and a continuous seven miles over the rolling hills along the crest of the range was driven within twenty-six minutes. The loss of such exhilarating experience is enough to put the traveler out of conceit with superseding railroads.[4]

Between the Bidwell party's stumbles through the wilderness and the Massachusetts editor's breezy jaunt lay a period of vigorous exploration and road building, which is the subject of this book.

Though the Sierra Nevada today retains many officially recognized wilderness areas and has been less obviously altered by human activity than the adjacent Central Valley, the human imprint is nevertheless pervasive. In recent years investigations by geographers have tended to remove the notion of a pristine pre-Columbian America, unaltered by human hands or feet, into the realm of myth.[5] Aboriginal populations were substantial, and their actions, particularly the setting of fires, must have been a major determinant in the distribution of plant communities. Even so, the Indian impact was relatively slight compared with what began with the gold rush.

The increase in activity was almost explosive after 1849. With mining, logging, ranching, and water development, the population of the Sierra rose to much higher densities than prevailed before, in many places higher than today. Great flows of people and goods throughout the mountains created a volume of traffic vastly larger and more environment altering than the Indian trade in back-packed food items and decorative objects.

Yet it should not be assumed that all these movements simply appropriated existing routes. Despite folklore about the tendency of animal paths, Indians trails, wagon roads, railroads, and interstate highways to succeed each other in historical sequence along the same alignment, the demands of each form of overland transport were different, and the study of trans-Sierra routes shows many discontinuities. A good example is the Truckee route. It is a commonplace that this has always been the primary overland route connecting California with the rest of the country.[6] In actual fact the Truckee route lapsed into disuse well before the end of the gold rush. Most overland transportation in the 1850s and early 1860s used other, easier passes across the mountains. Only with the construction of the Central Pacific Railroad in the late 1860s did the Truckee route regain its importance.

The principle of least effort suggests that a lower mountain pass will be preferred to a higher one, other things being equal. Other things are usually not equal, however, and that is what makes the story interesting. The changing importance of the Truckee route shows how transportation channels may be determined by technology as much as by the physical configuration of the earth's surface. The Truckee route quickly got a bad reputation because it was so difficult for wagon trains to climb up from the east. Yet it became the favored route fifteen years later because it offered the easiest way for the railroad to climb up from the west, and difficulties on the east side could now be overcome with improved technology and a large labor force. There had been a radical reevaluation of topography.

Other important determining factors in creating the pattern of roads in the Sierra Nevada were the real or imagined appeal of certain destinations and promotional activities carried out by local businessmen and governments. Most emigrants did not wait until they had crossed the mountains before deciding where in California to go. On the contrary, they began to angle toward a particular California destination before they reached Humboldt Sink, well out in the Nevada desert. Boosters of nascent towns were aware of this and took steps to attract emigrants their way by improving mountain roads and making them easier to use (or at least claiming that they had done so). At first such promotional activities were carried out by ad hoc coalitions of businessmen, real estate speculators, and trail guides, with some individuals playing all three roles. But it was not long before government got into the act. Throughout the period between the gold rush and the completion of the Pacific railroad, road projects were a subject of intense political activity at local, state, and federal levels.

The combination of topographic, technological, political, and economic factors had the effect of encouraging the use of some of the many possible routes and leaving others undeveloped, or favoring a particular route for a time only to abandon it later. As a result, today there are passes in the Sierra where roads might cross but do not, and passes where once-busy roads have lapsed into near-invisibility.

Significant growth of geographic knowledge accompanied these road-building efforts. Surveys that sought no more than the best alignment for roads provided much additional information in the process, from the rough-and-ready knowledge summarized in the handwritten "waybills" that wagon drivers exchanged to the printed surveyors' reports sent out by state and local governments and by toll road entrepreneurs trying to raise funds. Formal exploration of the Sierra Nevada, by the Whitney survey, for example, came later, in the 1860s.

Beyond the local economic rivalries of competing California towns lay much larger geopolitical concerns. The historical geography of roads for wagons and stagecoaches over the Sierra must to some degree be only a part of a wider view of all overland transport between the Pacific Coast and a frontier of settlement that remained at the eastern edge of the Great Plains from the early 1840s to the late 1860s. Federal policies decided in Washington, D.C., were an important part of the story.

The still broader landscape of the affairs of nations is important as well. Road building and the accumulation of geographic knowledge in the Sierra Nevada were part of a larger geopolitical movement in which the United States acquired and absorbed vast western territories formerly held by others. To understand many of the actions and speeches reported here, the mental map of the actors and speakers must be familiar. On this map, the block of territory formed by the present lower forty-eight states did not have the ancient solidity it seems to have today. Britain and France were still seen as contenders for the Pacific coast of North America in the 1840s. California's permanent adherence to the Union was not taken for granted by everyone in the 1850s. In the 1860s California gold and Comstock silver were prizes that had to be kept out of the hands of the seceding South.

Chapter 1 provides an overview of the physiography of the Sierra and its approaches and pays some attention to the chief climatic problem for transportation, heavy winter snow. Chapter 2 relates traverses of the range by parties on foot or on horseback that established an important body of knowledge for the subjects of chapter 3, the emigrants who crossed the mountains, beginning in 1844, in trains of ox- or mule-drawn covered wagons. The several transmountain tracks of the wagon train emigration formed the transportation inheritance of California's first road builders, mostly small-town entrepreneurs and politicians, whose efforts are the subject of chapter 4.

Chapter 5 looks at the new state government of California and its first halting efforts to survey and build a road over the Sierra. Chapter 6 shifts the focus to Washington, D.C., to cover a national transportation question that colored all Californians' thinking about trans-Sierra roads: the long-awaited Pacific railroad and the sectional rivalry that delayed its completion. Chapter 7 reviews a series of federal initiatives in the late 1850s that sought to encourage overland stagecoach and fast mail service by building roads from the Missouri frontier to California. Chapter 8 is concerned with the mail contractors and stagecoach operators who used trans-Sierra routes. Renewed road-building efforts within California, stimulated by this federal activity, forms the material of chapter 9. Chapter 10 examines the way the Central Pacific Railroad was projected as a commercial challenge to already existing roads and road traffic. The final chapter traces the fate of the trans-Sierra roads after they had been supplanted in many of their functions by the railroad and before the automobile brought about their dramatic revival.

CHAPTER 1

Mountain Wall, Snow, Basins, and Rivers

In the usage of the early American period, "the Sierras" denoted the great mountain barrier between the Central Valley of California and the "sagebrush plains" and "alkali flats"—these too were common designations on the maps of the time—that lay off to the east. It took a while for the ends of the range to be clearly defined and for the name "Great Basin" to catch on.

In essence the Sierra consists of a rotational granite block with a steep fault scarp on the east and a gradual slope west to the flat Central Valley. Over wide areas in the northern Sierra eroded remnants of basalt flows overlie the granite. The basic structure is fairly simple, but erosion, by ice as well as by running water, has greatly complicated the surface as we see it today.[1]

At the north end, the dividing line between the Sierra and the Cascade Range is easy to specify in the abstract but hard to find on the ground. Mount Lassen is clearly one of the Cascade volcanoes, but lava flows from it and its predecessors have buried part of the older Sierra block. The valley of the Feather River can be taken as a transition zone. At the other end, the Sierra was once considered to run south to a junction with the Coast Ranges in the vicinity of Tejon Pass. Later the range came to be thought of as ending on the south at Tehachapi Pass, and the mountains from there to Tejon Pass were designated the Tehachapi Range.

Elevations rise toward the south end, with the highest point at Mount Whitney (14,495 ft.), about 100 miles north of Tehachapi Pass. The 160 miles between Tioga Pass and Walker Pass—the High Sierra—remain an effective barrier to ground transportation even today, and a large area of the agriculturally rich and densely populated San Joaquin Valley has only circuitous overland links to the east. An account of roads over the Sierra Nevada must therefore be concerned chiefly with the northern Sierra, between Yosemite and Mount Lassen. Here elevations are lower, though still formidable enough for wagon drivers and railroad builders, with passes between 6,000 and 9,000 feet.

Though the gradual rise of the western slope does contrast with the steep escarpment of the eastern slope, the gradualness of the western slope is only an average. Erosion has dissected the surface into deep canyons, separated by remnant ridges that run roughly parallel to each other as they climb from the Central Valley to the Sierra crest. This is a landscape that both constrains and facilitates the building of roads. The ridges form natural ramps between the Sierra crest and the Central Valley. Along the top of such a ridge a road can be built in a fairly straight line for miles with little earthmoving. The disadvantage is that the higher elevations on the ridges may accumulate heavy snow for much, indeed most, of the year. The alternative strategy of following the canyons allows the Sierra to be deeply penetrated below the snow line, but then a great deal of earthmoving may be required to carve a roadbed out of steep slopes.

Ridge roads came before canyon roads, because emigrants in wagons found the ridges a convenient line of descent to the Central Valley and they crossed the Sierra in late summer, when snow was not a problem. Modern examples of ridge roads are Interstate 80, running atop the dividing ridge between the Bear River and the North Fork of the American River, and State Highway 4, in a similar setting between the Mokelumne and Stanislaus rivers. The former is kept open all year, at some considerable expense, while the latter is simply closed when the first heavy snowfall of the season occurs.

The increasing importance of year-round traffic, together with improvements in earthmoving equipment, made canyon routes more attractive. By laying out a road along the river at the bottom of a canyon, the miles subject to the snow problems of higher elevations were minimized. Total mileage might have to be increased, though, because of the sinuosity of the river. Excavating a stable roadbed out of steep valley sides entailed a further expense. Modern examples of such canyon roads are U.S. 50 east of Placerville along the South Fork of the American River and State Highway 49 through Downieville along the North Fork of the Yuba River.

Ridge routes were possible only on the western slope of the Sierra. The steep eastern face, always daunting in the era of animal-drawn vehicles, had to be climbed in a series of switchbacks, aided perhaps by a frontal assault that required wagons to be disassembled and pulled up over ledges on ropes. The approach to these arduous tasks was along the streambed of a river such as the Truckee, Carson, or Walker. Down in the gorge the feet of men and animals might be in the water for hours at a time. The ease of travel today on the eastern escarpment has come about through mechanized earthmoving on a scale far beyond the powers of earlier generations of travelers.

Another terrain feature of great importance for early transportation was the deep fault-block depression, technically called a graben, that contains Lake Tahoe and splits the central Sierra crest into two roughly parallel ranges, thus creating a double summit for transmountain routes near the lake. This accounts for the references to "eastern summit" and "western summit," or "first summit" and "second summit," so common in writings from the 1850s and 1860s. The terms are less intelligible today because many California drivers go only as far as Lake Tahoe and so are aware only of the western summit. Even through travelers on Interstate 80 or Amtrak may not notice the eastern range, because both the highway and the railroad follow the gorge of the Truckee River, which cuts through it from Lake Tahoe down to terminal Pyramid Lake. Travelers on U.S. 50, however, do climb over both ranges, at Echo Summit (7,382 ft.) on the west and Spooner Summit (7,146 ft.) on the east, dipping down to the shore of Lake Tahoe (6,229 ft.) in between.

The drainage pattern of the western slope has given double summits to transmountain highways farther south as well, though not because of the Lake Tahoe graben. Highway 88 has a western summit at Carson Spur (7,900 ft.) and an eastern one at Carson Pass (8,573 ft.), with an intermediate low point at Kirkwood (7,682 ft.). Highway 4 rises to Pacific Grade Summit (8,050 ft.) on the west and Ebbetts Pass (8,730 ft.) on the east, with a descent in the middle to Hermit Valley (7,060 ft.). The next two transmountain roads south have single summits: Highway 108 at Sonora Pass (9,624 ft.) and Highway 120 at Tioga Pass (9,941 ft.).

Climate

It was snow that gave the Sierra Nevada its name, and snow has always been the most important climatic feature affecting transportation there. For a time in the nineteenth century it was thought that the Sierra had the heaviest snow accumulation in the world. Further exploration and measurement eventually found even snowier places, but the passes and their approaches, particularly on the west side, do record some of the highest yearly snowfall totals in the United States. The paralyzing effect of heavy snowfall remains a threat to trans-Sierra transportation even today.

Most snow falls in storms associated with the passage of wintertime cold fronts off the Pacific Ocean, when several feet can accumulate in a few hours. In a major storm, even with much labor and equipment devoted to snow removal, both highway and railroad transportation can be paralyzed. (More than a half century after publication, George Stewart's *Storm* [1941] is still eminently readable as a semificationalized account of what happens when a major winter storm blows into California off the broad Pacific.)

Sierra snow has been the object of intense study for many years because of the economic importance of the snowpack as a great natural water storage reservoir for irrigation in the Central Valley. It is sufficient here to say that annual totals average 35 to 40 feet at the 7,000- to 9,000-foot level where most of the passes described in this study lie. The ground is covered for half the year, on average, from November to May.

The Great Basin

The basin and range province extends some 400 miles east of the Sierra to the Wasatch Front in Utah. Tectonic movements have stretched and cracked the earth's crust across this region. Some of the resulting pieces have sunk relative to those on either side, producing a corduroy pattern of basin and mountain range. The whole region is in the rain shadow of the Sierra. Vegetation is sagebrush steppe grading into desert in the alkali flats of the basins and into piñon-juniper woodlands in the mountains.

The Humboldt River, cutting across the region approximately from northeast to southwest, looked more like a creek to emigrants from the eastern half of the United States, but it did contain some water, enough, along with grassy bottomlands, to make the Humboldt seem a providentially located migration route in the 1840s and 1850s. The Humboldt Valley later provided the best route for the railroad, and eventually for U.S. 40 and Interstate 80.[2]

This fortuitous alignment of the Humboldt with the Truckee and Carson created a natural route for wagon trains, much as the alignment of the Platte, the North Platte, and the Sweetwater did in the eastern part of the trail. It was not as easy a route as it might have been, however.

By accident of geologic history, the Humboldt River ends in a salt marsh 40 miles from both Pyramid Lake, the terminus of the Truckee River, and Carson Sink, the terminus of the Carson River. If the Humboldt on the east and either of these rivers on the west had flowed into the same low point in the bed of Pleistocene Lake Lahontan, the emigrants might have had a continuous water route to the base of the Sierra. But the settlings of the earth's crust left the ice age lake with a number of deep spots, and when a changing climate evaporated most of the water, these remnant puddles and marshes were separated by arid gaps. The gaps were crossable, though, if one planned carefully and traveled as much as possible at night.

On its way to disappearance in the desert, the Carson River flows out of the mountains south of Lake Tahoe through Carson Valley, a basin that will be mentioned many times in this book. It was probably better known to Californians in the mid-nineteenth century than it is today, especially because so many of them had passed through it to get to California. With lush meadows and ample water, Carson Valley was a kind of oasis where westbound wagon trains recuperated after crossing the desert from the Humboldt and before tackling the Sierra. Carson Valley lies mostly in Nevada and was the first part of that state-to-be to be settled by the invading Americans, who founded Nevada's oldest town, Mormon Station, there in 1851. (With the Mormon withdrawal in 1855, the place changed its name to Genoa.) Carson Valley acquired renewed importance around 1860 when, irrigated by water diverted from the Carson River, it supplied agricultural products to Comstock Lode miners.

In the 1860s long-distance stagecoaches, the Pony Express, and the first transcontinental telegraph line all found it advantageous to use a central Nevada route rather than the established wagon road along the Humboldt River. The total distance from Salt Lake was at least 100 miles shorter, and commercial transport required fewer animals and less water and fodder than wagon trains did. Stations with reliable wells and a few acres of hay fields were sufficient to keep things moving. This change made no difference in the route over the Sierra, however. The central Nevada route, too, passed through Carson Valley, connecting with exisiting transmountain routes rather than creating new ones.

Mineral Deposits

The rich deposits of gold and silver found on the slopes of the Sierra Nevada are an important part of the story of transmountain transportation. First to be exploited were the gold-bearing stream gravels, found in a long belt along the west side of the range at elevations of 1,000 to 3,000 feet. These were the basis of the California gold rush, bringing tens of thousands of small-scale miners to the goldfields. As the easily accessible stream deposits were exhausted, gold mining increasingly became the domain of highly capitalized corporate enterprise, which used hydraulic mining to attack ancient stream gravels from vanished rivers, or industrial underground mining techniques to get at the hardrock matrix from which gold had been eroded into streams in the first place.

A decade after the gold rush, immense silver deposits were discovered in the Virginia Range, east of Carson Valley. This was the fabulous Comstock Lode, site of a silver rush that was probably of an importance equal to the gold rush in the accumulation of wealth that powered the economic development of California and the West.

The two precious metals had rather different effects on the transportation network. Dozens of gold-mining settlements were spread for almost 200 miles along the Sierra's western flank, and, vying with each other to attract migrants and business, they generated a multiplicity of westbound trails and roads in the 1850s. In the 1860s, on the contrary, the overwhelming concentration of silver in one location tended to give a single focus to eastbound transportation. The competition was between different routes or stage lines in providing the fastest service to one destination, Virginia City. By coincidence silver had been concentrated in a place between two of the leading overland routes to California, virtually assuring that one of them would become the chief gateway to California, rather than other routes farther north or south.

CHAPTER 2

Trans-Sierra Transport before Wheeled Vehicles

Though this book is concerned mainly with wheeled transportation across the Sierra Nevada, we must pay some attention to the earlier era of foot traffic and pack animals. Much information, good and bad, about Sierra geography was accumulated in that period and used later by wagon train emigrants.

Indian trails have attracted the attention of historians and anthropologists, but the question of how important these routes were in guiding the movements of non-Indian explorers and emigrants remains open. Aboriginal inhabitants of the Central Valley, primarily the Yokuts, Miwok, and Maidu, as well as tribes east of the Sierra, such as the Washoe and Paiute, resorted to the high country in summer to hunt and to escape the heat of the lowlands. The distribution of artifacts from archaeological sites provides substantial evidence of cross-mountain trade as well.[1] John C. Frémont tells of buying salt from Indians in the vicinity of Carson Pass and being told that it came from "across the mountains."[2]

It seems reasonable to assume that if a trail existed in the right direction, the newcomers would probably have taken advantage of it rather than bushwhack their way across country. But it is important to remember that the requirements of human porters, pack trains, animal-drawn wagons, railroads, and motor vehicles are all rather different, and a line of travel that is good for one would not necessarily be good for another.

Nevertheless, the proposition that Indian trails (and before that buffalo and other animal trails) were the first and best indicators of the

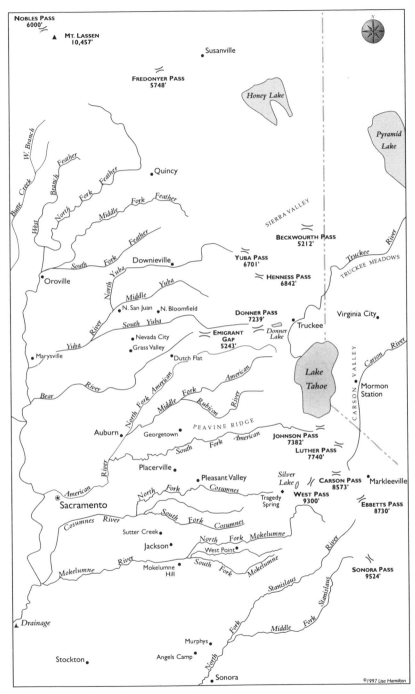

Map 1. The northern Sierra Nevada in the mid–nineteenth century.

alignments of future roads and railroads had already become a cliché by the middle of the nineteenth century. This is demonstrably wrong in a sufficient number of cases that we cannot simply assert that the emigrants must have followed Indian trails. The matter has to be looked into on a case-by-case basis; it is worthy of a research effort of its own but is tangential to the concerns of this book. Suffice it to say here that it does not appear from early travelers' accounts that Indian trails played an indispensable role in traverses of the Sierra by American emigrants, even if they did provide helpful leads in some situations. The one major exception, a case in which indigenous geographic knowledge did prove vital, was the information provided by a Paiute known to history as Truckee which allowed the Stevens party of 1844 to make the first wagon crossing of the Sierra, just as winter was closing in.

The Spanish and Mexicans

There is no evidence that Spaniards or Mexicans ever crossed the Sierra Nevada when they ruled California. Though the whole area south of 42 degrees and west of the continental divide was Spanish territory, according to treaty lines marked on somewhat speculative maps in faraway Europe, most of it was ignored by Spain as well as by its successor state, the Republic of Mexico.

There were a number of expeditions from the coast into the Central Valley to capture runaways from the missions, to scout for new mission sites, and to punish Indian raids, but even these limited ventures did not lead to permanent settlements. In 1806 Gabriel Moraga traveled along the eastern edge of the Central Valley and perhaps followed some rivers into the foothills, and in 1825 José Dolores Pico led a party into the lower Sierra along the San Joaquin and Kings rivers. But these expeditions seem to have been the high watermark of Spanish or Mexican exploration from the Pacific Coast. Despite apprehensions about British, Russian, and American incursions, Spanish and Mexican administrators in California made no attempt to cross the Sierra and stake an effective claim to territory in the continental interior that was nominally theirs.[3]

A Spanish expedition from New Mexico into what is now Utah was important in that it created a myth that confused geographic conceptions of the Sierra and the Great Basin for many years. In 1776 two Franciscan fathers, Francisco Atanasio Domínguez and Silvestre Vélez de Escalante, traveled northwest from Santa Fe in search of an overland route to Monterey. They reached the Green River in the vicinity of today's Di-

nosaur National Monument and named that stream in honor of Saint
Buenaventura, the great minister-general of the Franciscans in the mid–
thirteenth century. The Domínguez-Escalante expedition then went west
to Utah Lake and south to the big bend of what later became known as
the Sevier River, which they misidentified as the lower course of their
Buenaventura River.

The true nature of that vast area of interior drainage later called the
Great Basin was as yet unknown, and the cartographer of the Domínguez-
Escalante expedition, Bernardo Miera y Pacheco, reasonably guessed that
the Buenaventura probably came out somewhere on the California
coast. In this way a substantial river flowing west from the Rocky
Mountains through unknown country to the Pacific Ocean had been in-
vented. Alexander von Humboldt borrowed from Miera in his map for
the *Political Essay on the Kingdom of New Spain* and thus gave the
Buenaventura River respectability and worldwide publicity, which was
further extended when Meriwether Lewis and George Rogers Clark,
and Zebulon Pike in turn, relied on Humboldt's map in their widely
read works.[4]

Explorers of the Sierra

Jedediah Smith

The first non-Indian to cross the Sierra was the Yankee trapper Jedediah
Smith, who made the crossing from the west side. At the annual trappers' rendezvous in Cache Valley (vicinity of present Logan, Utah) in
the summer of 1826, William Ashley sold off the fur company he had
formed in 1822 with Andrew Henry. The buyers—David Jackson,
William Sublette, and Jedediah Smith—were curious about the beaver
potential of the unknown land between Salt Lake and California. They
decided that Smith would lead a party of fourteen trappers into that area
while Jackson and Sublette remained in the Rockies to trap on the upper Green River.

The Smith party set out south along the foot of the Wasatch Front in
what later became Utah. Smith's plan was to intersect the Buenaventura
River and follow it west to its mouth on the coast of California. The
party would then go north along the coast to the Columbia River, come
back inland along the Columbia and its tributary, the Snake, and so return to Bear Lake in time for the rendezvous of 1827.

When they encountered the Sevier River in its north-flowing reach,
before it bends around to the southwest, Smith guessed (reasonably but

incorrectly) that this stream continued north into Utah Lake and was therefore not the Buenaventura, so they pressed on south. Since there was no Buenaventura River to be found, the expedition went all the way to the Virgin River and then followed that stream south to the Colorado. They crossed the Colorado at some point now inundated by Lake Mead and passed along the river's east bank to the Mojave villages across from the vicinity of present-day Needles.

After two weeks' recuperation with the Mojaves, the Smith party crossed the desert toward the Mexican settlements near the coast with two Mojave guides and were hospitably received at San Gabriel Mission on November 26, 1826. Governor José Maria Echeandía at San Diego, however, refused them permission to travel north to San Francisco and instead ordered them to leave California by the way they had come.

Smith and his men retraced their steps over Cajon Pass and thus did leave the part of California that was effectively controlled by Mexico. Safely beyond the reach of the governor's writ, they abandoned their earlier path, traversed the western end of the Mojave Desert to Tehachapi Pass, and crossed into the San Joaquin Valley. They proceeded north up the east side of the valley, looking for the Buenaventura River and trapping as they went. Smith concluded that none of the many rivers issuing from the Sierra could be the Buenaventura. Smith was right, as we now know. But it would be interesting to know how he came to this conclusion. How could he know that a large river emerging from the Sierra through a deep canyon had *not* penetrated the range from the east side? In his 1823–24 travels in what later became Wyoming, Smith had visited the area of the Wind River Canyon.[5] Here he would have seen an example of a river flowing right through a mountain range, probably because the preexisting river had cut down through the mountains as fast as tectonic forces raised them up. What was it about the rivers emerging from the Sierra that made Smith realize that such was not the case here? Unfortunately any notes he may have made on this subject have been lost.

The Smith party's presence in the Central Valley somehow came to the notice of the authorities at Mission San Jose and the Presidio of San Francisco. A military detachment sallied forth but settled for a parley instead of a confrontation. Smith sent a letter to San José on May 19, 1827, explaining that he was just waiting for the snow to melt sufficiently to get across the Sierra. This was probably true enough; it was too late to make further progress toward the Columbia that year and still arrive at the rendezvous in time.

The Smith party first tried to cross the Sierra by going up the valley of the Kings River, but they found the snow too deep. They went north to the American River and tried again, but snow still blocked the way. Coming back south, Smith left most of his party in camp and, soon after sending his letter to San Jose, ascended the North Fork of the Stanislaus with two companions. They reached the Sierra crest in the vicinity of Ebbetts Pass after an eight-day trip. On their way across central Nevada, Smith and his two companions very nearly died of thirst. At length, after twenty days of extremely arduous travel, the three men reached Salt Lake and went on to that year's rendezvous at Bear Lake.[6]

Their trials are evidence of the sketchy state of knowledge concerning the Sierra and the Great Basin at this time. If Smith and his companions had gone north after crossing Ebbetts Pass, they could have reached the Carson River and followed it down to its sink, crossed to Humboldt Sink, and then followed the Humboldt River upstream to its headwaters. It seems clear that Smith had no idea that the Humboldt River existed. If snow had not prevented him from crossing the Sierra by going up one of the forks of the American River, he would surely have discovered Lake Tahoe, the Truckee River, and the Humboldt, and might thus have opened up the California Trail seventeen years before the Stevens party did.

When Smith returned from the Rockies to the rest of his party on the Stanislaus later in 1827, he took the same circuitous route south along the Wasatch Front to the Mojave villages. This time nine men were killed by the Mojaves, made hostile by the depredations of another band of trappers. Back in California, Smith resumed his original plan of pushing north along the coast to the Columbia. That adventurous and perilous journey is full of interest, but Smith never came back to the Sierra, so we must leave him at this point.

Joseph Walker

In 1833 the first non-Indians crossed the Sierra from east to west. They were a detachment of Captain Benjamin-Louis-Eulalie de Bonneville's expedition, led by Joseph Walker. Bonneville had left the army to go into the trapping business, although there has always been speculation that he retained some official ties and used trapping as a front for spying on the strength and activities of the Mexicans in the southwest and the British in the northwest. On the Green River in late summer of 1833,

Bonneville divided his trapping force of 165 men into three divisions, one of which was headed by Walker. The Walker party was to explore the country west and southwest of Salt Lake for beaver as far as California and return the following summer, according to Zenas Leonard, Walker's clerk and chronicler of the expedition.

This mission was obviously similar in its ambitions to Smith's trip seven years earlier. But Washington Irving, who wrote the as-told-to account of the Bonneville expedition, seems to have been unaware of Smith's travels, for he called the region southwest of Salt Lake "as yet almost unknown."[7] It seems highly unlikely, however, that in the small world of Rocky Mountain trappers Smith's travels would not have been widely known by 1833. It is possible that an outsider like Irving may simply have been uninformed, but if he got this information from Bonneville, the latter was being disingenuous. He and Walker must surely have been conversant with Smith's discoveries, as well as those of Peter Skene Ogden. Ogden, working for the Hudson's Bay Company, had in November 1828 made the first visit to the Humboldt River by a non-Indian and had revisited the area, with a large force of trappers, by the time of the Bonneville expedition.[8] Perhaps intelligence gathering really was Bonneville's ulterior motive.

Zenas Leonard gives no details of the Walker party's intended route, but it is clear that Walker had fuller geographic knowledge than Smith. He did not set off south along the Wasatch Front as Smith had done but went around Salt Lake on the north, evidently familiar with Ogden's discovery of the Humboldt River, which Ogden had called Mary's River, after the wife of one of the trappers in his party.

In the barren salt plains beyond Salt Lake the Walker party encountered Indians who told them that some distance to the southwest they would "come to a high mountain which was covered with snow at the top the whole year round, and on each side of which we would find a large river to head and descend into the sandy plains below, forming innumerable small lakes, and sinks into the earth and disappears."[9] The party came to this mountain in due course. Leonard's account continued: "It presents a most singular appearance—being entirely unconnected with any other chain. It is surrounded on either side by level plains, and rises abruptly to a great height, rugged and hard to ascend."[10]

The identity of this mountain is not clear. Pilot Peak, a prominent and isolated landmark from the south, as seen by travelers on today's Interstate 80, comes to mind. But the Walker party was approaching from the northeast, and from that direction Pilot Peak appears as the high

point at the far end of a short mountain range, not as an isolated peak.
And, with a summit elevation of 10,704 feet, it does not remain snow
covered through the summer. Another problem with Pilot Peak is that it
is separated from the headwaters of the Humboldt River by the Toana
Range and the Pequop Mountains. The Ruby Mountains, which do usually have patches of snow all summer, and are part of the headwaters
basin of the Humboldt, may have been what Leonard meant. But this is
a mountain range, not an isolated peak unconnected with any other
range. Perhaps Leonard remembered inaccurately what the Indians said,
or had a garbled translation, or got his memories confused. In any case
the import of these directions was clear enough: up ahead the Walker
party would find a mountain that fed a stream that would take them a
long way west. This, plus information floating around from Ogden's
travels, must have been enough, because the Walker party found the
Humboldt River without major incident and followed it down to Humboldt Sink by early October 1833.

Near the sink they were approached by a small army of Paiutes, 800
or 900 according to Leonard. Walker thought their behavior looked like
preattack maneuvering, and when a few demonstration shots—the
Paiutes had not yet acquired guns—failed to keep them from moving
closer, Walker gave the order to open fire. Thirty-nine Paiutes were killed
on the spot, and the rest fled. These deaths put Leonard on the defensive
in the account he published years later, in response to harsh criticism of
Walker in Washington Irving's account of the Bonneville expedition,
which had appeared in the meantime.

> The severity with which we dealt with these Indians may be revolting to the
> heart of the philanthropist; but the circumstances of the case altogether atones
> for the cruelty. It must be borne in mind that we were far removed from the
> hope of any succor in case we were surrounded, and that the country we were
> in was swarming with hostile savages, sufficiently numerous to devour us.
> Out object was to strike a decisive blow. This we did—even to a greater ex-
> tent than we had intended.[11]

The massacre was a disaster for more than those killed that day. A re-
venge clash with Walker's party on its return trip led to fourteen more
Paiute deaths, and the two encounters must have done much to create
the Paiute hostility that helped make life miserable and dangerous for
emigrants for many years, in a part of the journey where unaided nature
was capable of making life miserable and dangerous enough. But
Walker's apprehensions cannot be summarily dismissed: he had spent

much of his adult life among Indians and was married to a Crow woman.

Geographic knowledge as well was a loser here. If a peaceful meeting had occurred, a naturally curious man, as Walker seems to have been, quite possibly would have elicited in 1833 the information that the Stevens party got from "Truckee" in 1844. Geopolitical currents as well may have been affected. Walker was a man of influence and prestige in the West, and if he had learned of a central route over the Sierra in 1833, the American migration to California might have set in earlier and more strongly than it did.

From the neighborhood of Humboldt Sink the Walker party went south and eventually came to a large brackish lake, formed by a river descending from high snow-covered mountains, the Sierra Nevada. The next day they ascended the river and discovered a path that seemed to have come over the mountains from the west and had been traveled by horses. By following this path they reached the top of the range, but they then got lost and were unable to find a way down the west side. They saw a number of Indian trails, but none going in the right direction. For five days they wandered south through the high country, eventually arriving at a place where Leonard recorded something unusual: "many small streams which would shoot out from under . . . high snowbanks, and after running a short distance in deep chasms which they have through ages cut in the rocks, precipitate themselves from one lofty precipice to another, until they are exhausted in rain below. Some of these precipices appeared to us to be more than a mile high."[12]

This passage is considered by many to be the first written description of Yosemite, and the inference is that the Walker party at this point was on the divide between the Tuolumne and Merced rivers. With some difficulty they found their way down off this ridge and soon reached a grove of astoundingly large trees, allowing Leonard to write what became the first published description of *Sequoia gigantea*.[13]

Because Leonard's description is short on topographic detail, it is impossible to retrace the Walker party's route across the Sierra much more accurately than this. It seems likely that the brackish lake was Walker Lake, and the river one of the branches of Walker River. Yet in going south along the east side of the Sierra they would have encountered Walker River before coming to the lake. If their aim was to cross the mountains, they would logically have turned at this point to follow the river upstream. It is clear, however, that they went downstream to the shores of the lake, since Leonard does describe the water as brackish. This again brings up the mixed motives of the whole Bonneville venture. The Walker party may have been spying out the land, but still they were trappers and perhaps made a detour down to the lake to look for beaver.

The Walker party emerged from the Sierra Nevada into the Central Valley about the end of October 1833. They followed the San Joaquin River down to San Francisco Bay and then crossed the Santa Cruz Mountains to the beach somewhere near Año Nuevo Point. By chance they were able to hail a passing American merchant ship and spent an enjoyable two days eating and drinking with the crew. Walker took the group on to the San Juan Bautista Mission, then to Monterey. It was an amicable visit, so much so that the governor offered Walker a land grant. Walker and most of his party were not ready to settle down, however, and after several weeks they prepared to depart. Six of its members did succumb to the charms of California and decided to stay. The whole experience was most interesting and enjoyable for Leonard, and he wrote many pages about life among the *Californios*.

On February 14, 1834, the Walker party, now down to fifty-two members, left the coastal Mexican settlements for the Green River to rejoin Bonneville as planned. They traveled slowly south through the San Joaquin Valley and crossed the southern end of the Sierra about the first of May. Leonard's account remains vague on topography,[14] but they probably went through what later became known as Walker Pass. Walker was to travel that way many times later, and the pass had his name from an early date. Leonard does not mention the imposing gorge of the lower Kern River, which suggests that they may have cut across the Greenhorn Mountains from the San Joaquin Valley, reaching the Kern upstream from the gorge, at some point now submerged by the Lake Isabella reservoir.

Walker Pass was more important in the geographic imagination of the 1840s and 1850s than it ever became in reality. It is a low pass (only 5,250 ft.) across the Sierra divide between the Great Basin and the Central Valley, but the Walker Pass route as a whole does not provide easy passage through the mountains. Before coming out into the Central Valley, the westbound traveler must choose between a climb over the Greenhorn Range, with a road summit 852 feet higher than Walker Pass itself, or a passage down through the narrow and tortuous gorge of the Kern River. Still, until trans-Sierra routes were opened near Lake Tahoe, the Walker Pass route did offer a way around the most formidable part of the Sierra and was the destination of early travelers.

To jump ahead for a moment, let it be noted that Walker Pass could never have been a practical route for a railroad. Even the highway link today is relatively unimportant. Walker Pass was so much discussed in the 1850s as a crossing for the Pacific railroad because of a simple case of mistaken identity. Frémont, in his influential 1845 report, confused Walker Pass with Tehachapi Pass, about 45 miles to the southwest, and as a result Walker Pass was extolled for properties it did not possess. It was Tehachapi Pass that provided a passage for the railroad in 1876, and is today the main highway link out of the San Joaquin Valley to the east. None of this was Joseph Walker's fault, of course, and he deserves the credit for finding the shortest, if not the easiest, way to get around the main mass of the Sierra on the south.

Walker took his men back north along the eastern base of the Sierra, planning to find their previous year's trail and follow it in reverse back to Green River. They kept a watch for familiar landmarks along the mountain wall to the west and thought they saw several of them, but were repeatedly disappointed. Finally Walker decided to chance a cutoff across the desert to the Humboldt. No water could be found on this route, however, and Walker yielded to the thirsty company's desire to turn back. But now they were unable to find their own tracks of a day or two before and soon were lost in the desert. "At no time, either while crossing the rocky or California mountains, did our situation appear so desperate," remarked Leonard later.[15] Eventually the horses scented water; the party was saved and soon found their old trail. At Humboldt Sink the Walker party had another encounter with the Paiutes, with fourteen Indians killed this time.[16] The rest of the trip back up the Humboldt was apparently without major incident, and the party rejoined Bonneville in early July 1834.

Walker's chronicler Zenas Leonard has left us his own notions of western geography. Twice he describes the land between the Sierra and the Rockies as a vast plain,[17] a curious conclusion, since mountain ranges come into view one after another along the route he himself took down the Humboldt Valley. Presumably he meant that the individual ranges rose from a common level like islands in the sea rather than form broad areas of mountainous country. Leonard perceived that this was an area of internal drainage.

> There are numerous small rivers rising in either mountain [i.e., the Sierra and the Rockies], winding their way far towards the center of the plain, where they are emptied into lakes or reservoirs, and the water sinks in the sand. Further to the north where the sand is not so deep and loose, the streams rising in the spurs of the Rocky and those descending from the California mountains, flow on until their waters at length mingle together in the same lakes.[18]

(If the last were true, the overland migration would have been much easier than it was.)

Leonard did have a clear idea of the Sierra as an important water divide and ruled out the possibility of a Buenaventura River.

> The California Mountain extends from the Columbia to the Colorado River, running parallel with the coast about one hundred and fifty miles distant, and twelve or fifteen hundred miles in length with its peaks perpetually covered with eternal snows. There is a large number of water courses descending from this mountain on either side—those on the east side stretching out into the plain, and those on the west flow generally in a straight course until they empty into the Pacific; but in no place is there a water course through the mountain.[19]

Again, Leonard was half right. He evidently had no clear idea that the Coast Ranges form a western wall to the Central Valley and that streams descending the Sierra on its west side are tributaries of the San Joaquin or Sacramento and reach the Pacific through San Francisco Bay or else drain into sinks in the southern San Joaquin Valley. But he was clear on the fact that no river flowed through the Sierra from the interior to the Pacific.

Walker and his men were not the first to explore the Humboldt River Valley, but they were the first to demonstrate that the Humboldt offered a practical route for a sizable party to cross the Great Basin. The Humboldt River, pointed directly at the Tahoe Sierra, was a major portion later of the California Trail, even though Walker's own pass across the Sierra ultimately proved to be of minor importance.

The Bidwell Party

In 1841 the first group of California-bound emigrants, carrying their worldly goods in wagons, set out from the Missouri frontier. They had only the most rudimentary notions of western geography. As John Bidwell reminisced a half century later, "Our ignorance of the route was complete. We knew that California lay west, and that was the extent of our knowledge." He added that they consulted a map showing a large body of water in the approximate location of Salt Lake, with two rivers larger than the Mississippi flowing from it to the Pacific. An acquaintance in Missouri advised Bidwell to take boat-making tools so they could descend one of these rivers if the country turned out to be too rough for wagons.[20]

As Joseph Chiles, a member of the party, put it (in the third person), "Thus on they traveled seven long and weary months, with no guide no compass, nothing but the sun to direct them. They had learned through Dr. [John] Marsh's letters the latitude of San Francisco Bay, and they thought the sun was sufficient to guide them there."[21] Fortunately for them, just as they were getting started they encountered and joined a party of Jesuit missionaries led by Pierre-Jean De Smet and guided by Thomas Fitzpatrick, a veteran of the Rocky Mountain fur trade.

Fitzpatrick took them all as far as Soda Springs, in today's southeastern Idaho. Here it would be necessary for the California-bound party to take their leave and strike out on their own. Some thought better of it and changed their destination to Oregon. This was on August 11. The thirty-two men, one woman, and a child who were still determined to go to California tried to find a guide at Fort Hall, "a pilot to conduct us to the Gap in the California mountains, or at least to the head of Mary's river."[22] (In 1841 Mary's River was one of several designations for the stream to which Frémont later permanently fixed the name of Alexander von Humboldt.) Bidwell had evidently picked up the idea that a river provided a route through the wilderness. Doubtless he had taken advantage of his weeks of travel with Fitzpatrick to remedy his geographic ignorance. "The Gap" was probably a reference to Walker Pass.

There was no pilot to be had at Fort Hall, so the members of the Bidwell party were on their own. They were in a position to be the first to bring wagons across the Sierra Nevada, but after a number of misadventures they had to jettison the vehicles near the Ruby Mountains in what is now eastern Nevada. By the middle of October 1841 they had reached the eastern foot of the Sierra, traveling on foot with pack animals. Abandoning their plans to travel south along the east side of the Sierra to Walker Pass, they determined instead to cross the range farther north. Bidwell's account is too sketchy in topographic detail to allow an exact determination of where this was. They ascended a river that flowed down from the Sierra, convinced that it was somehow linked with the San Joaquin, which they knew to be in California. By the time they realized that it was probably not the San Joaquin they had gone too far into the mountains to be willing to turn back.[23]

In a retrospective account written nearly fifty years later, Bidwell says that they "ascended the mountains on the north side of Walker River to the summit, and there struck a stream running west which proved to be the extreme source of the Stanislaus River," which they followed down into deep canyons.[24] The Walker and Stanislaus basins border each other for some ten miles, and along this line are Sonora Pass (traversed today by Highway 108) and Emigrant Pass, used for a year or two in the 1850s by gold seekers bound for the southern mines.

Bidwell and his companions, no longer encumbered by wagons, had little trouble getting up the east side of the Sierra, but like the Walker party they had a long struggle down the west side. They did not recognize the Central Valley for what it was but thought they still had to cross the Coast Ranges to reach California. Soon they had the good luck to run across an Indian sporting a cloth jacket. The man knew John Marsh, whose letters back to Missouri had stimulated their adventure in the first place, and was willing to take them to Marsh's ranch at the foot of Mount Diablo. Only after reaching the ranch and talking with Marsh, on November 4, 1841, did Bidwell and his companions realize that they had arrived in California.[25]

The Bidwell party included a number of men who were to play prominent roles in California: Bidwell himself, founder of Chico and later a congressman; Charles Weber, founder of Stockton; Josiah Belden, first American mayor of San Jose; and Joseph Chiles, a thirty-one-year-old frontiersman who came to reconnoiter California and its opportunities.

Joseph Chiles

At the end of the trail, after the Bidwell party dispersed to seek their individual fortunes, Joseph Chiles made an extended tour of northern California: San Jose, Monterey, Santa Cruz, Yerba Buena (San Francisco's name at the time), Sonoma, Napa Valley, Suisun Valley, Vaca Valley, and Sutter's Fort. Later in life, based on this trip, he gave Hubert Howe Bancroft a brief but colorful description of California life in the days of the hide and tallow trade.[26]

In Napa Valley Chiles visited an old friend from Missouri, the trapper George Yount, who had settled there on a Mexican land grant after arriving in California in 1831 via Santa Fe and the Old Spanish Trail. Chiles was impressed with Napa and decided to acquire land and start a lumber mill. First it would be necessary to go back to Missouri to get his children—his wife had died and the children had been placed with various relatives—and the necessary milling equipment. Yount saw an opportunity here to be reunited with his own wife and children, whom he had not seen for seventeen years. Chiles made plans to go back the next spring and return with his family, Yount's family, other emigrants he might persuade to make the trip, and a load of mill machinery.

Waiting out the winter of 1841–42 in California, Chiles must have kept his ears open for travelers' tales and trail information. During a lengthy visit with Yount, part of the time soaking in the hot springs that later became famous as Calistoga, he would have had plenty of time to query his host about the details of the route to southern California from Santa Fe. He would have learned as well about the easy pass around the south end of the Sierra that Joseph Walker had found in 1834.

In April 1842 Chiles formed a party of fourteen bound east for the Missouri settlements. Most of them were members of the Bidwell party who, like Chiles, had come out just to look around or do some trapping and now were ready to go back. They went south through the San Joaquin Valley, but missed Walker Pass, leaving the valley by Tejon Pass instead. In the Mojave Desert they picked up the Old Spanish Trail to Santa Fe and then the Santa Fe Trail to Independence. Their only difficulty seems to have been a confrontation with some Apaches near Abiquiu, which Chiles was able to defuse without bloodshed.[27] They arrived in Missouri on September 9, 1842.

By late May 1843 Chiles was ready to head back west, his party assembled and the milling machinery packed. He did not bring his children with him as he had planned, not yet sure of being able to care for them in California. And Yount, it seems, had been rather complacent about the continuing loyalty of his long-neglected family. Only one of the three children, an eighteen-year-old daughter who had no recollection of her father, wanted to go. An older daughter was already married, and the son was so embittered by his father's absence that he had no interest in seeing him again. As for Yount's wife, she had divorced him and married another man.[28]

Chiles chose the central overland route up the valley of the Platte, the route he had taken to California with the Bidwell party in 1841, rather than the southern route by which he had returned in 1842, perhaps because the desert crossings would be more difficult with wagons than with a pack train. The party set out on May 20, 1843.

It is not certain how Chiles planned to cross the Sierra, but it seems unlikely that he would have wanted to retrace his difficult steps with the Bidwell party. He could always go south along the east side of the Sierra until he found the trail by which he had left the Central Valley on his eastbound trip the previous year. In any case that decision would not need to be made until later; they had to follow the Platte and Sweetwater to South Pass first. At the Kansas River, not far into the trip, they encountered a larger train bound for Oregon. Eighteen of the Oregon wagons joined the

Chiles party on July 6. On July 16 another member of the Oregon-bound group, Pierson Reading, came over to them.[29]

By chance Joseph Walker was at Fort Laramie when the Chiles party arrived, and Chiles induced him to sign on as guide for $300. Walker's plan seems to have been to cross the Great Basin via the Humboldt, travel south below the eastern wall of the Sierra, and enter the San Joaquin Valley by way of Walker Pass. This had been the Bidwell party's original travel plan, and now having the actual discoverer of Walker Pass along for the trip must have inspired confidence. Walker knew the entire route from his pioneering expedition of 1833 and could be expected to have stayed current with trapper lore about using the Humboldt River as a lifeline across the Great Basin. His opinions might be valuable also with regard to the interesting question of a possibly more direct way across the Sierra west of Humboldt Sink. Certainly his services were worth the $300.

The party went on to Fort Hall first, expecting to replenish their dwindling food supplies. Unable to procure as much as they needed, they decided to split into two groups. The women, children, and some of the men would go with the wagons and most of the food under Walker's guidance to Walker Pass as originally planned. Meanwhile, Chiles would take twelve men, along with twenty-six horses and mules, and traverse the unexplored country around the north end of the Sierra into the Sacramento Valley. Pierson Reading went with the northern detachment and kept a diary of the trip.[30]

The destination of the northern detachment seems to have been Sutter's Fort, where they could buy supplies and go east across the Sierra as a relief column to meet Walker somewhere near Humboldt Sink. Chiles would be able to explore for a pass across the middle of the Sierra from the west side. He could get local advice at Sutter's and would have rested and freshly provisioned men to cross the Sierra.

As it turned out, Chiles took much longer than he expected getting through the lava-encrusted desert country of what is now southeastern Oregon and northeastern California. Beyond Fort Boise all was terra incognita: Pierson Reading noted on October 1, "We will be the first party that ever attempted to pass through." (Actually, Peter Skene Ogden had been there, but he was working for the Hudson's Bay Company, and Reading probably would not have heard about him.)

When the Chiles party finally reached Sutter's Fort on November 10, snow was already piling up in the Sierra, and they had to abandon their plans to cross the mountains. They would have been too late anyway.

Walker and the wagon party had reached Humboldt Sink around October 22. Their supplies were running low, and after a week Walker decided to push on. He took the group south past Walker Lake and the Excelsior Mountains to Owens Valley, where they abandoned the wagons, cached Chiles's sawmill machinery, and reorganized themselves as a pack train. They came through Walker Pass on December 3. After recuperating their strength and that of their animals on the game and grass of the San Joaquin Valley, they went on north and were reunited with the rest of the party.

Chiles thus twice missed the chance to be in the first wagon train to cross the Sierra Nevada. He settled down in Napa Valley, where, realizing that the local penchant for building with adobe would mean low demand for construction timber, he decided to start a grist mill. This was probably a sound business decision; even three years later, Edwin Bryant noted the high price of flour in the Central Valley and attributed it to the "scarcity of flouring-mills in the country."[31] Chiles never went back to reclaim the sawmill machinery in Owens Valley, where it was found by some puzzled prospectors years later.

For a few years Chiles disappears from the annals of exploration, and in 1844 it was the Stevens party that was the first to bring wagons all the way from the Missouri frontier to the Sacramento Valley. But in the summer of 1847 Chiles stirred himself again and decided that his prosperity was sufficient for a trip to Missouri to get his children at last. He signed on as a guard for $2 a day with Commodore Robert F. Stockton's party, which was going to Washington, D.C., to testify at the court-martial of John C. Frémont (for having assumed the governorship of California in defiance of General Stephen Watts Kearney). Chiles, who had had some dealings with Frémont in the Bear Flag affair, went on to Washington to testify on his behalf and then returned as far west as Independence. After spending the winter in Independence, Chiles set out for California in the spring of 1848 as planned. The trip was uneventful until the party met a group of Mormons who told them of the gold discoveries and a new route across the mountains, a subject that is covered in the next chapter.

John C. Frémont

John C. Frémont, officer in the army's Corps of Topographical Engineers, was the last explorer of the Sierra before the wagon train era began. On his first expedition, in 1842, he had traveled up the Platte and

Sweetwater rivers as far as the Wind River Range and South Pass, with
Kit Carson as his guide. This region had long been known to trappers,
but Frémont was the first to describe it in scientific, or at least literary,
terms, and his report made him a national celebrity.

On May 29, 1843, Frémont set out on his second expedition, with instructions to extend his 1842 survey beyond South Pass to the coast of
Oregon. Frémont's father-in-law was Thomas Hart Benton, the powerful senator from Missouri who championed a thirty-eighth parallel route
for the Pacific railroad—straight west from St. Louis and Independence—despite mounting evidence that the Rockies in this latitude
would be an insuperable barrier. On the way to South Pass Frémont made
a side trip to the valley of the Arkansas River near the Front Range, to
look for alternatives to the Platte route that would more closely approximate Benton's wishes. There he ran into Kit Carson, his guide the
year before, and signed him up again.

A few words on Kit Carson may be in order here. He first appears in
the annals of western exploration in the summer of 1830, when he visited the San Joaquin Valley as a very junior member of a trapping party
of forty who came in on the southern route from Taos. In the San Joaquin
they met and joined forces with a group of Hudson's Bay Company trappers led by Ogden. The two parties traveled north through the valley and
then separated at the end of the trapping season. Ogden led his men back
to the Columbia River. The Taos trappers with Carson remained near
the Sacramento River, passing their time hunting. When Indians ran off
a herd of horses one night, Carson joined in a pursuit party that went
"upwards of one hundred miles into the Sierra Nevada Mountains." He
left no further geographic detail about these first experiences in California in his autobiography, written much later, but evidently Frémont
thought he was familiar enough with the Sierra to be useful as a guide.[32]

At first it may seem as though Frémont's expedition would have had
nothing to do with the Sierra, since Oregon was his destination. But Frémont was already thinking about the return journey. Once arrived on
the Oregon coast, Frémont would link his survey geodetically with surveys made along the Pacific Coast in 1841 by U.S. Navy Commander
Charles Wilkes. (These coastal reconnaissances were only a small part
of the agenda of the famous U.S. Exploring Expedition, which was concerned more with the far reaches of the South Pacific and included the
first definite sighting of Antarctica.) When Frémont reached Fort Van-
couver, across the Columbia from present-day Portland, about November 7, 1843, he had fulfilled the first part of his instructions, since Wilkes

had already reached that point from the ocean side and the two surveys could be tied together.

For his homeward journey, Frémont "contemplated a new route, and a great circuit to the south and southeast, and the exploration of the Great Basin between the Rocky mountains and the Sierra Nevada." In the course of this journey, Frémont wanted to determine the existence of three features that had been reported by others or shown on maps. These were Tlamath Lake, Mary's Lake, and the Buenaventura River.[33] Wilkes as well had been looking for the Buenaventura, having been ordered to scan the coast for any significant river flowing out from the interior south of the Columbia.

Traveling south from the Columbia up the valley of the Deschutes River, Frémont easily found Tlamath (now spelled Klamath) Lake and then headed east and south into the Great Basin. He soon realized that he had passed the probable location of Mary's Lake without seeing it, and gave it up without further ado. But the Buenaventura River still seemed to tantalize him.

Whether Frémont was seriously looking for this river or was using it as an excuse to ramble around and gather material is a good question. Unlike Wilkes, a seaman whose circle of acquaintances would have given him no reason to doubt maps published by the great Humboldt or by fellow military officer Zebulon Pike, Frémont had spent much time among people who had direct personal knowledge of the interior west. Jedediah Smith's explorations in 1826 and 1827 had put the existence of the Buenaventura much in doubt. Zenas Leonard had stated explicitly that there was no river running through the Sierra from the interior. In the world of trappers and mountain men the idea that there was no such thing as the Buenaventura River must have been a commonplace by 1843.

Was Frémont just being theatrical, then, when he made remarks such as the following?

[December 11, 1843] In our journey across the desert, Mary's lake, and the famous Buenaventura river, were two points on which I relied to recruit the animals, and repose the party. Forming, agreeably to the best maps in my possession, a connected water line from the Rocky mountains to the Pacific ocean, I felt no other anxiety than to pass safely across the intervening desert to the banks of the Buenaventura, where, in the softer climate of a more southern latitude, our horses might find grass to sustain them, and ourselves be sheltered from the rigors of winter and from the inhospitable desert.[34]

[January 3, 1844] We were evidently on the verge of the desert which had been reported to us; and the appearance of the country was so forbidding, that I was afraid to enter it, and determined to bear away to the southward, keeping close along the mountains, in the full expectation of reaching the Buenaventura River.[35]

In other words, this quest was not a matter only of gratifying curiosity; Frémont was betting the welfare of his expedition on the existence of this shadowy river. Writing some years later, Senator Benton stated that Frémont believed in the existence of the Buenaventura River and that his belief was bolstered by conversations with the Hudson's Bay Company's factor, John McLaughlin, a well-informed man who had made a "conjectural map" of the river for Frémont.[36]

Captain J. H. Simpson, of whom we will hear more later, was more critical of his fellow topographical engineer:

> Colonel Fremont's reports shows that in this expedition he had not seen, or did not care to give heed to, the previously published history and map of the explorations of Bonneville; for, had he done so, he would probably not have been led into the error to which he attributed a great deal of his hardships, of constantly looking for the hypothetical river of Buenaventura, which, as he supposed, taking its rise in the Rocky Mountains, emptied itself into the bay of San Francisco, and upon which he expected to winter.[37]

Frémont did fill in blank spaces on the map as he moved south. He reached and named Pyramid Lake. He reached the Truckee River, though his name for it, "Salmon Trout," did not stand the test of time. Not yet having found a west-flowing river, the Frémont party continued south through the arid landscape, first to the Carson River and then to the Walker River.

Apparently Frémont's plan had been to keep going south along the east side of the Sierra. But the snow and cold were too much. Charles Preuss, Frémont's cartographer, recorded the change of plans: "On the fourth of January . . . it was decided to seek refuge with Captain Sutter on the Sacramento River."[38] That snow and cold were likely to be much worse in the mountains than in the relatively warm and dry rain shadow at their eastern foot did not deter Frémont. His geographic knowledge of the Sierra was clearly limited—as was, to be fair, that of mountain men Kit Carson, Alex Godey, and Thomas Fitzpatrick as well.

Instead of taking the West Fork of Walker River, they followed up the East Fork to the vicinity of present Bridgeport, far south of where they should have been if their aim was simply to cross the mountains. From here they searched the mountains to the west for a pass. They went through Devil's Gate, thinking it was the divide, only to come down into the valley of the West Fork of the Walker, which they followed to a point only 20 miles from its confluence with the East Fork before Frémont realized they had gone around in a large circle east of the Sierra.

From this point on the West Fork of the Walker they cut across to the East Fork of the Carson in the vicinity of present-day Markleeville. Frémont and a few others went up Hot Springs Creek past Grover Springs through Charity Valley to Faith Valley, from which they had a clear view to the west of the summit ridge running from Round Top on the south to Red Lake Peak on the north, in the middle of which is Carson Pass.

Frémont's camp on the east side of Faith Valley, reached on February 5, served as a base camp for the next two weeks, as the rest of the party, animals, and baggage were slowly brought up through the snow from Grover Hot Springs. Frémont, Preuss, Carson, and Fitzpatrick used this time to scout the range ahead. As early as February 6, Frémont and Carson reached a point from which they could see the Sacramento Valley and Mount Diablo on the horizon. Preuss went to take a look for himself "at the promised land" on February 12.[39] On February 14 Frémont climbed Red Lake Peak and from the summit made the first recorded observation of Lake Tahoe.

Finally, struggling through deep snow, the entire party with their pack animals made it over the crest on February 20, 1844. Their line of approach from Faith Valley makes it unlikely that they went through the exact notch of Carson Pass, which is aligned with Hope Valley. They were more likely to have crossed a mile or so to the south, in the vicinity of Frog Lake. They did not descend to the Central Valley along the "Carson route," as it became established a few years later, but instead angled north to the South Fork of the American and followed that stream, with great difficulties, down to Sutter's Fort, which they reached on March 7.[40]

After a two-week stay at Sutter's Fort and a visit to Chiles in Napa Valley, the Frémont party set out on their return trip, on horseback and with pack animals, traveling south through the San Joaquin Valley. Frémont intended to leave the valley via Walker Pass, and later on, in present Utah, he clearly thought he *had* gone through Walker Pass. But it is obvious from his own descriptions that he traveled through Tehachapi Pass.[41] He encountered Walker and traveled with him for a while later in the trip, but if Walker corrected Frémont's geography, Frémont does not mention it. The confusion of Walker and Tehachapi passes continued for a long time. Right after the Pacific railroad surveys law was passed, nine years later, Thomas Hart Benton, no longer senator, wrote an impassioned plea for his "central national highway," that is, his St.

Louis to San Francisco route. The proposed route included "Walker's Pass," which Benton promoted using Frémont's description of 1844, evidently not aware even then that this was a description of Tehachapi and not Walker Pass.[42]

The party crossed the western Mojave, keeping the snow-covered San Gabriel Range on their right until they encountered the Old Spanish Trail running along the Mojave River. They followed the trail past the south end of Death Valley to the site of present Las Vegas, then went north via the Virgin River and the Wasatch Front to the vicinity of Utah Lake. Here they turned east for more exploration of the Colorado Rockies. It was this trip that led Frémont to pronounce that most of the area between the Salt Lake and the Sierra Nevada was in fact a "Great Basin" (his term), which Joseph Walker and many others probably already knew as a practical fact.

Frémont definitely had a flair for cartographic description. On the official map of his 1843–44 expedition, in a long arc from north to south across the western part of the United States, the Great Basin was labeled thus: "The Great Basin: diameter 11° of latitude, 10° of longitude, elevation above the sea between 4 and 5 thousand feet, surrounded by lofty mountains: contents almost unknown, but believed to be filled with rivers and lakes which have no communication with the sea, deserts and oases which have never been explored, and savage tribes which no traveler has seen or described."[43]

Frémont returned to the west in the fall of 1845 on his third expedition. He found his way back to the Truckee River and crossed over what later became Donner Pass, reaching Sutter's Fort on December 9. As Frémont passed over the summit he noticed ruts made by wagons. The age of wheeled-vehicle traffic over the Sierra had begun.

CHAPTER 3

Wagon Trains
across the Sierra

The first wheeled vehicles to cross the Sierra Nevada belonged to a party of emigrants from Council Bluffs, led by Elisha Stevens in the summer and fall of 1844. The Stevens party set the pattern for subsequent overland emigrants to California. They followed the Platte and its tributary, the Sweetwater, west to South Pass. This was the first and easier half of the trip. Then they cut across the valleys of the upper Green River and Bear River to reach Fort Hall on the Snake River, leaving Great Salt Lake far to the south. They ascended the Raft River, a tributary of the Snake, past a remarkable area of granite domes and pinnacles known as City of Rocks and crossed over into the valley of the Humboldt River. They followed this meager desert stream across the Great Basin to where it finally disappeared by seepage and evaporation in Humboldt Sink, just south of present Lovelock, Nevada, and still short of the Sierra Nevada by 50 miles or so.

From Humboldt Sink they made the short but difficult desert passage to one of the rivers draining the east side of the Sierra—the Truckee, in the case of the Stevens party, the Carson or the Walker for others—and ascended its valley to some point where a scramble up and over the summit was feasible. Finally, their destination almost in view, they would descend the gentler western slope, usually along the top of a ridge, to the great Central Valley of California. This was the California Trail.

The route was determined only partly by topography. Availability of water and grass for livestock was always a major consideration. As we shall see, stagecoach and freighting operations were later able to achieve shortcuts that seem topographically obvious but were feasible only because the repetitive, two-way nature of their business justified the building of way stations where employees maintained supplies of water and fodder. Wagon train emigrants, traveling one way, once and for all, had to depend entirely on what stingy nature provided, and this sometimes required departing from the shortest path.

Mountain man Caleb Greenwood, about eighty years old, was the Stevens party's guide as far as Fort Hall, but that was the limit of his personal experience. Along the Humboldt River they were all improvising, and their main guidance would have been the traces left the year before by the Walker division of Chiles's party.

The Truckee Route

Humboldt Sink was a decision point. Staying with Walker's trail far south to Walker Pass would have been the safest course, but some members of the party argued, purely on calculations of latitude, that they could save time by cutting west across the mountains, without knowing whether there was a pass through. Actually there were several. Sonora, Carson, Johnson, Donner, Henness, and Beckwourth passes were all possible gateways to California, as we can see today, but members of the Stevens party could only guess, and hope, that something of the sort might exist.

As they camped at Humboldt Sink and debated what to do, one of the stranger events of the trip occurred. An old man of the Paiute tribe appeared, and through sign language and diagrams drawn on the ground he made them understand how they could cross the desert to a stream that flowed out of the Sierra, follow this stream up into the mountains, and cross the range to the other side. As a result of this remarkable apparition, the "straight west" advocates won the day. The Stevens party took the old man's advice and crossed the desert to a small river in the vicinity of what is now Wadsworth, Nevada. Abundant water, forage, and firewood in the meadows and groves along this river must have been a welcome relief to them after the trip down the penurious and alkaline Humboldt and their subsequent haul across the desert. They did not forget the informant who directed them there and gave the stream his name, which they understood to be Truckee.[1]

Following the Truckee River upstream brought the Stevens party to a wide valley, later to be known as Truckee Meadows (and a quarter century later the site of the new Central Pacific Railroad town of Reno).

Truckee Meadows, at 4,500 feet, was still on the east side of the Sierra crest. Following the river farther upstream brought them to another difficult canyon. By following this natural passageway carved by the river, they could pass through the eastern range of the Sierra. But it was not an easy passage. The Truckee gorge narrowed to the point that the emigrants had to travel in the actual bed of the river. Rocks and prolonged exposure to water was hard on the feet of cattle and humans alike. As if this were not enough trouble, snow began to fall.

Above this canyon the Stevens party came out into rolling pine and sagebrush country, in the vicinity of the later town of Truckee, where the going was easier. Soon they reached Donner Lake and faced the western summit, a mountain wall that looked (and still looks) like an impossible path for wheeled vehicles even on the balmiest summer day. This was November, however, with snow already on the ground and no time to backtrack in search of an easier route.

At this difficult point the Stevens party decided to enhance their chances of survival by diversifying. One party of six would go on ahead to Sutter's Fort, traveling light with packhorses and no wagons. This would ensure that the presence of an overland party at the gates of California would at least be known to people already inside. The others consolidated vital provisions in five of the wagons, leaving the remaining six at Donner Lake with a guard of three men until spring. Getting the five wagons and their teams over the mountain crest was an epic struggle, requiring the wagons to be dismantled and hoisted up cliffs by rope in a foot of snow. Despite the difficulties all five wagons were hauled across the summit on or about November 25, 1844. This place eventually acquired the name Donner Pass because of the notorious events of two years later, but as E Clampus Vitus and others have correctly but vainly asserted, it ought to be known as Stevens Pass.

Three days later, going down the west side of the Sierra but still some 6,000 feet above sea level, this group was stopped by a major snowstorm in the area of Big Bend, a dozen miles west of the summit. They built a makeshift shelter there and agreed on another split: the women, children, and two men would stay with the wagons while the other men slogged on down to Sutter's Fort. They made the trip in a week, arriving about December 13, 1844. The packhorse party of six had already arrived, having gone south to about the midpoint of the west shore of Lake Tahoe, where McKinney Creek enters. They climbed the creek valley to the crest, descended tributaries of the American River, and reached Sutter's Fort without serious mishap.

All now wanted to refit quickly and go back for the women and children, but Sutter argued that the snow was too deep and that with shelter and the supplies in the wagons the people stranded at Big Bend would be safe until conditions improved. Evidently Sutter wanted the emigrants and their rifles on his side during the unsettled conditions that the revolt against Governor Manuel Micheltorena had created. They must have trusted Sutter, because they were persuaded to leave their families and friends at Big Bend and go off soldiering.

Meanwhile, the three men left at Donner Lake realized that the snow was relentlessly accumulating and not melting down between storms as it usually did back east. Hunting was becoming difficult and the prospects of survival dim. They decided to abandon the wagons and try to get across the mountains on improvised snowshoes. But one of them, Moses Schallenberger, found he was already too weakened to make this arduous journey and returned, knowing that he probably would not last out the winter.

Sutter's recruits returned from their adventures in the Micheltorena affair (some going as far as Santa Barbara), and by March 1 they had rescued the Big Bend contingent. One member of the rescue party, Dennis Martin, having assured himself about his father's well-being at Big Bend, went on across the summit on snowshoes to check on the fate of Schallenberger, knowing that the chances he had survived to this point were slight. But Schallenberger was miraculously still alive at Donner Lake, having subsisted mostly on trapped foxes. In fact, he lived another fifty-five years and as an old man wrote, or dictated, what became one of the main sources of information about the Stevens party.[2] Despite the many dark moments, everyone who set out from Council Bluffs in this first party to take wagons across the mountains survived the trip. With this series of events the Truckee route was established.

In the 1845 travel season several parties totaling about fifty wagons used the Truckee route.[3] By the time Frémont passed this way on December 4, he noted the route as an established fact: "The emigrant road now passes here, following down a fork of the Bear River, which leads from the pass into the Sacramento Valley."[4]

From the summit the emigrant road's course approximated that of the Central Pacific Railroad (and today's Interstate 80) as far west as Emigrant Gap.[5] Thence it went sharply downhill into the Bear River valley, climbed Lowell Hill Ridge, and then followed its crest down toward the Central Valley. This course was approximately parallel to the ridge later followed by the railroad and highways and within view of it, but the two routes were separated by the deep valley of the Bear River. The wagon road stayed north of the river all the way down to Johnson's Ranch, in the vicinity of today's Wheatland, about 32 miles north of Sutter's Fort.

Promoting a New Route

Doughty old Caleb Greenwood did not spend much time in California, considering the trouble he had taken to get there. On May 12, 1845, he returned east with his two sons in a party totaling thirteen. The others were going all the way to the Missouri settlements, but the Greenwoods planned to stop at the point near Fort Hall where the California and Oregon trails diverged. Their plan was to station themselves at the parting of the ways and persuade Oregon-bound emigrants to change their destination to California, and they had a fair amount of success in this. Benjamin Franklin Bonney, only a child at the time, left a vivid account of Greenwood coming around to his family's campfire at Fort Hall to warn them of the perils of Oregon and beguile them with the charms of California.[6]

A by-product of the Greenwoods' trip east was the discovery of an easier alternative to the arduous passage through the upper Truckee River gorge. This "Dog Valley route," in the mountains west of Truckee Meadows, required a steep climb over a ridge summit of 6,155 feet between today's towns of Verdi (4,840 ft.) and Truckee (5,800 ft.), but it was easier than the tortuous and boulder-strewn canyon. The Dog Valley route became the main emigrant trail and later the primary wagon and stagecoach road west of the Truckee Meadows area and remained the main road into the early automobile age. In the late 1860s the Central Pacific built down through the river gorge, because the ridge between Dog Valley and Verdi was too steep. In 1925 the state of California built a new highway paralleling the railroad, and the Dog Valley route dwindled into a gravel road for ranch traffic and recreational access to three reservoirs.[7] It was the original Stevens party route that later became U.S. 40 and eventually Interstate 80.

Two members of the Greenwood return party to the States, William H. Winter and E. A. Farwell, wrote travel accounts that were read by many would-be emigrants. Winter returned to Lafayette, Indiana, and wrote *Route Across the Rocky Mountains, with a Description of Oregon and California.* Farwell went to New Orleans and on April 22, 1845, saw a report in the *Picayune* that motivated him to put pen to paper. The report, based on an interview with a traveler just arrived from

California via Mazatlán and Mexico City, reported Frémont's arrival
in California with sixty mounted men via a new pass. Farwell sus-
pected, correctly, that this was the Truckee route and wrote a letter to
the editor, giving a short history of the Stevens party, including the
meeting with "Truckee" and a description of their route. The letter was
reprinted by Missouri papers in May and so received wide circulation
among people planning to make the trip in the 1846 travel season.[8]

The Dog Valley shortcut eliminated the upper part of the Truckee
gorge, but it brought emigrants to Donner Lake, where they faced the
same difficult haul over the steep granite slopes of the western summit.
Parties who arrived early enough in the season had the opportunity to
reconnoiter for alternative routes. Two were soon found a mile or two
south of the pass that the Stevens party had pioneered. One of the alternatives acquired the name Roller Pass, because of a log made to serve
as a pulley for the rope or chain by which combined teams of oxen hauled
the wagons up the last few hundred yards. The eastern slope of Roller
Pass is, if anything, steeper than the Stevens route, though the crumbling
rhyolite may have been easier than hard, slick granite for hooves and
wheels to grip. Another gap in the crest, between Roller Pass and the
Stevens route, was thought by some to look a little less difficult than the
other two; this acquired the name Coldstream Pass. (Coldstream Pass
and Roller Pass are easily accessible on foot via the Pacific Crest Trail
south from Donner Pass Road at the summit.)

Within 2 miles of each other, these three passes were but local variants in what was basically one route over the Sierra. The emigrants of
1845, 1846 (including the ill-fated Donner party), 1847, and 1848 came
into California this way. Then, in the summer of 1848, a quite different
route was opened up.

The Carson Route

In 1848 the renowned frontiersmen James Clyman and Joseph Chiles
brought emigrant parties into California by passing over the Sierra crest
south of Lake Tahoe. This was an improvement sufficient to change the
whole course of the emigration. As it became more publicized, the Carson route, as it was known, became the primary entrance to California,
and the notorious Truckee route with its variants fell into disuse, so
much so that when Theodore D. Judah was examining possible trans-
Sierra railroad routes a decade later, he apparently did not even consider
the Truckee route a leading candidate until the Dutch Flat pharmacist

Daniel Strong drew his attention to it. But that is material for a later chapter. First, let us see how this new Carson route came into use.

The Carson River is the next substantial stream south of the Truckee River that flows down the east side of the Sierra. The West Fork of the Carson drains Hope Valley, a grassy intermontane flat at the 7,000-foot level just across the Carson Range from the south end of Lake Tahoe, and has carved a rugged canyon to Carson Valley, where it meets the East Fork. Like the Truckee, the Carson then runs east into the bed of Pleistocene Lake Lahontan and disappears by seepage and evaporation. Also like the Truckee, the Carson River attracted a flow of emigrants. The emigrant wagon road ran south through the length of Carson Valley, up the river's deep canyon to Hope Valley, and then sharply up from the south end of Hope Valley to Carson Pass.

Unlike the Truckee route, however, the Carson route was pioneered by a party leaving California and traveling east. Frémont had publicized the fact that it was possible to get across the mountains south of Lake Tahoe, but California-bound emigrants did not immediately search this locale out, possibly because Frémont's account was short on the topographic detail that might have provided guidance. The event that put it on the emigrants' map was a crossing in 1848 by a group of Mormons traveling east to rejoin their coreligionists at Salt Lake City after a brush with the Mexican War and a spell of working for John Sutter. Clyman and Chiles encountered these Mormons east of the mountains and changed course for the new route.

These eastbound Mormons of 1848 were members of the Mormon Battalion, a body of 536 men who had been recruited into the U.S. Army at Council Bluffs to fight in the Mexican War. They were marched through the Southwest to San Diego by Lieutenant Colonel Philip St. George Cooke without ever actually seeing battle, then demobilized in Los Angeles on July 16, 1847, and left to fend for themselves.[9] Many were eager to rejoin their families and friends, though it was not clear where in the vast continental interior these familiar faces were to be found.

A large contingent of battalion veterans crossed into the Central Valley through Tejon Pass. They had picked up a map and travel instructions of some kind in Los Angeles and tried to cross the Sierra by ascending the Kings River. This proved impossible, so they returned to the valley and headed north to Sutter's Fort. At the Mokelumne River they encountered Martin Murphy and his family, who had come to California as part of the Stevens party. Here the Mormons learned for the first time that the main Mormon emigration led by Brigham Young had settled near Salt Lake. After arriving at Sutter's Fort on August 26, a number decided to remain until spring to accumulate some money.

The rest set out toward Salt Lake along the Truckee route, now established as the way to California. Crossing the summit on September 5, they noticed a "windlass" used to haul wagons up the east side of the mountain, which suggests that they traveled via Roller Pass. At Donner Lake they found makeshift shelters and some skeletal remains of the Donner party, still unburned and unburied despite orders given by General Kearney on his march east earlier that summer.

On September 6 this group encountered Sam Brannan, who was passing through on his way back to San Francisco after a meeting with Brigham Young. Brannan had tried unsuccessfully to persuade Young that the Mormons should keep moving west and settle in San Francisco. If he had succeeded, the history of the western United States would have been quite different, but Young had already decided that Salt Lake Valley was the place.

Riding a day behind the disgruntled Brannan was Captain James Brown of the Mormon Battalion, with letters to the men from their families and a general epistle from Brigham Young admonishing them that "it would be wisdom for [single men] to return to California and go to work and fit themselves out with plenty of clothing, stock, provision, etc. and come up next season to the valley [i.e., Salt Lake]."[10] So the battalion veterans turned around and crossed the mountains back to California.

Some of them hired on with John Sutter and were part of the crew at the famous mill construction site where James Marshall discovered gold in late January 1848. Despite the lure of easy money—at this time gold nuggets were being dug out of stream banks with pocket knives—many were determined to go on to Salt Lake when the snows in the Sierra melted. Meeting on April 9, 1848, they agreed to be ready to go on June 1. It is a testimony to the power of family ties and religious beliefs that these men left the goldfields just as multitudes elsewhere were sparing no effort to get there. Evidently they regarded their adventures on the fringe of the Mexican War and their discovery of gold as mere diversions on the way to Zion.

Among those at Sutter's mill were Henry William Bigler and Azariah Smith, who kept diaries of the trip east.[11] The Mormon party resolved to try to improve on the existing route: "It was further decided that we send out a few men to pioneer out a route across the Sierra Nevada and if possible find a much nearer way than to go the Truckee route and thus shun crossing the very deep and rapid Truckee River twenty-seven times. We were informed by Mr. Brannan we would have to do so if we went that route."[12] This decision was of great significance, in that it led directly to the opening of the Carson route across the Sierra.

The Mormons were not ready to go on June 1, and there was still too much snow in the high country anyway, but by the first of July the travel party was assembled in Pleasant Valley, near Placerville. There were forty-five men and one woman, traveling with seventeen wagons, three hundred horses and cattle, and two small brass cannons bought from Sutter.[13] On July 3, 1848, this procession set out east toward the Sierra crest, following Iron Mountain Ridge, which forms a natural ramp up to the area of Carson Pass between the South Fork of the American River and the Cosumnes River. Three men were sent out to scout the route ahead.

The topography of the Sierra gave the Mormon party every reason to expect it would be fairly easy to find a way up to the crest. In fact, crossing the Sierra Nevada west to east would be easier than east to west for any pioneering party. Streams flowing west down the tilted granite block that forms the range have etched out deep canyons with high ridges rising between them. Interfluves between upper tributaries are pinched out where the tributaries converge, but those that form the divide between one major river and another extend far down toward the Central Valley. Eastbound travelers leaving the valley can start uphill with a good chance of rising fairly steadily toward the summit of the Sierra; westbound travelers may pick a promising descent only to find it ending in some canyon still deep within the mountains.

Frémont, describing his descent from Carson Pass in February 1844, left a vivid account of how frustrating the trip down the west side of the Sierra could be even for a party traveling with pack animals and not encumbered with wagons. At one point they had followed a descending ridge only to find themselves deep in a tributary canyon of the South Fork of the American, with nothing to do but climb back up. Frémont's account of his expedition's long and painful descent from Carson Pass to the Central Valley is a reminder that even with Mount Diablo already sighted on the horizon, early travelers were far from being out of the woods when they crossed the western summit.[14]

Some members of the Mormon party must have read Frémont's widely distributed report of this 1844 expedition and knew he had crossed the Sierra crest somewhere along their own projected line of march. But they could have had no very exact idea where this crossing point was in relation to their position, since Frémont had not descended along the

ridge the Mormons were following but had angled north from Carson
Pass to the headwaters of the South Fork of the American and somehow
descended it to the Central Valley. Frémont's account would have been
of little help to the Mormons other than to inspire confidence that it was
possible to get over the mountain crest somewhere up ahead.

When the Mormon party set out, the three scouts had been gone about
a month, and their friends were beginning to worry. On July 5 a second
scouting party went out. They reached Carson Pass and returned to the
main group on July 14 with much useful trail information but no news
about the missing three. On July 19 the Mormon party reached a spring
at the 7,900-foot level, to find bloodstains on the ground, a pouch of
gold that had belonged to one of the missing men, and a mound of recently disturbed earth. Soon they unearthed the bodies of the three missing scouts. Indian attack was presumed, though there were doubts; the
party left an inscription on a fir tree near the grave that read "supposed
to have been killed by Indians."[15] These, the only fatalities of the trip,
are commemorated in the name Tragedy Spring.[16]

On July 22, 1848, the Mormon party crossed the western summit, slogging through snowbanks two feet deep and with drifts up to fifteen feet
nearby. "This day I gathered flowers with one hand and snow with the
other," Bigler remarked. The next few days were spent in the vicinity of
the western summit, repairing equipment and clearing the trail for those
coming on behind. On July 26 they camped at what is now Caples Lake.
Ten men went out "to explore and hunt a pass across the mountain."
They returned to camp the next day having made "no new discovery."[17]

From the western summit there is a sweeping view to the east, and it
is obvious where the trail must go: through a broad saddle between
Round Top on the south and Red Lake Peak on the north, just as Highway 88 does today. This is Carson Pass, and members of the Mormon
party could hardly have failed to study it closely as they wended their
way down from the western summit to Caples Lake. Probably the hoped-
for "new discovery" concerned not the pass itself, therefore, but an easy
way down the eastern slope to Red Lake. As they learned, there *was* no
easy way; the steep slope above Red Lake was to remain one of the notorious hard places on the Carson route until a highway grade was
blasted out of the mountainside many decades later.

On July 27 the Mormons moved 3 miles and made camp "near or at
the summit of the great Sierra Nevada," that is, near Carson Pass. Bigler
was aware that this eastern summit was the divide between the Pacific
slope and the Great Basin and thus "the" summit, even though it was

almost a thousand feet lower than the western summit. On July 28 they moved another 1.5 miles and camped at the head of what they named Hope Valley.[18] Evidently moving the wagons and cattle over Carson Pass and down the steep slope to Red Lake took all day, which is not surprising in light of the many later descriptions of this short but precipitous stretch. It is curious that Bigler had no more to say about the feat.

On the evening of July 30 the Mormon party reached the upper end of Carson Canyon, having evidently taken the previous day to rest and recuperate the animals in Hope Valley, since it would not have taken them more than a day to get through the valley. They spent the next four days creating a rough road down through the canyon for the wagons— building up fording places, rolling rocks out of the way, and digging— though not neglecting the opportunity to do some trout fishing in the Carson River. After emerging from Carson Canyon, the Mormon party went north through Carson Valley to the Truckee River, where they picked up the well-worn emigrant trail and followed it in reverse, crossing the desert via Boiling Springs to Humboldt Sink.

Traveling east along the Humboldt, the Mormons met at least five parties of emigrants. On August 16, 1848, Azariah Smith noted in his diary: "In the after noon yesterday, some sixteen wagons came in, on the way to California, from the States, and they got a waybill of us—calculating to take our trail over the mountains."[19] A waybill was a set of written travel instructions, a rudimentary guidebook warning about tricky fords, good places to camp, and so forth. Bigler too mentioned this party, counting eighteen wagons, but said nothing about waybills or destinations. Neither diarist identified the leader. It may have been James Clyman, in which case his would have been the first westbound train to cross Carson Pass.[20]

Bigler and Smith mentioned meeting four other parties.[21] On August 16 both diarists noted briefly the passing of a train of twenty-five wagons. This may have been Pierre Barlow Cornwall's party. On August 26 both noted a party of ten wagons, led by Peter Lassen to his highly speculative northern route, as related in the next chapter. On August 27 they passed a pack team of ten men led by Samuel R. Hensley. (This group was mentioned by Bigler but not by Smith.) The Clyman, Cornwall, and Hensley parties are not well documented; it is possible that they used Carson Pass, but there is no record of it. (Clyman, a most literate frontiersman and a prolific writer on other periods of his life, left no description of this particular trip, and there seem to have been no diarists in his party either.) So it was the last group the Mormons encountered that occupies a more prominent place in history. "On the thirtieth [of August 1848] we met Captain Chiles and Company of forty-eight wagons: emigrants," wrote Bigler.[22] The Chiles party had dedicated diarists, so even if they came behind Clyman they were the first clearly documented emigrant party to enter California along the new route the Mormons had just blazed, henceforth known as the Carson Pass route.

The Chiles Party

This was Chiles's third westbound overland trip to California. His first was with the Bidwell party of 1841; his second, the 1843 venture when Joseph Walker acted as guide over the Sierra for part of the group while he went around the north end of the range. By the time Chiles led this 1848 party west down the Humboldt, the Truckee route had become well established, and most probably that was the way he intended to go. On July 26, eight days west of South Pass, the party encountered Walker at their noon halt, and he accompanied them for the rest of the day.[23] Doubtless Walker and Chiles rode together and talked about trail geography.

One member of the Chiles party, Richard May, left a detailed account of the trip and mentioned two encounters with returning Mormons.

> August 25, 1848 [at a point 30 to 40 miles east of the Humboldt River canyon near Carlin]: We met a train of packs from California, 23 in number. Several of them had specimens of gold lately discovered in that country about 70 miles above Sutters establishment. They represented the mines as being very rich yielding on an average of two ozs. of gold to the days labor and that one particular man had made 700 dollars in a day. The train giving us this information were Mormons bound for the Salt Lake Valley.[24]

This group of Mormons, however, was not Bigler's party, who came along four days later, on the evening of August 29:

> At our encampment we met 17 wagons from California. They had near 100 head of horses and some cattle bound for the Salt Lake being a part of Cooks Battalion. They were returning from the services of their country and had with them a small piece of ordinance. I did not inquire but expected it was a trophy they were carrying along won by their arms.[25]

Bigler's party had evidently lost or eaten quite a bit of livestock, but had gotten all seventeen wagons across the mountains and still had at least one of the cannons bought from Sutter. The first Mormon parties had left Pleasant Valley after Bigler's group but, traveling with pack animals instead of wagons, took the lead in Carson Valley. Either or both would have been able to tell Chiles about the new route. It would be helpful to know what they advised, but no written record has surfaced. We may have an approximation, however, in the "Mormon Guide," a half sheet of foolscap folded into four pages, which J. Goldsborough Bruff found being sold by two Mormons at City of Rocks the following year. The last portion of the guide, from Carson Valley on, reads as follows:[26]

Through the cañon—rough road	5
Thence to *Red Lake,* or foot of dividing ridge	11
Good campg. near by Lake, valley excellent camp	6
Over big hill, to *Rock Valley,* good campg.	10
To *Leak Springs,* good campg & good by the way	13
Camp Creek—poor camp	10
Down the ridge	16
Turn your animals into a valley 2 ms. from the road on the left	
To *Pleasant Valley.* (First mining)	12
Thence to Sutter's Fort	55

These directions, though rudimentary, can easily be traced. Some of the place-names—Red Lake, Leak Springs, Camp Creek, Pleasant Valley—are still found on today's maps. The canyon with the rough road is Carson Canyon. The lake with "good campg" is Caples Lake, or rather its natural and smaller predecessor. The "big hill" is the climb over Carson Spur, that is, the western summit.

Chiles surely got more precise information than this in campfire conversations with the Mormons, though for him the salient point may have been the bare fact that wagons had been brought over the mountains from Placerville to Hope Valley and then down the Carson River, details of the route being secondary. Seventeen wagons and hundreds of cattle would have left a trail easy to follow. Running into these Mormons and learning about an alternative to the notorious Truckee route must have seemed like an uncommon piece of good luck.

Chiles did not follow the Mormon trails exactly, however. The Mormons had stayed close to the eastern base of the Sierra after crossing the range, going north to the Truckee River at Truckee Meadows (Reno) before turning east into the desert. Chiles turned his party more directly south from Humboldt Sink, cut across to the Carson River in the vicinity of today's Lahontan Reservoir, and then followed the Carson upstream. He thus lost no time in following a time-honored custom: es-

tablishing a cutoff in the original route. Following the Carson River upstream, Chiles reached Carson Valley. ("Carson Valley" in the usage of
1848 as well as today is actually a structural basin, the westernmost in
the basin and range country that extends from the Sierra Nevada to the
Wasatch Front in Utah. From a hydrological point of view, Chiles was
of course already within the valley of the Carson River when he reached
its banks far downstream from the "valley.")

Once in Carson Valley, Chiles simply followed the Mormon trail in
reverse: the easy procession south through the valley, then the struggle
up rocky Carson Canyon, the lush and restful environment of Hope Valley, the steep climb from Red Lake to Carson Pass, and an easy four-mile
descent to Caples Lake. Leaving Caples Lake the trail climbed steeply up
the valley of Emigrant Creek toward two low points in Carson Spur, a
craggy ridge that dominates the southwest skyline as seen from the lake.
The broad saddle on the right is actually lower by some 250 feet but
drops off too steeply on the far side to have been convenient for wagons. The higher left-hand notch, by contrast, led the emigrants onto
Squaw Ridge, which abuts Carson Spur at a right angle and provided a
convenient onward path southwest and west around Silver Lake.

It is worth emphasizing that the emigrant wagon route went up from
Caples Lake right over the top of Carson Spur, in contrast to Highway
88, which goes around it about 1,600 feet lower. The western summit,
the "big hill" of the Mormon guide, is 9,500 feet above sea level and is
the highest elevation reached by significant numbers of covered wagons
on the old trails. The Walker River Emigrant Road to Columbia and
Sonora, which is discussed in the next chapter, probably crossed at Emigrant Pass, about 9,700 feet elevation, somewhat higher than West Pass.
But it was used for only one or two years because it was so difficult.[27]

To many emigrants West Pass was the gateway to California. The political boundary of the state was some four or five days back, but that
boundary had not yet been surveyed on the ground, and in the minds of
tired travelers this high point, with the gradual descent to the Sacramento
Valley hinted at in the view off to the west, was the beginning of the
home stretch. The descent from the summit onto Squaw Ridge had some
steep rocky places, but then for several miles the ridge offered easy going, with extensive meadows, lush from recent snowmelt, where stock
could be fed.

At first glance the Carson route would seem to have had several strikes
against it. There were two summits instead of one, and both were considerably higher than the highest point of the Truckee route, one by

1,500 feet and the other by 2,500 feet, with a dip between that had to be descended and then climbed all over again. On the higher western summit deep snow might linger into July, and some years even into August. All the same, the Carson Pass route quickly became the main road into California.

There were good reasons for this. Evidently the wagon haul over both summits, though steep, was less hellish than on the Truckee route. Only three fords of the Carson River were required, compared with the two dozen zigzag crossings of the Truckee. Beyond West Pass the ridge road down to the Placerville area was easier than the route down to Sutter's Fort, and it brought emigrants into the heart of the gold diggings. From 1851 on, the trading post at Mormon Station (renamed Genoa after 1855) provided a chance to replace depleted supplies and gave evidence that California was almost in sight. A less material but perhaps potent factor was the sinister reputation that enshrouded the Truckee route for years after the Donner party disaster. For a variety of reasons, then, the Carson route replaced the Truckee route as the most frequented overland entrance to California just as the gold rush was getting under way.

Use of the Carson Route

Because the Carson route is less familiar to the modern reader than the Truckee route, let us look at the experience of traveling over it, as shown in some accounts from the early years.

Emigrant parties bound for Carson Pass crossed the Great Basin along the Humboldt River, just like those headed for the Truckee route. The parting of the ways was near Humboldt Sink. There both routes had to leave the comparative security of the river's meager and alkaline flow and strike out into the desert. The Truckee route bore slightly south of west until it reached the Truckee River and then followed the river upstream to Truckee Meadows, whereas the Carson route went straight south to the Carson River and then upstream to Carson Valley. Carson Valley offered plenty of water and grass and, after 1851, a chance to buy provisions at Mormon Station. At the south end of Carson Valley, across the line in California (though the exact location of the border on the ground was a matter of conjecture in the early 1850s), the trail entered an opening in the mountains. This was the lower end of the canyon formed by the West Fork of the Carson River.

Carson Canyon remained for several years a notoriously difficult part of the trip, often mentioned in travel diaries and official reports. It was "the most wild looking chasm eye ever rested upon, and the worst road the human imagination can conceive," wrote one, who, like all the others, had had plenty of comparative experience in the long trek from the Missouri River.[28] The difficulty was the chaos of boulders, running water, and vegetation that choked the canyon. Added psychological stress, very often mentioned, was produced by the vertical walls of the canyon high above, from which, it was obvious to all, the boulders had dropped.

> The principal obstructions that interposed themselves to our march was the large piles of granit that had broken off the walls of the Mountains which stood on either side thousands of feet above us—and over hanging us as it ware—and rolled down into the gorge, forming piles from 1 to 300 feet high. These we were compelled to find our way through by circuitous routs and winding ways, Ascending and descending over steep craggy cliffs and precipices. We were compelled to force our wagons over, around, and through many of these places by manual labour the turns being too short to be made with the team hitched on.[29]

Travel conditions in Carson Canyon have been so much improved that such old descriptions would seem colorful exaggerations, were they not unanimous in saying how dreadful the canyon was. The obstructions that so intimidated early travelers have been blasted and bulldozed out of the way, and today's blacktop road winds smoothly through the canyon. The car roof keeps most travelers from even noticing the canyon walls that so greatly oppressed travelers like Sarah Royce: "As the cañon narrowed, the rocky walls towered nearly perpendicular, hundreds of feet; and seemed in some places almost to meet above our heads."[30]

Despite the impediments, most emigrants got through Carson Canyon in one day, and their reward was Hope Valley, a relatively flat grassy intermontane valley at 7,000 feet. Many emigrants found this a good place to rest for a day, though late in the season they were likely to want to push right on through. At the south end of Hope Valley, about 5 miles farther on, was Red Lake, and there the going got difficult again. The problem here was simple steepness. The elevation gain from the lake to Carson Pass was only about 800 feet, but the climb was arduous.

> Immediately after passing [Red Lake] we came to the foot of an immense elevation. We first looked at the high, steep and rough mountain road, then at the wagons, and then at the mules, and lastly we looked at one another, but twas no use looking; the work had to be done.[31]

What the work was like is related by another.

> We have to go nearly (that is the general direction) strait up it winding first
> to the right & then to the left, gaining by gradual approaches. Large trees
> have been fell to the ground & a kind of road made above it by throwing
> brush & dirt on it, to gain the upper side of some large stone which forms a
> kind of road again until another turn can be effected. We have to lift our wag-
> ons round frequently and make a square tact to the right or left. Many of the
> places have such perpendicular falls, that, if a mule were thrown off or wagon
> & team they would fall from 50 to 100 feet without touching anything.[32]

Eventually Carson Pass was reached, and from there the trail descended easily, about 900 feet in 4 miles, to a body of water variously
known as Summit Lake, Mountain Lake, Clear Lake, and Twin Lakes.
There seem to have been two lakes in this location, in dry years at least,
with an intervening strip of land that served emigrants as a causeway.
(The two lakes have been raised and consolidated into one by a dam to
form a Pacific Gas & Electric reservoir now known as Caples Lake.)

> This is a handsome Valley with several beautiful little streams putting in from
> the mountains and running through it, emptying their waters into a beauti-
> ful Lake. . . . Here we found good grass & encamped for the day at the foot
> of the next high ridge of Mountains that we have to ascend.[33]

This was another place to take a well-earned rest.

> [We] camped for the night upon the shores of Mountain Lake, where the
> mules and Horses fared well upon good mountain grass. This encampment
> was in a beautiful place, high Towering mountains surrounding a beautiful
> Lake upon whose banks the green grass grew so bountifully, and where the
> tall pine trees gave us such a welcome shade. There were many lying in camp
> about us; feeding their teams and making preparations for the ascent of the
> second and last summit.[34]

The 3-mile climb from Caples Lake to West Pass is steep, but it is not
as arduous as the climb up from Red Lake, and many diarists reported
that with an early morning start they could reach the top by midday. Farther back in their journey from Missouri, emigrants had marveled at seeing snow in the middle of the summer, but it had always been off in the
distance on mountain slopes. Now for the first time on the trip they found
themselves slogging right through it.

> Near the top is a large snow bank, the melting of which makes the ground
> very swampy just below it. After we had gained the summit we were then in
> the region of perpetual snows. We were forced to drive our teams across one
> of these banks of snow that must have been 20 or 30 feet deep.[35]

We are now ascending the second summit and have to pass over a great
quantity of snow almost perpendicular the horses sinking almost up to their
bodies in the snow.[36]

Some emigrants enjoyed the novelty of this alpine experience.

We soon got ready for our mountain excursion, and started upward amid the
tall pines and large rocks, the latter impeeded our progress at first, but the
higher we got the scarcer they became, untill at length the road got quite
smooth. We left camp at 8 in the morning and reached the summit at 12
oclock, passing by the side of a tremendous snow bank near the highest point
of elevation. Here is mountain country to our hearts content, great banks of
snow, large and sterile rocks. . . . We have now lifted ourselves to a great elevation, thousands of feet above the great desert we have left so far behind,
and were it not that these mountains are topped off with such high and lofty
peaks, and so many of them, we could see and traverse with eye, many a weary
mile of our late travel, but as it is, so many rocks, trees and lofty peaks inter-
vene, our vision reached but little way. But as the scene around us is so very
interesting we have plenty to employ our eyesight.[37]

Few others, however, showed the geographic sensibility of Sarah Royce
(mother of the philosopher Josiah Royce, to be born a few years later in
Grass Valley):

I had purposely hastened, that morning, to start ahead of the rest; and not
far from noon, I was rewarded by coming out, in advance of all the others,
on a rocky height whence I looked, *down,* far over constantly descending
hills, to where a soft haze sent up a warm, rosey glow that seemed to me a
smile of welcome; while beyond, occasional faint outlines of other mountains
appeared; and I knew I was looking across the Sacramento Valley.[38]

The westbound trail descending from West Pass ran along the top of
Squaw Ridge, south of Silver Lake, and remained above 8,000 feet for
at least 10 miles, affording panoramic views north to Pyramid Peak and
south along the main range of the Sierra toward Yosemite.

We are now upon the topmost ridges of the Sierra Nevada Mountains. Language is inadequate to describe, the striking contrast between this grand and
magnificent Alpine and Elysian Scenery. Nothing in nature I am sure can present Scenery more wild, more rugged more bold, more grand, more romantic, and picturesquely beautiful than this mountain scenery. The tall craggy
rocks that would discover themselves as walls on either side of the deep
Canons & Gorges that would lead off, from the snowy peaks (in which we
would frequently discover small Lakes or basons, into which the waters
teemcd) Would prcscnt an interest to the admirer of nature which he would
scearce get tired of dwelling upon. While upon the other Slope of the mountain: the umbrageous foliage of the tall and stately pines, furrs and cedars,

deepening in verdue, and density as the forest approaches the more gentle and grassy slopes, presenting a most liveing landscape until they gradually recede from the view. The tops of thise mountains are Carpted with a heavy coat of fine bladed green Blue Grass. And along the small branches many kinds of wild flowers are to be found. These contributed in calling to mind assosiations which melted the sensibilities blunted as they were by long exposier by heardships and privations, and forced upon the memory the endearments of home, & the pleasures of civilization.[39]

A few miles farther along to the west, the spring where the three scouts of the 1848 Mormon party were mysteriously murdered was a landmark along the trail, though the details of the event had become somewhat blurred in the retelling: "Camped near sundown at Tragedy Springs, so called from the circumstances of two white men being murdered by Indians near the spot."[40]

After the Carson route was established by Chiles and others in 1848, it rapidly became the leading route across the Sierra. One register of the arrivals in the summer of 1854 showed 808 wagons, 30,015 head of cattle, 1,903 horses and mules, and 8,550 sheep.[41]

Difficulties of the Carson Route

As a summer-only wagon entryway to California, the Carson route was not easy, but it was easier than any other route among those that gave direct access to the goldfields. Though Beckwourth Pass and the Nobles routes (see below) might be less difficult, they did not bring the traveler down out of the mountains right into the middle of the gold diggings.

Some of the hard places could be, and were, smoothed by the construction techniques of the time; Carson Canyon began to attract such efforts from the early 1850s. But the problem of the climb up from Red Lake was really solved only a century later by blasting a completely new grade out of the mountain wall on the other side of the lake. And nothing was ever done about the climb up to West Pass and the long, slow descent along Squaw Ridge. Only steady use by commercial vehicles such as freight wagons and stagecoaches could have paid for serious improvements on those heights, but the Carson route posed one insuperable obstacle to year-round commercial traffic: a very long snow season. Thirty-five miles of it were over 7,000 feet, with 13 miles above 8,000 feet and 3 miles above 9,000 feet in the vicinity of West Pass. This meant long stretches where snow lay deep well into the summer.

Remnant snowbanks were more of an inconvenience than a hazard for summer emigrant traffic, but they provided a powerful reminder of what the area must be like during the winter. When mining and trade east of the Sierra increased demand for two-way, year-round transportation, it was obvious that a less snow-clogged route would have to be found.

The Carson route dwindled in importance as better routes were opened up during the 1850s, but before West Pass fell into complete disuse it had been the scene of the struggles of tens of thousands of emigrants. In 1862 the Amador and Nevada Wagon Road was constructed around rather than over Carson Spur, along the line of today's Highway 88. Along with the pass itself, close to 20 miles of the old emigrant trail were abandoned, left to suffer the slow erasures of nature rather than the more vigorous ones of transportation improvements, which have made it impossible to trace the exact route over Donner Pass. Today the 20 miles of the old trail over West Pass can be explored on foot, and the experienced eye can still detect traces of that immense traffic of a century and a half ago.

From Tragedy Spring west to Corral Flat, Highway 88 is approximately congruent with the emigrant route for about 5 miles. At Corral Flat the emigrant route turned somewhat to the northwest and followed Iron Mountain Ridge to Sly Park, approximating the alignment of today's two-lane blacktop aptly named Mormon Emigrant Trail. Highway 88, descendant of the Amador and Nevada Wagon Road, heads off southwest from Corral Flat to the Amador County mining districts around Jackson and Sutter Creek.

CHAPTER 4

Local Initiatives in Road Building

B efore the gold rush most emigrants to California were on a one-way trip, moving themselves and their goods to California with the intention of settling down there. For this they needed only the rudiments of a road, just enough to allow passage of a team and wagon at something like 15 miles per day. They might complain bitterly about arduous slopes and treacherous fords, but there was little effective demand for improved roads, simply because most emigrants did not expect to pass that way again.

The gold rush and statehood worked a change in attitude regarding improved roads. At least four groups of Californians had an interest in faster and more reliable transport: homesick recent arrivals, California boosters among the political and business classes, merchants desiring a more reliable supply of goods, and entrepreneurs who foresaw California's economic sway over much of the interior West.

Newer residents of the state, especially single men lured by gold, were less prepared to cut old ties than those, often family groups, who had earlier come out to start a new life. The difficulties, expense, and danger of the trip made such sojourners acutely aware of their isolation and distance from "home." They knew that if communications were left at the same level of organization that had brought them out west, they would be able to do little more than entrust a letter to the occasional eastbound traveler.

California businessmen had a stake in making travel easier for emigrants who were ready to put down roots. A common complaint in the

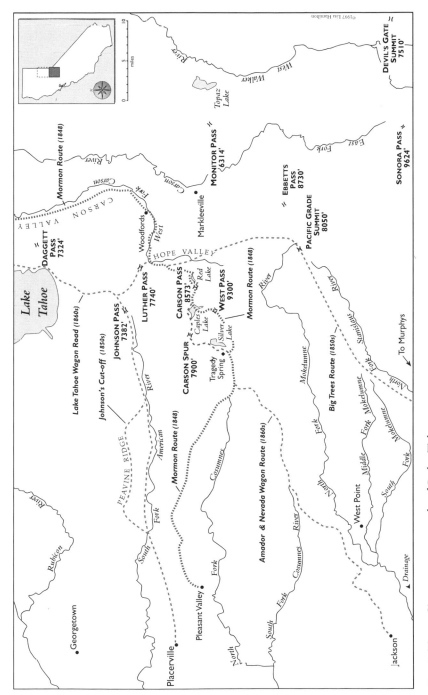

Map 2. Trans-Sierra routes south of Lake Tahoe.

1850s was that the state had entirely too many single male drifters seeking instant wealth and not nearly enough steady workers with families. Better roads, it was thought, would encourage more women and children to come to the state. Sherman Day, the road surveyor and state senator whose activities are reviewed in detail later, put the matter clearly:

> The most important demand of the State is for population—not for such as usually comes to us by sea, composed either of the trading or adventurous classes, whose main object is to make their "pile" and retire; or of the Asiatic race who design, perhaps, to make but a temporary residence, and whose permanent residence is certainly not to be coveted;—but we need precisely that class of population that usually takes the land route—the farmers and the free laborers of the Western States, who bring with them their wives and their little ones, their flocks and herds of cattle, their wagons and working teams, and who, almost from their entrance are ready and able to enter upon the cultivation of the soil, or the development of mineral wealth, and come intending "to dwell in the land."[1]

Merchants whose stock-in-trade consisted largely of goods from the eastern states were always being starved of one kind of commodity and glutted with another because communication was slow and erratic. They were thus eager for improved roads so that they could adjust supply to demand.[2]

By the middle of the 1850s California was becoming an important center with its own periphery of settlement and economic development, eventually as far east as the Colorado Rockies and the Black Hills. There was growing awareness of California's opportunities in the interior west. At first, servicing travelers' needs at trans-Sierra rest stops like Carson Valley created settlements on the east side of the Sierra.[3] In the 1850s the agricultural population of Carson Valley was augmented by mining camps. In 1859 the silver boom on the Comstock Lode and the sudden growth of Virginia City tremendously increased freight, express, and postal traffic over the mountains. Meanwhile the population of Utah had been growing steadily since the first Mormon settlement in 1847. The Denver area boomed with a gold rush at the end of the 1850s. And the plains of Kansas and Nebraska began to fill up as the "Great American Desert" shrank on the Americans' mental map.

Transport by Sea

Roads over the mountains were not the only possible connection between California and the East. The long voyage around South America was an important route for people and freight until the transcontinental railroad was finished in 1869. (For certain kinds of freight, such as grain bound for Europe, ocean shipping around the Horn remained important long after that.)

Another important maritime competitor of the overland route was the combination sea and land journey via the Isthmus of Panama, which actually antedated the gold rush. By act of Congress on March 3, 1847, the secretary of the navy was directed to contract for mail transport twice a month via steamship from New York to Chagres and once a month from Panama to Astoria, Oregon. William Aspinwall of New York took over from the original contractor on November 19, 1847, and incorporated the Pacific Mail Steamship Company on April 12, 1848. Aspinwall later built the Panama Railroad across the isthmus and became the major figure in transportation via Panama. His only serious competitor was Cornelius Vanderbilt, and eventually the two men formed a partnership.[4]

The Pacific Mail Steamship Company remained an important economic and political power in California until the completion of the railroad in 1869 doomed the isthmus route. The firm was viewed by the public, however, as a grasping monopoly offering poor and dangerous service. On September 12, 1857, the ocean steamer *Central America* went down off Florida, with a loss of 423 lives, including James Birch, the California stagecoach magnate, and $8 million in gold. The cause of the disaster was a mysterious engine failure in the middle of a gale.[5] The ill-fated ship belonged to the U.S. Mail Steamship Company, the Atlantic half of the detested monopoly. It is true that this disaster was not typical, being in fact the worst in the two decades of the isthmus route, but there had been other, smaller shipwrecks, and the wreck of the *Central America* inflamed popular opinion. A mass meeting in San Francisco on October 31, 1857, produced resolutions that demanded an end to the monopoly.[6]

Another hazard was the threat to health posed by the trip across Panama. Mysterious tropical fevers lurked in the rain forest and in the towns on either shore where transit passengers waited for ships. The danger was somewhat abated when Aspinwall finished his railroad across the isthmus in 1855. The railroad reduced the trip to four hours from as many days, but the traveler was still taking a chance. For an example we need not look beyond the dramatis personae of this book. The brilliant career of Theodore D. Judah, tireless promoter of the Pacific railroad and the man who surveyed its course over the Sierra, was cut short at the age of thirty-eight when Judah contracted typhoid fever while crossing

Panama on a trip to New York. And this happened at the relatively late date of 1863, when the isthmian passage had become routine.

This is not to say that there were no dangers on the overland route, for there were many, including diseases, such as cholera, that could be as deadly as any in Panama. But just as there are people today whose fear of flying leads them to undertake long automobile journeys instead, heedless of highway mortality, so there must have been many who unhesitatingly chose the dangers and hardships of the overland journey rather than commit their lives to the open sea.

For all these reasons the prospect of improved transportation across the Sierra Nevada was a matter of intense public interest in California from the earliest days, and remained so until the long-delayed transcontinental railroad became a reality in 1869. One has only to look through the main San Francisco or Sacramento newspapers from the 1850s and 1860s to notice the space devoted to transportation matters: reports on weather conditions affecting movement across the mountains, actual or threatened Indian disruptions, new routes, changes in the schedules of stage and express services, proposals for new road surveys, progress of construction on old ones, and so forth. The stagecoach station seems to have been the beat of at least one reporter on every paper, for routine arrivals and departures were covered, complete with the names of passengers and anecdotes about anything out of the ordinary.

The First Overland Mail

The first overland mail shipment may be said to have left the West Coast on April 17, 1848, when military authorities in San Francisco sent Kit Carson east with dispatches. Regularly scheduled overland service had to wait another three years. On January 27, 1851, the U.S. Post Office advertised that it would accept bids for a contract to carry mail on horseback between California and Salt Lake, via Carson Valley. George Chorpenning and Absolom Woodward submitted the lowest of thirty-seven bids, a modest $14,000 a year, and on April 25, 1851, they signed a contract with the Post Office, to run until June 30, 1854. Trips were to be made monthly, within thirty days' travel time one way. On May 1, 1851, Chorpenning left Sacramento for Salt Lake with the first mailbag to cross the continent.[7] This was the first scheduled transportation of any kind across the Sierra Nevada.

On his first trip Chorpenning encountered snowdrifts 15 miles above Placerville, which suggests that he used the Carson Pass emigrant trail. He described the rigors of traversing them: "By tramping and beating the snow down with wooden mauls made for the purpose, we could open a trail for our animals, and we were enabled to travel from six to eight miles per day."[8] This can be compared with the two to three days it took to make the whole trip from Placerville to Carson Valley in the summer.

This first trans-Sierra mail service cannot be counted a great success. Chorpenning and Woodward had run-ins with Indians in the summer of 1851, and Woodward was killed by Indians in November. In December and January heavy snow blocked service completely. The February 1852 mail went via the Feather River Valley and reached Salt Lake only with great difficulty. Chorpenning sent the March mail via ship to San Pedro and thence overland to Salt Lake via Cajon Pass and the Mojave Desert. In the summer of 1852 he was back on the central overland route, but that winter he returned to the warmer and drier southern route, maintaining service to Carson Valley by employing the redoubtable Snowshoe Thompson. In the summer of 1853 he returned to the central route, and again went back south in the winter. When Chorpenning's contract expired in the summer of 1854, he gave up on the central route entirely, bid successfully on the San Diego/Salt Lake route, and moved operations there year-round.[9]

Chorpenning's troubles on the Carson route were well publicized, and his experience was a clear indication, if any were needed, that emigrant wagon roads used in summer would not suffice for year-round travel in both directions. Improvements to existing emigrant roads were pointless, since they would continue to be buried in snow every winter. Could some better way through the mountains be found?

A new route was partly a matter of finding a lower pass, but the snow problem involved considerations other than elevation alone. Ridges might get more snow than adjacent valleys yet benefit from the scouring effects of winds. On shaded northern slopes snow lay deeper and longer into the spring than at higher elevations facing south. Staying low by running along a river at the bottom of a canyon was a way of minimizing snow problems but would necessitate earthmoving operations in narrow canyons and building bridges over tributary streams, which would be expensive. All in all, establishing a year-round road would require a higher level of organization and investment, such as a professional survey and at least semiprofessional construction work, than had been devoted to road building in the mountains up to this point. It would be a project full of opportunities for business and political entrepreneurs.

California Express and Stagecoach Firms

Entrepreneurs with the greatest interest in improving roads over the mountains were probably those in the express and stagecoach businesses. Both types of enterprise had sprouted in California almost at the beginning of the gold rush. Gold miners could use dust and nuggets as a medium of exchange in the gold camps, but many wanted to send money home or convert their gleanings into a more standardized medium such as gold coin. They craved mail from home but grudged the lengthy absences from their claims that a trip to the nearest post office might require. This was where the expressman came in.

The first of these businesses was that of Alexander H. Todd, in operation as early as the summer of 1849, and soon there were many others. Little capital was required to get into the express business in the early days, basically a team of horses and a wagon, or even a single pack mule. An express entrepreneur had only to show up at an unserved gold camp, get the names of people who were expecting letters at the nearest post office, and collect outgoing letters and gold dust for delivery to banks. He might also take orders for town goods if he had the capacity for transporting them back.

An initial period of competition among many small express operators was followed by consolidation into fewer and larger firms, which could offer a wider range of services. In 1851 Todd sold his interests to Newell & Company, which later became the Stockton agents for Adams & Company, a New York–based firm that was on its way to dominating the California express business. Todd started another concern and then sold out to Wells Fargo, soon to be Adams's chief competitor.[10]

The two express companies had had similar beginnings back east. Alvin Adams got his start carrying valuable documents back and forth between Boston and New York in 1840. In 1850 Adams & Company set up a California subsidiary that went after the gold rush express business with vigor. The fact that it could provide through service from California gold camps to East Coast financial centers under one management gave it an edge over smaller California companies, many of which eventually gave up and sold out to Adams. By 1852 Adams & Company was a $12 million concern, with an early version of the pony express linking San Francisco to the larger gold camps, a semimonthly accompanied gold shipment via the isthmus to New York, and its own banking business. That year it built San Francisco's first stone office building, the Parrott Building, at the northwest corner of California and Montgomery streets, and soon was regarded as the leading business firm in California.

The beginnings of Wells Fargo were as humble as those of Adams & Company. In 1841 Henry Wells started an express service between Albany and Buffalo, carrying packages himself. He brought William Fargo into the business as a messenger in 1843 and made him partner in 1845. By this time their service area extended as far west as Cincinnati and Chicago. The partnership prospered and in 1850 merged with an express service in New York City operated by John Butterfield, who had started in the business in much the same small way as Adams, Wells, and Fargo. The merged firm was called American Express.

Fargo and Wells wanted American Express to expand to California and take advantage of business opportunities created by the gold rush, but Butterfield and other directors balked at the idea, thinking it too risky: Adams & Company was known to be already well established there. Fargo and Wells then found financial backers in New York and set up their own firm on the side, without leaving American Express. The sole purpose of Wells, Fargo & Company was to enter the express business on the West Coast. The firm opened its first office in San Francisco in July 1852.[11] Henry Wells, who made a single inspection trip to San Francisco, and William Fargo, who never saw the West at all, ran the business from New York through trusted agents. From early on the company offered a wide range of banking and express services. Through aggressive management and by undercutting Adams's rates, it prospered.[12] One by one, the firm of Wells Fargo bought out other express operations in California, much as Adams was doing. In 1855 Wells Fargo had twenty-four branch offices, and Adams was its only serious rival.

At that time the leading bank in San Francisco was Page, Bacon & Company, and it was closely associated with Adams & Company. The two firms shared the Parrott Building. News arrived in San Francisco on February 18, 1855, that Page Bacon's parent bank in St. Louis had failed after overspeculation in railroad construction. It was known that the San Francisco branch had sent large amounts of gold to St. Louis, and many feared that the branch might not be able to cover local deposits. The fears were well founded. In the ensuing bank panic both Page

Bacon and Adams were bankrupted. In contrast, Wells Fargo was able to cover its deposits and survived the panic with remaining cash assets of more than $100,000. Wells Fargo took over the Parrott Building and went on to dominate San Francisco banking and the California express business for decades.[13]

As the express business had grown during the 1850s so had stage-coaching. The two were symbiotic but distinct fields of enterprise. Many small stagecoach lines came into being early in the American period, as soon as the coaches could be shipped around the Horn to San Francisco. The leading man in staging was James Birch, who came to California in 1849 from Providence, Rhode Island, at the age of twenty-one. Birch had learned the business in New England and promptly launched his West Coast career in Sacramento by buying a freight wagon and carrying men to the mines. A man of great enterprise and energy, Birch began to buy out small stage operators in the Central Valley and the gold country. By the end of five years he had acquired most of the stagecoach lines in California and consolidated them into the California Stage Company, which he directed from Sacramento.[14] When Wells Fargo achieved a virtual monopoly of the express business in California, it did so not by operating stagecoaches of its own, though it did have a few, but by sending express shipments on vehicles operated by others, chiefly Birch's organization.

One important line that James Birch did not acquire was the Pioneer Stage Company, started by J. B. Crandall, another transplant from New England. Crandall had been driver and co-proprietor of one of California's first stagecoach lines, which operated between San Francisco and San Jose in 1850. The following year he launched the Pioneer Stage, to run between Sacramento and Placerville. True to the company name, Crandall was to drive the first stagecoach over the Sierra in 1857. The first later maintained a high level of service between Sacramento and Virginia City along the Lake Tahoe Wagon Road.[15]

The First Made Road: The Johnson Cut-off

In 1852 the first trans-Sierra road entrepreneur appeared. He was John Calhoun Johnson, a rancher near Placerville who had come overland from Ohio to California in 1849. Johnson surveyed and in some rudimentary way cleared a new route between Carson Valley and Placerville, crossing the Sierra between the Truckee route on the north and the Carson route on the south. Known as Johnson's Cut-off, this was the first of a series of roads following approximately the alignment of today's U.S. 50. The great attraction of Johnson's Cut-off was that it crossed the Sierra at summits of about 7,400 feet and about 7,150 feet, considerably lower elevations than the Carson route's 9,500 and 8,573 feet and so less plagued by snow.

In operation by the summer of 1852, the Cut-off had features of both ridge roads and valley roads. Johnson's basic strategy going up from Placerville toward the western summit seems to have been to stay low by following the South Fork of the American River as closely as possible, though to avoid a rocky and tortuous reach of the river he had to go high along Peavine Ridge, on the north side of the river. That portion entailed some steep slopes and snow problems, but it was an unavoidable compromise for a small entrepreneur without access to an earth-moving labor force. Johnson blazed his "road" down off the east end of Peavine Ridge about 4 miles west of Strawberry and then followed the river some 12 miles to its headwaters, making a final steep climb to a saddle in the western summit ridge. This acquired the name Johnson Pass. Many travelers were to comment on the view from this point. Lake Valley lay at their feet, and Lake Tahoe was off in the middle distance about 8 miles away. (U.S. 50 went through Johnson Pass until the present highway over Echo Summit, 7,382 feet, about a mile to the south, was completed some time before 1950.[16] The old road is still maintained for access to summer cabins and Echo Lake.)

Eastbound from Johnson Pass the Cut-off descended steeply about 1,000 feet to Lake Valley and skirted the southeast part of Lake Tahoe, staying away from the lakeshore to avoid rocky spurs alternating with swampy ground. The road climbed the Carson Range to Eagle Ranch Pass, now Spooner Summit (7,146 ft.), at about the midpoint of the east side of the lake, and descended the east side of the Carson Range to the vicinity of today's Carson City. In this way Johnson's road "cut off" most of Carson Valley by crossing its narrow north end, whereas travelers on the emigrant trail had traversed the valley for its entire length.

Johnson's Cut-off was the first trans-Sierra route that was laid out in advance, rather than coming into being through the passage of successive wagons wearing ruts into the ground. The new route had some steep grades, but only 6 miles were above 7,000 feet, compared with 34 miles of the Carson emigrant route. It was shorter was well: 103 miles between

Sacramento and Carson Valley, as opposed to 120.5 miles.[17] Still, calling Johnson's Cut-off a road may be stretching things. One traveler in 1852 described it as "a pack road, a little track like a foot path."[18] Another traveler, John Riker of Piqua, Ohio, left the following account of a passage along it on July 27–28, 1852, westbound from Tahoe Valley toward Placerville:

> Soon after leaving camp we came to a very high mountain, which seemed inaccessible on account of its perpendicularity, together with the immense quantity of detached rocks which literally covers its sides. Presently a trail was discovered, leading towards the summit, which was sufficient evidence that others had passed before us, and why should not we? The ascent was commenced,—from rock to rock we were forced to climb until, weary and worn down by the constant exertions essential to the advancement of our desires to reach the summit, where we arrived in safety. [This is the climb from Tahoe Valley to Johnson Pass.]
>
> I am now quite unwell, which renders traveling a double task to me. After leaving the summit, the road was good for some distance; then we descended another steep and stony mountain to the first waters of the American River [Slippery Ford], down which we followed a short distance, and then began the ascent of another very high mountain [Peavine Ridge], up which we traveled until night put a stop to our toils for the day.[19]

Johnson's Cut-off was an improvement over the Carson route, but it was only a first step toward a road fit for regular stagecoach service. Probably most of the traffic on it was incoming emigrant wagons and pack trains. George Chorpenning does not seem to have been impressed with it as a year-round route. As we have seen, he moved his mail route south in the winter of 1852–53, and again the following winter.

Spontaneous route changes soon occurred, showing how tentative the road system was. As we have seen, Johnson's Cut-off crossed the eastern summit at Eagle Ranch Pass. But before long travelers bound for Carson Valley found that it was easier to turn away from Lake Tahoe after descending from Johnson Pass and push on southeast over Luther Pass (7,740 ft.) to Hope Valley, where they connected with the now well-worn emigrant route. This they followed down through the canyon of the West Fork of the Carson River to Carson Valley. The shift away from Johnson's route seems to have been encouraged by improvements to the old (i.e., three or four years old) road through Carson Canyon, which, as we saw, was infamous for its huge obstructing boulders. These were cleared away, or bridged to some degree, in the early 1850s, apparently by inhabitants of Carson Valley to encourage traffic to come their way.

Improvements in Carson Canyon did not steal away all the traffic from Johnson's Cut-off over Eagle Ranch Pass, however, and both remained in use. To some degree the traveler's choice seems to have turned on tolls. Evidence on tolls is fragmentary and elusive. The facility for which a toll might be charged was not the road as such but rather some improvement such as a bridge or a properly banked and surfaced shortcut. Entrepreneurs who created these improvements might be in business for a single season, pocket the proceeds, and go on to something else.

At various times there were tolls on many routes. According to one account, John Reese and Israel Mott, early settlers near Mormon Station, received a five-year franchise from Utah Territory on December 1, 1852, to build a bridge over the Carson River and charge a toll for its use. They were expected to keep the canyon road in repair and to spend $1,000 for this purpose over five years. Toll road segments through Carson Canyon remained in business until the late 1870s, according to one source.[20] But according to another account the competition of Johnson's Cut-off made the inhabitants of Carson Valley worry about losing traffic, and this would create pressure against tolls. There must have been a chronic conflict of interest pitting toll road entrepreneurs against local businessmen who would thrive on the increased traffic a free road would attract. Residents of Carson Valley met on November 11, 1854, and decided that the road through Carson Canyon should be a free road, that a company collecting tolls should be requested to stop, and that maintenance should be paid for from taxes.[21]

Public Roads

The summer of 1853 saw the beginning of what might be called public sector involvement with the trans-Sierra roads question. In July a citizens' meeting at the Empire Hotel in Placerville appointed a committee to obtain subscriptions for making Johnson's Cut-off the best road between Carson Valley and California. The committee raised $1,600 in three days and sent a party of sixteen men with equipment to blast and grade what were said, optimistically, to be "the only two bad places" on the route. Three weeks later the men returned, having improved the road enough to aid a large number of emigrants finding their way into California.[22]

Placerville would never be able to attract all the traffic, however. Routes crossing the Sierra near Lake Tahoe were inconveniently far north for the booming southern mines around Sonora and Columbia, which organized their own efforts at road building. Columbia showed initiative in the summer of 1852 by bringing in emigrant parties on what they proclaimed the Walker River Emigrant Road. An item in the *Sacramento Daily Union* in September described the arrival of fourteen mule-drawn wagons with seventy-five emigrants from Ohio and Indiana. A deputation of Columbia citizens met them at the head of the Tuolumne and brought them down a road along the divide between the Stanislaus and Tuolumne rivers, a road described by the correspondent as one that "could be rendered good with a little labor." When they arrived in Columbia the weary travelers were welcome with a public dinner, complete with speeches by local notables.[23]

The same summer citizens of nearby Sonora went even further to attract emigrants to this route. They subscribed funds to support a relief party for struggling emigrants and sent out their mayor to Humboldt Sink to draw in wagon trains over what they called Sonora Pass. The Sonora delegation did attract some emigrants over this new route, which crossed the crest somewhat to the south of what is called Sonora Pass today.

Despite great difficulties the Sonora route attracted a lot of traffic in the following year, 1853. A correspondent of the *Daily Alta California* stationed at Relief Camp west of the pass reported on October 30 that "475 wagons, 1900 souls, and 15,000 head of cattle" had passed by since September 25. He added that he was leaving the spot, as snow was falling and the travel season appeared to be over.[24] He did not report what state of mind the 1,900 souls were in. In fact, emigrants experienced serious difficulties with the steep slopes on this road, and its heavy use in 1853 must be credited to the selling job carried out by the major and his delegation and to the fact that the flow of discouraging trail information in an easterly direction was too slow to deter parties following behind. The October snow caught some of them still on the trail and almost brought disaster. Over the winter there was plenty of time for word of these difficulties to reach the eastern United States by ship, and traffic on the Walker River Emigrant Road declined sharply in following years. (West of Pinecrest, the Walker River Emigrant Road closely approximated the alignment of today's California 108, but east of there it passed through what is now the Emigrant Wilderness and crossed the Sierra crest at Emigrant Pass, several miles to the south of California 108.)

At least three other towns near the western slope of the Sierra—Marysville, Sacramento, and Georgetown—also began to make efforts to draw in new residents. Civil rivalry had much influence on road projects. Local businessmen and promoters pushed projects for roads to attract emigrants and benefit their own towns and counties. Towns sent out promotion agents to woo emigrants still toiling through the valley of the Humboldt. The Placerville *Herald*'s Carson Valley correspondent sent in a warning about this practice.

> Couldn't you Placervillians send some good truthful men out here to represent your interest in some way? There are several "runners" on the Humboldt, who are praising up Marysville, and the Truckee route, and any number of traders can be found in Carson Valley who praise up the Volcano route, and both at the expense of the old Carson route to Placerville. You had better look to your interest.[25]

Ebbetts Pass

About midway between Carson Pass and Sonora Pass is Ebbetts Pass, 8,730 feet, now traversed by State Highway 4. No road was built through this pass until 1863, although the Big Trees route, which is considered in the next chapter, came within a few miles of it.

Ebbetts Pass was put on the map as the result of an 1853 expedition led by "Major" John Ebbetts. Ebbetts was backed by a group of San Franciscans who had formed the Atlantic & Pacific Company. This enterprise held three public meetings, in August, September, and October 1853, to voice dissatisfaction with Jefferson Davis's refusal to consider a route over the central Sierra Nevada in his instructions to the Pacific Railroad Survey. The company resolved to build a rail connection from San Francisco to join with Thomas Hart Benton's proposed line through what is now southern Colorado, Utah, and Nevada to Walker Pass. The meetings raised enough money to send Ebbetts out to locate a route between San Francisco Bay and the Virgin River of southern Utah, somewhere in the neighborhood of Las Vegas, which was expected to be a point on the Benton line.[26]

The Atlantic & Pacific Company chose Ebbetts to lead the expedition because he had crossed the Sierra crest with mules on a prospecting expedition in April 1850 from the headwaters of the Mokelumne to those of the East Carson, over a pass that he found free of snow. His instructions were to explore "toward the head of the Stanislaus, penetrating the Sierra at the 'most available point,' . . . returning, if possible, via the headwaters of the Tuolumne."[27]

The Ebbetts party left Stockton on October 7, 1853, and headed east up the Sonora route. This was the year that so many emigrant parties were in trouble as a result of overblown promotion by the mayor of Sonora, and the difficulty of this route made an impression on Ebbetts. His trip diary contains many references to remnants of abandoned wagons and dead livestock. Twelve days into the trip he lost patience with the Sonora boomers who had seen him and his party off: "road strewn with dead cattle, horses, remnants of wagons, & c.; in fact this route is the worst that could possibly be found; it is called the Walker river route, and I advise no emigrants to take it when others so far preferable are known."[28]

After crossing the Sierra at Emigrant Pass, the Ebbetts party passed down the valley of the West Walker River to Wellington, Nevada, and eventually to the termination of the Walker River in Walker Lake. On October 21, while in Antelope Valley on the upper West Walker River, Ebbetts and George Henry Goddard, his assistant engineer, climbed Antelope Peak (10,241 ft.), and from there Ebbetts identified a pass to the northwest as the one he had crossed in April 1851 and found free of snow. He said it might be 2,000 feet lower than the one they had just used. According to Goddard this was what later became known as Ebbetts Pass.

It is claimed, however, that intervening ridges make it impossible to see Ebbetts Pass from the top of Antelope Peak and that Ebbetts must have been pointing to a nearby pass that connects the head of the Mokelumne with the Wolf Creek tributary of the East Carson.[29] In any case, it is clear that Ebbetts thought there was a low pass suitable for a railroad *somewhere* in the vicinity of what we now call Ebbetts Pass, and this erroneous notion persisted for a few years. Ebbetts decided to save the pass for detailed exploration later and turned the group southeast to look for a feasible rail alignment through the basins and ranges of what is now southern Nevada.

They explored far to the southeast before returning to the east side of the Sierra Nevada in Carson Valley, where they joined the established emigrant trail. Ebbetts returned to Placerville via Johnson's Cut-off and left Goddard in Carson Valley to recuperate the mules. Goddard decided that the pass he and Ebbetts had seen from Antelope Peak must be the "lowest and easiest of access between the 37th and 39th parallels" and that he would spend the winter in Carson Valley an explore this "Ebbetts' Pass" as the weather allowed. But Ebbetts sent back word that for the moment Johnson Pass offered no obstacles to winter travel and that Goddard should push on across the mountain at once.[30] Goddard thus missed his chance to explore the new pass. So did Ebbetts; he was killed in a steamboat explosion on San Francisco Bay soon after his return.

The Ebbetts expedition did not establish a significant route across the Sierra, but it did add to geographic knowledge of the range. It also launched the surveying career of George Henry Goddard, until then a struggling artist and architect. Goddard had arrived from England at the age of thirty-three, and spent the rest of his long and active life in California. He was the cartographer of the first map of California to be based on actual surveys (now usually referred to as the Britton and Rey map, after the publishers). We will meet him again later as a surveyor of a state road through Johnson Pass in 1855 and of a road from the Feather River to Beckwourth Pass in 1856. He also worked with Theodore Judah in surveying possible routes for the Pacific railroad. Goddard would probably be better known today if his large collection of maps, drawings, and natural history specimens, the result of extensive travels throughout California, had not been lost in the San Francisco earthquake and fire of 1906.[31]

Henness Pass

The northern mines, in the Bear, Yuba, and Feather River valleys, were, like the southern mines, inconveniently far from the centrally located Truckee and Carson routes. In the early 1850s gold seekers found a more direct way to enter this region. Leaving the Truckee route in Dog Valley, they went west along the valleys of Davies Creek and the Little Truckee River, a landscape of open vegetation in which sagebrush and pine predominated, and without too many steep slopes. At the head of the Little Truckee they traversed an inconspicuous summit to the headwaters of Pass Creek, a tributary of the Middle Fork of the Yuba River.

The summit, which acquired the name Henness Pass, was, at 6,842 feet, a remarkably easy crossing of the continental divide between the Great Basin and the Pacific slope. But to the west remained many miles of ridge road down to the diggings. The main Henness Pass route came down the ridge between the North and Middle forks of the Yuba River, passing through North San Juan and eventually on to Marysville. At Jackson Meadows, 8 miles west of the pass, another trail branched off and descended the ridge between the Middle and South forks of the Yuba to Nevada City and Grass Valley. Further bifurcations of these trails led to various mining camps in the rugged hill country of Nevada and Sierra counties. (Jackson Meadows today is covered by the waters of Jackson Meadows Reservoir, owned by the Nevada Irrigation District.)

Through the 1850s Henness Pass remained primarily a route for emigrants who were heading for the northern mines. It was not the beneficiary of any organized attempts at improvement and as late as

1859, according to the memoirs of an early settler in the area, was still "nothing but an emigrant road and an extremely poor one at that."[32] Not until the Comstock silver rush was there effective interest in upgrading the Henness route to a two-story stagecoach road.

Beckwourth Pass

North of the Henness Pass route was an even lower shortcut from the Great Basin to the northern mines: Beckwourth Pass, at 5,212 feet. But describing Beckwourth as a pass across the Sierra requires even more qualification than is necessary for Henness Pass. Beckwourth is the lowest pass from the Great Basin into the Sacramento Valley, but in this region the watershed divide between the Sacramento Valley and the Great Basin is far east of the main mass of the Sierra. Beckwourth Pass leads west into broad, flat-bottomed Sierra Valley, which is still east of the Sierra crest but is drained by the Middle Fork of the Feather River through a deep gorge down to the Central Valley.[33]

Discovery of this pass is usually credited to James Beckwourth, in the spring of 1851, and part of the interest of the route comes from the picaresque figure of Beckwourth himself. He was born in 1798 in Virginia, the son of planter Jennings "Beckwith" and a slave woman of mixed race. He established a reputation as a trapper, lived for several years with the Crow Indians, and claimed to have become one of their war chiefs. In 1851 he led the first immigrant party across the pass named for him. In that party was the poet Ina Coolbrith, then ten years old, who recalled him later:

> [He was] one of the most beautiful creatures that ever lived. He was rather dark and wore his hair in two long braids, twisted with colored cord that gave him a picturesque appearance. He wore a leather coat and moccasins and rode his horse without a saddle. . . . And when Jim Beckwourth said he would like to have my mother's little girls ride into California on his horse in front of him, I was the happiest little girl in the world.[34]

In 1851 Beckwourth entered into a partnership with businessmen in Marysville, Oroville, and Quincy to develop a route from Truckee Meadows through Beckwourth Pass, Sierra Valley, and Long Valley to the Quincy area. West of Quincy a trail into the Sacramento Valley was already in use, passing down the ridge between the Middle and North forks of the Feather River, crossing the Middle Fork at Bidwell Bar, and going on to Marysville.[35] The east side of Beckwourth Pass was easily accessible from Truckee Meadows, 28 miles away via Long Valley and a low pass across the Granite Hills.

Beckwourth successfully promoted this approach to Marysville among emigrants arriving at Truckee Meadows, but fate cut short his efforts. Marysville suffered a major conflagration, and Beckwourth's backers were burned out before he was paid. Dejected and swearing never again to pioneer a road without being paid for it, Beckwourth went back to Sierra Valley, where as the first settler he opened a store and inn catering to the emigrant trade.[36] Beckwourth Pass was most active from 1851 to 1856. Like the Henness Pass route, however, it brought emigrants down into what was then the northern periphery of the active gold mining region and so failed to draw such large numbers as the routes south of Lake Tahoe.

Beckwourth Pass was so far east that it fed at least two other routes to the Central Valley, though these remained fairly minor in terms of numbers of travelers. The first was a route from the pass southwest across Sierra Valley and over the mountains to Downieville (approximately along the line of today's Highway 49), which was promoted by a Downieville resident, A. P. Chapman.[37] The other was a shortcut to Marysville through the Johnsville mining district (now Plumas Eureka State Park) and down the Gibsonville Ridge separating the South Fork of the Feather from the North Fork of the Yuba. Goddard surveyed the northern part of this second route in late August 1856 and found it steep in places but capable of much improvement at the cost of only some $3,000. He took elevations and found many stretches of the road to be over 6,000 feet and thus susceptible to snow problems. There is no sign that he recommended this as a major transmountain thoroughfare.[38]

On the whole it seems safe to say that Beckwourth Pass, despite its low elevation, was used primarily by emigrants bound for the backcountry mining and ranching districts of interior northern California. It was only after the wagon and stagecoach era that Beckwourth Pass became a major gateway to the state. In 1909 the second trans-Sierra railroad, the Western Pacific, today part of the Union Pacific, built its line from San Francisco to Salt Lake City through the pass. Today it is also traversed by State Highway 70, putting Beckwourth Pass on the most direct route between the Pacific Northwest and Reno.

The Nobles Routes

As we have seen, reaching California by going all the way around the Sierra on the north was attempted as early as 1843, when Joseph Chiles took a detachment west from Fort Hall across what is now southeastern Oregon, leaving the rest of the party with Joseph Walker to follow the Humboldt route. Chiles followed the Oregon Trail along the Snake River to the vicinity of Boise, Idaho, and then cut across the northwest corner of the Great Basin. The Chiles party got through but discovered no easy route that attracted others in their footsteps.

The idea of using the Humboldt as a way of getting across most of the Great Basin and then making a detour around the Sierra on the north continued to attract explorers. In 1846 Jesse Applegate led a party in blazing a trail intended to give emigrants an easier way into Oregon than the existing trails through the Columbia gorge or south of Mount Hood. The Applegate party cut across from the Willamette Valley of Oregon southeast to the Humboldt near today's Rye Patch Reservoir between Winnemucca and Lovelock, Nevada.

Applegate's aim was to make it easier to get to Oregon, but California-bound travelers tried to take advantage of part of the trail his party had blazed. In 1848 Peter Lassen, a Dane who had arrived in California by sea in 1840 and acquired a land grant in the northern Sacramento Valley, took a notion to bring in emigrants to his land and set himself up in the baronial style of John Sutter. Lassen was somewhat familiar with northeastern California, and his idea was to follow the Applegate Trail from the Humboldt through Fandango Pass in the Warner Range and then leave it to angle back to the southwest. In the summer of 1848 he journeyed east to a point on the Humboldt, apparently after crossing the Sierra via the Truckee route rather than by giving his own route a trial run in reverse (which might have saved him a lot of trouble later), and intercepted some emigrants whom he persuaded to take his "shortcut" to the Central Valley.

Traveling west somewhere along the Humboldt, Lassen and his followers met Henry Bigler and an eastbound Mormon party (discussed in chapter 3). After that meeting they left the Humboldt at what became known as Lassen's Meadows, now the site of Rye Patch Reservoir, and set out on the Applegate Trail. Lassen's mental map was defective; he greatly underestimated how far out of the way to the north this route would take them and failed to realize that it would be vastly shorter and easier to head southwest from the Black Rock Desert. The first half of the trip, as far as the Warner Range, went well, since they had the Applegate Trail to follow, but the second half was almost a disaster. Lassen did not know where he was going, and the party was saved only when a large well-provisioned group of gold seekers from Oregon overtook them and provided food. The Lassen party reached the Sacramento Valley in late October.

One might think that Lassen would have quit while he was ahead—members of his party were muttering about hanging him when the Oregon party showed up—but he quickly recovered his confidence and somehow managed to convince some of the party to sign a statement praising him and his route, the Lassen-Applegate Trail. This was published back east in time for the 1849 travel season, so many travelers in the gold rush year had the idea that there was a cutoff in the vicinity of Lassen's Meadows. The first part of the migration ignored it and headed on toward Humboldt Sink. But on August 11, 1849, an influential party chief named Milton McGee turned off onto the Lassen route and was then followed by thousands of others. Thus a large segment went so far out of their way that they were still on the road when winter weather struck, and a rescue operation had to be mounted from San Francisco.[39]

After this well-publicized fiasco, the Lassen route was thoroughly discredited and little used. But the concept of going around the north end of the Sierra still attracted road entrepreneurs. In 1851 a miner named William H. Nobles pioneered a more sensible route from Lassen's Meadows on the Humboldt to the north end of the Sacramento Valley. He followed the Applegate Trail as far as Black Rock but then turned southwest through the Black Rock Desert and the Smoke Creek Desert to Honey Lake Valley, later the site of Susanville. Thus far Nobles's work consisted chiefly in finding a line of reliable springs, since the country was relatively level and with sparse vegetation, offering little difficulty to wagons. West of Susanville the route traversed more rugged and wooded country as it cut closely around the north side of Mount Lassen. Even so, the slopes were not as steep as on routes near Lake Tahoe, and the high point was under 6,000 feet.

Since Mount Lassen marks the south end of the Cascades, the Nobles route is only a marginal member of the set of trans-Sierra roads. But it is important for us because from the viewpoint of emigrants, it offered a way out of the Great Basin and over the mountains to the Central Valley of California. In 1856 the route was shortened by the discovery of a spring that allowed a cutoff straight west along the south edge of the Black Rock Desert. The Nobles route was vigorously promoted by the town of Shasta. (Then an important gold town, it died when the railroad built through Redding, 6 miles to the east. Remnants survive as a state historic park.) This was perhaps the easiest overland route to the Central Valley and did get some use in the 1850s and 1860s. But it was a very indirect route to the principal gold diggings and main population centers of the state. (The Nobles route between Susanville and Redding approximates today's Highway 44, although the wagon road cut in considerably closer to Lassen Peak than the modern road does. Segments of it are now an attraction in Lassen Volcanic National Park. East of Honey Lake Valley toward the Humboldt the line of the Nobles route is approximated by unpaved county and ranch roads.)

CHAPTER 5

State Government
Road Measures

The early 1850s had seen competitive road improvement efforts by ad hoc coalitions of local government and businessmen trying to attract emigrants to their corner of California. A new chapter in Sierra Nevada transportation development opened toward the end of 1854 when Californians began to exert pressure on the state government to play a role in surveying and constructing roads. The business decisions of George Chorpenning, who in the early 1850s had provided northern California's monthly overland mail link to the East, were a likely catalyst. Residents of northern California could not have been very happy when Chorpenning decided to abandon San Francisco's direct route and relocate to southern California. They were already far from the terminus of any proposed Pacific railroad—Jefferson Davis having failed to provide for a survey across the Sierra—and now even the existing horse-powered mail service was shifting to the south.

On December 12, 1854, there was a mass meeting in San Francisco, ostensibly to promote a Pacific railroad with a western terminus at San Francisco. With this San Francisco meeting, isolated efforts in smaller towns such as Placerville and Marysville began to be supplemented by big-city interests working at the state level. Reports of the meeting and its participants suggest that there was something of an overland transport coalition within the upper levels of San Francisco politicians and businessmen.

The San Francisco *Daily Alta California* reported the next day that "the Hall was crowded on the occasion with a large and respectable audience, who appeared to manifest a great deal of interest in the proceedings." Dr. Oliver M. Wozencraft called the meeting to order at 7:30. (Wozencraft was a member of California's first constitutional convention and is perhaps best remembered today as an early promoter of irrigation in the Imperial Valley.)

After a welcoming speech by the mayor, Wozencraft presented a number of resolutions to be adopted by the meeting. One exhorted the federal government to build a railroad, though this was somewhat ritualistic, since the Pacific Railroad Survey was then under way and nothing further could be expected until it was finished. Among the more practical resolutions was the following:

> That we petition our Legislature to instruct our Senators and invite our Representatives to favor and procure the passage of a bill to plant military posts at suitable locations on the present central immigrant road, and improve the road at such places where it may be required, . . . [and] a bill which shall secure to us at an early day the postal and telegraphic facilities through our domains.

Wozencraft inveighed against "bloated steamship companies" and argued at length for the constitutionality of internal improvements to provide an overland alternative. He predicted "fearful loss of life and property on the emigrant trail and the probability of its increase until the Government should see fit to establish military posts." Though Wozencraft had been born and raised in Louisiana, he "was decidedly in favor of the Central route."[1] Evidently this was not a strict constructionist crowd, because one of the resolutions asked for federal assistance in the states as well as the territories.

The meeting appointed a committee of twenty-five to investigate the practicability of a road between San Francisco and Missouri and report back at a future meeting. Wozencraft said that he would interview stage owners. "He believed it would result in a line of stages being placed upon that road by the middle of next year." The meeting adjourned until December 20.[2]

The membership of the twenty-five-man steering committee, as we would probably call it today, included prominent San Francisco businessmen, lawyers, and politicians. These were not politically marginal road enthusiasts but the city's power elite, or at least one faction of it. Thomas Larkin was an American businessman in Mexican California and U.S. consul at Monterey before and during the American takeover of California. Henry Haight was a San Francisco lawyer and politician, later governor of the state (1867–71). Isaiah C. Woods was one of the two general partners in Adams & Company. W. J. Pardee was manager of Wells Fargo's express department and treasurer of the Sacramento Valley Railroad. Colonel E. D. Baker defeated Abraham Lincoln in the congressional election in Illinois in 1844 and later became a prominent California lawyer and political figure. He was killed in the Civil War, and Fort Baker in the Marin Headlands was named after him. Frank Pixley was a lawyer and journalist who later became attorney general of California under Leland Stanford and of the United States under President Ulysses S. Grant. Gabriel B. Post was a businessman who became a member of the San Francisco city council in 1849 and later a state senator. Frank Soulé was a prominent San Francisco journalist, editor of the *Daily Alta California*. Eugene Casserly was a lawyer, publisher, and officer of Adams & Company. James Birch was the prominent stagecoach entrepreneur. Frederick Billings was a partner in California's leading law firm, state attorney general, and later president of the Northern Pacific Railroad. (The Montana city was named after him.) John M. Horner, one of the Mormons on Sam Brannan's boat, was a farmer and land speculator in Alameda and San Mateo counties. John T. Doyle was a lawyer and founding president of the California Historical Society. William Tecumseh Sherman, later of Civil War fame, was at this time a banker in San Francisco. Washington Bartlett was a printer who became mayor of San Francisco and governor of the state in the 1880s.

Was this meeting, and others that followed, convened to advocate a road or a railroad? Today we think of roads and railroads as two quite different modes of transportation, but in the early 1850s the distinction was less sharp. The railroad had not yet impressed itself on the public mind as a radically new transportation technology (just as it took a few years for the automobile to be considered something other than a horseless carriage). Railroads were often discussed as a peculiar and specialized type of road. In 1849 Thomas Hart Benton had proposed a transportation corridor to the West Coast in which roads and railroads were to be substituted for each other depending on terrain. Probably for many Californians in 1854 the primary issue was overland transportation to "the States," the technology being distinctly secondary. In the long run there would surely be a railroad all the way across; in the meantime a road or some mix of roads and rails would do.

The lead editorial in the December 14 *Daily Alta California* commented favorably on the December 12 meeting. After noting that there
were two or three thousand in the audience, the writer said that the only
real fault of the meeting was the insufficient attention paid to the wagon
road, a necessary preliminary to the railroad, and one that might by itself bring some of the railroad's benefits within a year.[3] On the same page
a small notice requested the Committee of 25 to meet that day at 3:00
P.M. at the office of Wainwright and Randall on Merchant Street, to consider the emigrant wagon road and other matters tending to promote
emigration. This December 14 committee meeting was reported in the
Alta two days later under the headline "Pacific and Atlantic Railroad."
The report described the purpose of the meeting as improving "the present emigrant wagon road." The committee decided to solicit views and
suggestions from the public on the wagon road and the railroad, and a
"committee of five" was appointed to draft an address to the people to
awaken interest in the issue.[4]

The next meeting of the Committee of 25 was held on the evening of
Wednesday, December 19, also at Wainwright and Randall's offices. As
reported in the December 20 *Alta,* nearly all members were in attendance. Colonel Turner and John T. Doyle discoursed at length on the
route. Doyle suggested that the federal government be urged to issue
bonds for $1 million to aid in the establishment of a line of stages. In the
opinion of the *Alta*'s reporter, "The route as discussed by the Committee seemed to settle upon the present northern emigrant trail."

The committee instructed the (sub)committee of five working on the
public address to get facts and statistics, set out all such information in
detail, and prepare petitions to Congress. It created another subcommittee, with four members, to help with this research and, apparently,
work on route selection. The meeting resolved to encourage the mayors
of Sacramento, Marysville, Stockton, and other California cities to ap-
point similar committees.

The Committee of 25 met again on December 28, 1854. The subcommittee of four had conferred with stage owners in Sacramento and
reported back that a wagon road/stage line was eminently practicable
along the central route. All that was needed were military stations and
provision depots. A subcommittee of three was formed to prepare resolutions for a mass meeting to be held on January 2, 1855.

Meanwhile the subcommittee working on route selection was preparing a questionnaire directed to people who had made the overland trip
in the past six years. In the December 20 *Alta* Eugene Casserly published

a letter denying rumors that the northern route had already been selected and mentioning continuing efforts to gather information.[5] The questionnaire consisted of ten rather lengthy questions covering, among other things, route, dates of trip, pass taken through the Sierra, numbers of others using the same route and pass, qualities of soil, grass, and terrain noticed along the way, nature of repairs needed along the road, and practicability of setting up supply stations. It was published in the *Alta* on January 22, 1855, and again on January 25 and was also printed separately as a broadside or flyer to be distributed in some manner.[6] Answers were to be sent to Eugene Casserly at Adams & Company, then California's leading express company but within a month to go dramatically bankrupt.

Although most interest at this time was focused on government support, the potential of the private sector was not entirely neglected. The December 29 *Alta* ran a lead editorial promoting a road to be built by a stock corporation.

> If the subject can be divested of the visionary and speculative theories always attendant upon a new enterprise, and can be treated as a practical common sense business transaction, the Overland Mail and Immigrant Rod can be established and put into operation within a year and a half, and that too without costing the General Government and the State of California together one-fourth of the money that is now paid by the United States for the transportation of mails by way of Panama.[7]

The Emigrant Road Committee, as it had now come to be called by the press, held its next mass meeting as planned on January 2, 1855, with Mayor Stephen Webb of San Francisco presiding. The meeting was evidently intended partly as a vehicle to focus political pressure on President Franklin Pierce, a strict constructionist opposed to federal funding of internal improvements, and partly to get the state legislature to do something. Frank Pixley reported that the necessary investigations were proceeding and that similar organizations were forming in Sacramento and Marysville. The governor and legislature had shown interest. Resolutions were passed to the effect that although the Pacific railroad was the grand enterprise of the age, it would not be the work of a day, and that what was needed in the interim was an emigrant road from the valley of the Mississippi across the territories to California, easy to travel and protected by military posts. The state of California should appropriate money to build a wagon road to the eastern boundary of the state to meet the federal road. The rest of the evening was taken up by personal accounts of overland travel.[8]

Wozencraft remained a leading promoter of the overland road and soon took his campaign to Sacramento. On January 10 he addressed an emigrant road meeting in the capital, presided over by the mayor. A committee of fifteen was formed to carry on the work there.

San Francisco's Emigrant Road Committee met again on January 16, 1855, and voted to incorporate itself as the Pacific Emigrant Society, with the following aims: (1) to facilitate overland travel to California and promote permanent settlement of families; (2) to diffuse correct information about routes, seasons, and modes of conveyance; (3) to aid suffering emigrants and protect them from Indians; and (4) to cooperate with companies or individuals to open or improve roads.[9]

Governor John Bigler, who was among those present at the January 16 meeting, seemed to be working in harmony with the Emigrant Road Committee. His annual message to the legislature, delivered on January 5, had contained two pages (out of a total of 35) on the "Overland Route to California." With respect to the Pacific railroad, he said that "owing to the magnitude of the undertaking and the perplexing questions mooted, many years must elapse before this desirable and highly important project will be fully consummated." Until that time, he went on, Congress should establish military posts at intervals of 75 or 100 miles, with fifty men at each post, along the entire route from Missouri to California, guarding a road that would be suitable for stage travel from Fort Kearney to the Sierra Nevada. Bigler's main argument for improved transportation was that it would ease the way for families to be reunited in California and thus reduce the flow of remittances to the eastern United States, which he calculated at some $10 million per year.

There were constitutional limits, however, to what the federal government could provide for California, said Bigler. It would be hard enough to get Congress to vote for roads in the territories; support for roads within California was out of the question. And he conceded, "In truth, the portion of the entire route most difficult to be rendered fit for stage travel is that lying between California and the points on the Humboldt where the different trails leave the river." California's eastern boundary had not been surveyed at this time, and Bigler probably had in mind the portion between the Humboldt and the mining districts, which included the Sierra Nevada. Most emigrants felt that they had truly entered California only after crossing the Sierra. At the same time he was leading the call for federal aid for a road across the territories, Bigler realized that the state would have to take the initiative on the difficult western end of any such road. He asked the state legislature to adopt measures for road improvements over the Sierra Nevada.[10]

Passage of a Road Bill

On January 9, 1855, four days after the governor's message, Assemblymen W. B. Farwell of San Francisco and Edgar Bogardus of El Dorado County announced that they would introduce bills for construction of roads across the Sierra Nevada.[11] The next day Asa Kinney of Plumas County made a similar announcement. These bills were consolidated by January 15 and titled *An Act to Provide for the Survey and Construction of a Wagon Road from the Sacramento Valley to the Eastern Boundary of the State*.[12] It was referred to the Committee on Internal Improvements, C. T. Ryland of Santa Clara, chairman.

That the state was starting to move on the road question did not mean any diminution in local rivalries. A public meeting in Placerville on January 25, 1855, considered the probability that the legislature would soon appropriate money to build an "improved highway" to Carson Valley and discussed what might be done to make sure it went through Placerville. Placervillians were certain that Johnson's Cut-off would, with slight deviations and improvements, be the best route to follow. The city council was requested to appropriate $500 to hire an engineer and assistant.[13] On January 31, 1855, the county surveyor, William Henderson, and "Dr. Shober, a practical engineer," went up to survey a route.

Henderson and Shober surveyed from Placerville up the valley of the South Fork of the American River to Johnson Pass, thence down into Lake Valley, and on via Daggett Pass to Carson Valley. They seem to have followed Johnson's Cut-off east of Placerville to the place where it crossed over to the north bank of the South Fork of the American River and began to climb Peavine Ridge. Here they departed from the Cut-off and looked for a route closer to the river, that is, very low on the south flank of Peavine Ridge, with the idea of rejoining Johnson's Cut-off higher up on the South Fork. Henderson and Shober thus made a preliminary reconnaissance of what later became known as the Day route. They noted that there would be much timber to clear and several rock bluffs to deal with.

Henderson and Shober crossed the Carson Range from Lake Valley to Carson Valley at Daggett Pass instead of staying on the Johnson Cut-off to Spooner Summit. They came through Carson Canyon on the way back and evidently had no great trouble there; Henderson mentioned that there was a bridge at the canyon mouth but said nothing about how it was maintained.

It is interesting to note that Henderson introduced his report on this trip as a response to a request from Ryland for information, sent on November 13, 1854. This shows that state aid for trans-Sierra roads was already under consideration in the legislature a month before the beginning of the series of San Francisco road meetings.

On March 12, 1855, Ryland reported back to the assembly on the road bill. His opening remarks reflect differing opinions in the state regarding roads.

> They [i.e., the committee] have had much difficulty in arriving at anything like satisfactory conclusions of the manner of obtaining the end sought. All see the necessity of such a road, and but few doubt its practicability. The immigration to the Pacific demands it; our progress and prosperity as a State demands it; the exorbitant price of passage on the ocean steamers demands it; our connection with the rest of the Union, our safety in war and subsistence in dearth, demand it. Yea, everything demands it, and demands it now; but how to get it is the difficulty.
>
> In the first place we have not that unanimity in our own councils that should prevail. Men are differing. The various sections of the country are advocating not only different modes of constructing the road, but different routes upon which to construct it. The people of the north desire a northern route; the center a central route; and the south, a southern route. Some think that private enterprise, with a little assistance from the State, would build a toll road; others think that the State should construct it entire, and let it be free.
>
> All the difficulties can be easily overcome, we apprehend, except the one as to the most convenient practicable route.
>
> Our state is so new and unsettled, its mountain gorges and cañons are so little explored, and its waste places and deserts so little known, that your Committee have not been able to agree unanimously upon any particular route.[14]

Ryland went on to discuss six possibilities, which he outlined as follows:

1.   The Nobles route, which offered easy terrain and plentiful grass and water but was too far north of the main centers of population and principal mining districts.

2.   The Beckwourth route, from Marysville through Bidwell's Bar and American Valley to Beckwourth's Valley. A road existed but would need improvement. Private interests were planning to have stagecoaches running by the spring of 1856.

3. From Marysville up the Gibsonville Ridge. This road too was already traveled by stages as far as Gibsonville. Beyond that point the road could be made much better, but there were about 30 miles of high stony chaparral-covered ridges where grazing would be difficult for emigrant teams.

4. The existing Carson route, that is, the Mormon/emigrant route.

5. A far southern route via Tejon Pass, which was much too circuitous.

6. Up the South Fork of the American River via Johnson's Cut-off and then via Luther Pass and Hope Valley into Carson Valley.

Ryland devoted more space in his report to the Johnson's Cut-off/Hope Valley route than to the other five, and that is the one he recommended to the assembly. It was already much traveled and would need relatively little work, and it led to Carson Valley, an important way station between California and Salt Lake and soon to be thickly settled. Ryland's choice showed the influence of Henderson's report. There was already a good road from Sacramento to Placerville—50 miles out of the total 110—with daily stagecoaches making the trip in five to six hours. The road was somewhat improved for 16 miles east of Placerville. The next 25 miles would need work owing to "points or ledges of rock running in close to river." Some rerouting and bridging would be necessary at Slippery Ford. Over on the Lake Tahoe side of the western summit, some 3 miles of side-hill grading would be necessary, this being the greatest difficulty on the whole route. Carson Canyon would need some more work, but this would be done by the people in Carson Valley without charge to California. Total mileage from Placerville to Carson Valley would be 59.5, with only 7 miles likely to have snow problems. The estimated total cost of the road would probably be $30,000 to $75,000. (This amount can be compared with the per mile cost of railroads, which Senator William Gwin had estimated as $27,300 when he introduced his railroad bill.)

On April 2, 1855, the road bill came up for debate in the assembly. Some members proposed that the state should take no action until the federal government had located and surveyed a road to the eastern boundary of California, so that California's road might connect with the federal one. The assembly rejected that proposal; a majority wanted to get moving right away. They also voted to change the name of the measure from *An Act to Construct a Wagon Road from the Sacramento Val-*

ley to the Eastern Boundary of the State to the more direct *An Act to Construct a Wagon Road over the Sierra Nevada Mountains.*[15]

In the final bill the route was not specified other than to say that it should begin "at the western foot of the steep slope of the Sierra Nevada." The bill further stipulated that no expenditure was to be made for improving existing roads in the Sacramento Valley or the Sierra foothills if such roads were already capable of carrying loaded wagons. It was to be a free public road, not a toll road. (This would change later.) The act created the Board of Commissioners, consisting of the governor, the secretary of state, and the surveyor general. These three commissioners were to determine the route and "if possible to have said road so far completed as to make it beneficial to the emigration of the present year."[16] The cost for this project was not to exceed $105,000, including $5,000 for the survey.

On April 5 the assembly passed the road bill 48 to 16. The distribution of the "no" votes is interesting. Some were from coastal counties—Los Angeles, San Francisco, Sonoma, Alameda—where maritime interests were strong. Many others came from the delegates of mountain or foothill counties—Tuolumne, Tulare, Calaveras, Nevada, Mariposa, San Joaquin—where one would expect great enthusiasm for the project, unless of course there was some suspicion that the fix was already in for a route through Placerville. All three of Calaveras County's delegates, for example, voted against the bill.[17]

Later in the year, when surveys along the Placerville route were well advanced, the *Marysville Daily Herald* inveighed against the "El Dorado Route," calling it a flagrant example of pork-barrel favoritism and threatening an injunction to stop the work. Nothing came of these fumings at the time, but they portended trouble ahead.[18]

The senate version of the bill was submitted to the Committee on Internal Improvements. The committee's chairman, Sherman Day, reported on it with a well-reasoned eleven-page overview of the road situation in early 1855. Day, who was both politician and surveyor, allowed that sound policy usually looked to private enterprise to build roads but held that the difficult terrain and uninhabitable nature of the Sierra, and the fact that benefits would accrue to the entire state, justified state action in this case. He reviewed the many routes used by emigrants, from Lassen's in the north to Cajon Pass in the south, with attention to their individual advantages and problems. The extreme northern and southern routes would need less work but would also be less useful in relation to existing needs. The state should concentrate its support on a central route between San Francisco and Salt Lake via Carson Valley and especially on the mountains just south of Lake Tahoe.

Day reviewed the possible routes in this area.

> It is said there is a good route from Georgetown up and along one of the spurs of the Sierra to some pass near the southwest corner of Bigler Lake [Tahoe]. Johnson's Cut-off, and the route up the South Fork, surveyed by Mr. Henderson . . . come next in order going south. The next is route proposed by Mr. Taylor, who lives near the old Carson trail, to cross the Sierra some two or three miles south of Henderson's crossing, where Mr. Taylor says the Sierra presents but one ridge to cross instead of two, as on the other routes, passing near Red Lake and following into the old Carson trail on top of the mountain, which is here about 7,500 feet above the sea. The next route going south is the old Carson emigrant trail, which forks both to Placerville and Diamond Springs or to Volcano and Jackson.

In these remarks Day outlined the surveying program he would follow that summer. He could not say how much the cost would be until there had been a regular survey, but he believed that it would be fully within the $100,000 provided for in the assembly bill.[19]

On April 19 and 20, the senate debated the bill. Members proposed various amendments calling for more than one road and having surveys run through their own counties, but all failed. Day offered an amendment to strengthen the provision that no money would be spent in the Central Valley or in the foothills where wagon roads already existed; this passed. On a final vote, the road bill passed 15 to 12.[20] On April 28, Governor Bigler signed it into law.

The State Road Bill in Trouble

It would appear that great progress was being made, but the *Act to Construct a Wagon Road over the Sierra Nevada Mountains* was in trouble from the beginning. Even as Governor Bigler signed the bill, he declared that it should have provided a means of paying the interest on the bonds and should have had a provision for submitting the proposed expenditure to the voters. He advised the legislature to pass a supplementary act remedying these defects.

On April 23, 1855, while the bill was still waiting for Bigler's signature, the surveyor general, Seneca Hunt Marlette, sent a letter to the legislature pointing out that it would be impossible to carry out a competent, professional job of surveying the proposed route for only $5,000.[21] The legislature ignored the suggestion. In fact, there was doubt as to whether even this inadequate amount could be disbursed by the state treasury, because the legislature had not actually used the word *authorize* with regard to the $5,000 survey. On May 23, 1855, Marlette asked the attorney general, J. R. McConnell, for an opinion and was told that the $5,000 was probably covered by the overall appropriation of the act but that the constitutionality of the act itself was in question and no steps should be taken without a favorable judicial decision.[22]

Nothing daunted, Marlette went ahead and bought supplies for the survey. He submitted his accounts to the office of Controller Samuel Bell on June 4, 1855, only to be told that the latter had left town. When Bell did respond to Marlette in early July, it was to say that he would not audit the accounts, because the act contained no specific appropriations for the survey.[23]

But Marlette had not waited around for this answer. On June 6, 1855, the Board of Wagon Road Commissioners met in Sacramento and directed Marlette to "make such explorations as may be necessary to enable him to estimate the expense of constructing a good wagon road" but said nothing specific about money. In other words Marlette got together with the governor and the secretary of state, and these three (comprising the total membership of the Board of Wagon Road Commissioners) decided to go ahead with the surveys without worrying about the appropriation. According to the historian Theodore Hittell, it was characteristic of Bigler to take actions of dubious constitutionality and then challenge the legislature to pass measures that would bring them into compliance.[24]

To get started with the survey, Marlette appealed for support from three jurisdictions that could expect to benefit directly from a new road. He pointed out that $5,000 was insufficient for the survey work and suggested that the friends of the various possible routes organize reconnaissance parties on their own account. Marlette or his representatives would accompany these and make a choice. The $5,000 would then be concentrated on a complete survey of the chosen route.[25]

Placerville seems to have been the most vigorous in taking up Marlette on his offer. As we have seen, that town had already begun its own efforts at the public meeting of January 25, by sending Henderson and Shober to Carson Valley and back. On June 11, 1855, Dr. L. Bradley of Diamond Springs, 3 miles south of Placerville, began a road survey along the South Fork of the American River. Bradley was a successful promoter of canals and had built a 75-mile irrigation and miners' ditch in the Pleasant Valley area, about 10 miles southeast of Placerville.[26] He returned on July 3 from his road survey, saying he had been driven off by Indians but had laid out much of the route anyway. He submitted bills totaling $2,704.34, which Marlette thought excessive (he said he would pay $500).[27]

Sherman Day's Georgetown-Tahoe Exploration

The senate had ended its session on May 7, and Senator Day was now free to follow his profession. (The legislature met only a few months a year then, and being a member was not a full-time job.) Sherman Day was a surveyor, secretary of the Pacific & Atlantic Railroad Company, and a state senator, perhaps in that order. He signed up for the wagon road project and on June 11, 1855, left for Georgetown, to begin a survey of a Georgetown-Tahoe route. Residents of Georgetown had raised the money to pay for this trip.

Day proceeded east along the ridge south of the Rubicon River, a tributary of the Middle Fork of the American River, and reached the Sierra crest above the west side of Lake Tahoe. Most of the ridge, as it rose steadily to the east, was satisfactory for a road, but the final climb to the top of the range was too rugged, in Day's opinion. Furthermore, it would then be necessary to go around Lake Tahoe, and this would make the route from Georgetown too circuitous.

The *Sacramento Daily Union*'s Georgetown correspondent wrote of Day's return to Georgetown, "Mr. Day brings back a very favorable report, having found the route more feasible than anticipated . . . over the worst places wagons pass daily."[28] Whether this was blind boosterism on the part of the correspondent or whether Day just wanted to say something nice to people who had funded his expedition is not clear. In his official report he stated quite clearly that although the Rubicon ridge would be good for a road, he had found no practicable pass over the mountains just west of Lake Tahoe.

Nearly thirty years later, in a letter to his son, Day reminisced about this trip, with details that did not appear in his official report, but which give a more vivid picture of what early-day surveying in the Sierra was like.

John Conness, formerly U.S. Senator from California . . . and I made a wagon road exploration trip from Georgetown across the Sierra Nevada by way of the headwaters of the South Fork of the Middle Fork American River, crossing the high range of snowy peaks, a platoon of which Pyramid Peak is the

Corporal. We ran plumb against the broadside of Lake Bigler, and slept there one night by the side of a huge yellow pine prostrate and on fire—no blankets—scant supper only the remnants of the morning's ration and to keep warm we slept alternately on each side an hour at a time, turning ourselves like fowls on spit at a rotisserie. We had plenty of arms and ammunition but if we shot ducks in the lake we could not "retrieve" them. Conness gave me for my allowance as breakfast a piece of meat as large as my hand; and I am not at all sure that he did not do without himself.

This was to sustain us while returning to camp over four ranges of mountain. Conness, Old Wimmer the gold finder of Coloma, a Mr. Parker of Georgetown & myself formed the party. On top of the mountain pass Wimmer and I separated from the other two to explore a more northerly pass; and again I separated from Wimmer, I still keeping further north. Having satisfied myself about the pass, I descended the steep wall of the backbone of the Sierra, and tried to wade the American, clear and cold, about half a mile above one of its falls. After going in to my vest pockets I saw that refraction was deceiving me, and that I might be lifted off my feet and taken down over the falls. This would not have been pleasant news to your mother. So I retraced my steps, and ascended the river 1 1/2 miles to a bridge of driftwood, and crossed it. When I had crossed the last ridge, very tired and nearly exhausted, Conness and party came out to meet me. They had previously found Wimmer, lying down, exhausted, and refreshed him, and got him into camp. Canned peaches tasted nice when I got into camp, and possibly I may have taken something stronger, but not much, if any. Alcohol on such occasions is not so good as rest and a moderate amount of plain food.

We descended to Georgetown without having discovered our wagon road: and rested a day or two at Conness' house. He was then an Expressman, Miner, and politician.[29]

Day and Marlette's Joint Exploration

On July 16, 1855, Day, having eliminated the Georgetown route, moved on to explore the mountains between Placerville and Carson Valley. Marlette joined him for this trip. They first examined the route that Dr. Bradley had surveyed at such exorbitant cost. Bradley's route was to have come into California by following the old Mormon/emigrant route from Carson Valley over Carson Pass as far as Caples Lake and then gone around the north end of Carson Spur somewhat as Highway 88 does today, to descend along the south side of the valley of the South Fork of the American River to the Placerville ridge in the vicinity of Sly Park. Marlette and Day traveled over a part of this route and viewed the rest of it from a distance. The obvious problem was its location on a north-facing slope, where snowdrifts would remain late into the spring. Furthermore, the benefits of going around Carson Spur rather than climbing over it would be largely negated by having to ascend and descend a series of smaller ridges in approaching the South Fork. Time has supported Marlette and Day's verdict; no thoroughfare has ever been built along this alignment, only logging roads.

Day and Marlette now turned their attention to the "old Carson Pass trail." It needed some improvement on the west side of Carson Pass, and on the east side would have to be "entirely regraded on a new route." (Evidently they meant an alternative to the notorious pull up to the pass from Red Lake, one of the most difficult parts of the trail.) Carson Canyon they found to be already much improved by the removal of boulders and the construction of two bridges, though capable of still more amelioration.

Improvements to the road through Carson Canyon were especially significant because the canyon was a common link in three routes between California and Carson Valley: the Carson Pass route, the road from Lake Valley over Luther Pass, and the Big Trees route up from Stockton. All three converged on Hope Valley, eastbound, and in common passed down through Carson Canyon to Carson Valley.

Day explored the various "eastern summits"—passes over the Carson Range—and determined that the one known today as Spooner Summit, traversed by U.S. 50, was the lowest. (He was right. Spooner Summit is at 7,146 feet. The others are Daggett Pass, 7,334 feet; Luther Pass, 7,740 feet; and Carson Pass, 8,573 feet.) Day then headed back west from Spooner Summit. (By this point of the trip, Marlette had evidently gone back to Sacramento, leaving Day on his own.)

Johnson's Cut-off ran along at a rather high elevation on the west side of the Carson Range as it rounded the southeast quadrant of Lake Tahoe (rather than descending to run closer to the lakeshore as U.S. 50 does today), to avoid the rougher lower slopes. As a result, it seemed to Day, the road actually went higher than the pass (Spooner Summit) at several points, which increased the number of miles with snow problems. Day concluded that the only reason this part of Johnson's Cut-off had been attractive in the past was that it allowed travelers an alternative to passing through Carson Canyon in its unimproved state. Now that boulders were being removed and bridges built in Carson Canyon, even Johnson would probably prefer it over his own route.

Consequently, Day decided to recommend a route that would not go near Lake Tahoe at all but instead make a sharp turn south as soon as possible after getting down from Johnson Pass, go up the valley of the Upper Truckee River, and cross over Luther Pass to Hope Valley to meet the improved road through Carson Canyon (approximately the alignment of State Highways 89 and 88). In this Day was simply confirming the way two or three years of travelers had been voting with their feet and wheels.

There was still the problem of the steep slope between Lake Valley and Johnson Pass, the western summit. Johnson's Cut-off, a road mostly by courtesy title, was obstructed by chaparral and boulders and rose 1,000 feet in three-quarters of a mile, a grade that was three and a half to four times what Day thought it should be. It was impossible to avoid the grade completely. Any road that went up the valley of the South Fork of the American from Placerville would have to come out somewhere on top of this ridge, high over Lake Valley. But the road down to Lake Valley could be stretched farther along the mountainside so as to get a more reasonable grade, and that is what Day proposed to do, opining that $15,000 would probably be enough to pay for it. (Day toyed in print with the idea of building a high viaduct from the western summit across the Upper Truckee valley to an equivalent elevation on the approach to Luther Pass, so as to reduce or eliminate the dip down to Lake Valley and back up to Luther Pass, but he realized that this was a bit too visionary for the technology and money available at the time.)

West of Johnson Pass, headed back to Placerville, Day descended along Johnson's route only as far as the point where it began to climb Peavine Ridge. He wanted to improve on Johnson's route by avoiding the heights of Peavine Ridge and staying closer to the South Fork of the American River, as Henderson had suggested. He laid out a provisional alignment along the lower slopes of the ridge, above the more difficult rock outcrops in the depths of the canyon but still below the snow zone atop the ridge, and on the north (sunny) side of the valley. Building a road on this line would involve some digging and blasting along the hillside, but state money would make that possible.

Day's route approached Johnson's Cut-off again farther down, around the 3,200-foot contour. This is about as far west (downstream) on the South Fork as travelers can go and still conveniently climb away from the river onto the interfluve ridge on which Placerville and environs are located. Below this point the South Fork enters a deep canyon on its way down to Coloma and Folsom. (One reason Frémont's 1844 expedition had such trouble getting down the western slope is that he followed the South Fork through the canyon, popular today for whitewater rafting, rather than cross over onto the Placerville ridge south of the river.)

In his final report Day proposed the following route to be the recipient of state funds under the *Act to Construct a Wagon Road over the Sierra Nevada Mountains:* (1) follow Johnson's Cut-off from Placerville as far east as the crossing of the South Fork of the American, (2) stay low on the south side of Peavine Ridge (this was where a large amount of the new construction would be required), (3) follow the upper course of the South Fork to its headwaters near Johnson Pass, (4) descend into Lake Valley along a new alignment (more construction work), (5) take the Luther Pass/Hope Valley route over the Carson Range. This is the route that for the rest of the 1850s was referred to in the newspapers and government reports as the "Day route" or "Day survey."

The two other possibilities, according to Day, were not very attractive. The Carson/emigrant route could be improved into a good road between Placerville and Carson Valley, if there were no other choices, but snow would always make it impassable in winter. And the new route proposed by Dr. Bradley also would have snow problems, because of its many north-facing slopes.

George Goddard's Survey

Later in the summer of 1855 Marlette found a reason for further Sierra road surveying when Brigham Young appointed Orson Hyde to be district judge of Carson Valley. (Nevada Territory was not created until 1861, so California adjoined Utah Territory on the east). Some valley residents objected to Hyde's appointment, claiming that Carson Valley was within the eastern boundary of California. The border had been defined abstractly in terms of latitude and longitude but had not yet been demarcated on the ground. Judge Hyde came to Sacramento and conferred with Governor Bigler on the matter.

Bigler agreed to have Marlette carry out the boundary survey, and Hyde was to provide men, animals, and provisions. Marlette in turn directed Goddard on August 3 to do the fieldwork, and while he was at it to gather more information on passes in the Carson Range east of Johnson Pass.

Goddard set out from Placerville on August 26, 1855. For the first 14 miles east from Placerville the emigrant road, Johnson's Cut-off, and the Day survey approximately coincided. Instead of descending into the South Fork valley to cross the river, Goddard stuck to the emigrant route, turned southeast, and ascended a long ridge, today called Iron Mountain Ridge, to Tragedy Spring and on to West Pass. Goddard noted the turnoff to "Dr. Bradley's proposed new road" and described it as a great improvement on the old road, except that its position on a north-facing slope would mean snow problems in winter. No doubt Day and Marlette had already briefed Goddard on this point, but he was enough of a practical geographer to have come to the same conclusion on his own. Goddard noted in passing that the grade along Iron Mountain Ridge would probably be too steep for a railroad. Considerations touching on the route of the inevitable railroad were never far from the minds of road builders.

Approaching West Pass Goddard could see a mountain near Ebbetts Pass that he recognized as the same one he had seen from the eastern side with Ebbetts in October 1853. Regarding Ebbetts Pass, he again opined that "there is reason to believe it is the lowest and most suitable one for the Pacific Railway in the central portion of California."[30] This remark by an accomplished surveyor shows how much was still unknown about the Sierra: Ebbetts Pass was much higher than Goddard thought, and the approaches to it are hopelessly steep and tortuous for a railroad.

Goddard spent several days in the vicinity of the two Carson summits and the Clear (Caples) Lake valley between. His report contains much commentary of geographic interest, but as far as determining routes was concerned, he only confirmed Day's conclusions. He commented on the precipitous slope between the eastern summit (Carson Pass) and Red Lake as "certainly the worst and least easy of improvement on the road . . . and of itself sufficient reason for the rejection of [this] route, for the intended Immigrant Wagon Road."[31]

Selection of the Day Route

On August 26, 1855, the Board of Wagon Road Commissioners selected Sherman Day's survey as the route of the official wagon road over the mountains under the *Act to Construct a Wagon Road over the Sierra Nevada Mountains.* (This board, it will be remembered, consisted of the governor, the secretary of state, and the surveyor general.) As winter settled over the mountains, the board accepted construction bids. The *Daily Alta California* in San Francisco inveighed in a November 3 editorial against this solicitation of bids, claiming that citizens wished to have no more debts incurred except for actual necessities and that government officials should stop this outlay, which was illegal, in the editor's opinion, because the measure had not been submitted to a vote of the people.[32] The bidding closed on December 28, "quite a number of bids" being received, according to the *Alta*. Because the governor was absent, they had not yet been opened.[33]

On January 11, 1856, the *Alta* ran a story that must have surprised many readers. When the bids were opened on January 5, one L. B. Leach of Stockton was found to have submitted the low bid of $58,000, well below the $100,000 limit set by the legislature. But no such person turned up in Sacramento to pursue the matter, and therefore no contract had been entered into before January 8, the last day of Governor Bigler's term. The *Alta* commented, "It was not improbable that the design was to defeat any actions towards building the road. It now rests with Gov. [Neely] Johnson and the new Board of Commissioners to decide whether another effort shall be made to let out a contract under the clearly unconstitutional law of the last session."[34]

Some have suggested that Stockton interests were behind the fictitious Leach bid, that it was a ploy to sabotage a road seemingly designed to benefit Sacramento, though no hard evidence was produced. It certainly seems possible, but as we have seen, all of northern California was agitating for transportation links across the Sierra. Stockton businessmen would benefit from such a link even if it came through Sacramento, so why should they take such a dog-in-the-manger attitude?

Why indeed unless they had an alternative route of their own. It helps to remember that Sacramento had been the state capital for only four years and was less clearly preeminent over Stockton than it is today. Stockton was a tidewater port, like Sacramento, and already an important stagecoach center for the southern gold mining region and the northern San Joaquin Valley. It may have appeared quite plausible to aggressive Stocktonians in 1855 that they could wrest away from Sacramento the role of metropolis of the Central Valley, and having the main trans-Sierra route leading directly to their city would certainly help. There was such a route, or so they thought, called the Big Trees route.

The Big Trees Route

Probably the most serious competitor to Johnson's Cut-off or to any other proposed route via Placerville or Sacramento, the Big Trees route was promoted by businessmen in Stockton and a number of gold camps in Calaveras County, particularly Murphys. Improved roads and coach service already existed on its west end, due to early touristic interest in what is now the North Grove of Calaveras Big Trees State Park. The first hotel there was built in 1854.[35] All that was needed, they thought, was to push the road beyond the Big Trees, up the slope and over the crest to Carson Valley.

In Sacramento on July 26, 1855, Surveyor General Marlette had received a letter from Calaveras County, requesting state support for a survey along this route. As we saw earlier, the *Act to Construct a Wagon Road over the Sierra Nevada Mountains* did not specify a route. But the Ryland report recommended a route approximating Johnson's Cut-off, and the surveyor general had followed this recommendation in his instructions to Day and Goddard. There was not enough money for a Big Trees route survey as well, Marlette replied to Calaveras County; they must take the initiative themselves.

The town of Murphys raised $500 and on August 8, 1855, sent out O. B. Powers to survey the Big Trees route. (Murphys took its name from members of the extended Murphy family who formed a large contingent of the 1844 Stevens party, the first emigrants to cross the Sierra with wagons.) The Powers party found a wagon road, used for hauling logs, already open as far up as Big Meadow, at about 6,500 feet. They continued along the south side of the dividing ridge between the Stanislaus and Mokelumne rivers to the Pacific Grade summit (8,050 ft.), where they noted a small lake (Mosquito Lake). At this point they were 40 miles from Murphys, and 31 of those miles were already a satisfactory wagon road. The Powers party descended to Pacific Valley, where they saw a number of Indians who were too fearful to approach closely, and went on to Mokelumne Valley (Hermit Valley), where they stayed for several days.

Up to this point the Powers survey had followed, in a general way, the alignment of today's Highway 4. From Hermit Valley the present-day road continues east another 5 miles to Ebbetts Pass. Powers and his party did not go this way, however; they pushed their Big Trees route north instead, to another valley, walled on the east side by a high ridge of "conglomerate" (volcanic breccia). Here the Indians were more numerous and much bolder, but then they began to call out such expressions as "How do you do?" learned no doubt from emigrants. Tensions eased, and the Indians, who proved to be Washoes, agreed to serve as guides across the mountains. The valley thus acquired the name Indian Valley, by which it is still known.

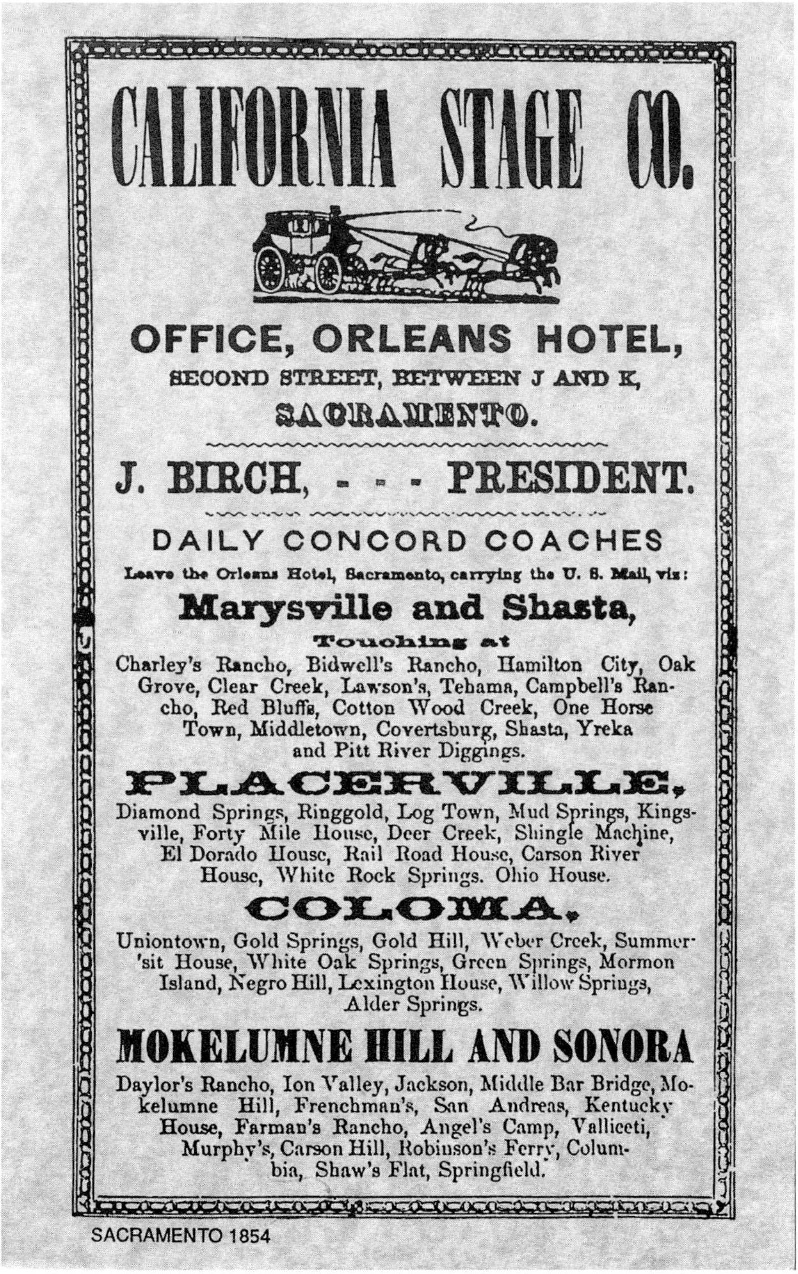

CALIFORNIA STAGE CO.

OFFICE, ORLEANS HOTEL,

SECOND STREET, BETWEEN J AND K,

SACRAMENTO.

J. BIRCH, - - - PRESIDENT.

DAILY CONCORD COACHES

Leave the Orleans Hotel, Sacramento, carrying the U. S. Mail, viz:

Marysville and Shasta,

Touching at

Charley's Rancho, Bidwell's Rancho, Hamilton City, Oak
Grove, Clear Creek, Lawson's, Tehama, Campbell's Rancho, Red Bluffs, Cotton Wood Creek, One Horse
Town, Middletown, Covertsburg, Shasta, Yreka
and Pitt River Diggings.

PLACERVILLE,

Diamond Springs, Ringgold, Log Town, Mud Springs, Kings-
ville, Forty Mile House, Deer Creek, Shingle Machine,
El Dorado House, Rail Road House, Carson River
House, White Rock Springs. Ohio House.

COLOMA,

Uniontown, Gold Springs, Gold Hill, Weber Creek, Summer-
'sit House, White Oak Springs, Green Springs, Mormon
Island, Negro Hill, Lexington House, Willow Springs,
Alder Springs.

MOKELUMNE HILL AND SONORA

Daylor's Rancho, Ion Valley, Jackson, Middle Bar Bridge, Mokelumne Hill, Frenchman's, San Andreas, Kentucky
House, Farman's Rancho, Angel's Camp, Valliceti,
Murphy's, Carson Hill, Robinson's Ferry, Columbia, Shaw's Flat, Springfield.

SACRAMENTO 1854

Figure 1.   Advertising flyer of the California Stage Company, 1854. By
this time, James Birch had largely consolidated his stagecoach empire in
California. Service was extensive throughout the gold diggings, but had
not yet been established over the Sierra Nevada.

Figure 2. Brockliss Bridge as shown in *Vischer's Pictorial of California: Landscape, Trees and Forest Scenes: Grand Featurs of California Scenery, Life, Traffic and Customs* (1870). This was one of several bridges that have carried road traffic across the South Fork (mistakenly called the North Fork here) of the American River. On the south side was the broad interfluve ridge, site of Placerville, separating the basins of the American and Cosumnes rivers. On the north was Peavine Ridge, followed by the Johnson Cut-off, and the newer road surveyed by Sherman Day along the valley of the South Fork. (California State Library)

Figure 3.   Business card issued by the Pioneer Stage Company. The small print reads, "This route affords a fine view of Lake Bigler or Tahoe running for twenty miles along its shores." (Wells Fargo Bank)

Pioneer Stage Route,

Via **LAKE BIGLER**, or **TAHOE**,

SACRAMENTO to VIRGINIA CITY

ESMERALDA REESE RIVER AND HUMBOLDT.

Via S. V. R. R'ds & P. & V. R. R'ds.

		Miles.	
Sacramento,	- - -	0	
Folsom,	by Rail Road,	22	
Latrobe,	" " "	15	37
Placerville,	by Stage,	16	
Sportman's Hall,	" "	11	
River-Side Station,	" "	10	
Webster's,	" "	9½	
Strawberry Valley,	" "	11	
Yank's,	" "	11	
Lake Bigler,	" "	9	
Glenbrook,	" "	9	
Carson,	" "	13½	
Virginia City,	" "	16	116
Geneva to Markleeville,	"	25	
" " Esmeralda,	"	94	
Carson to Reese River,	"	170	
" " Star City,	"	165	

WILLIAM SHEW,

PHOTOGRAPHER,

No. 423 Montgomery Street,

SAN FRANCISCO.

Figure 4.   Reverse side of Pioneer Stage Company business card shown in figure 3, listing major station stops between Sacramento and Virginia City, as well as branch lines to other mining districts east of the Sierra. The appearance of Glenbrook, about midway along the eastern shore of Lake Tahoe, shows that the Pioneer was following the northernmost of the three alternative routes east from Johnson Pass (Echo Summit), the route that approximates today's US 50. The other two were the middle route over Daggett Pass and the southern route through Luther Pass and Hope Valley. (Wells Fargo Bank)

Figure 5.   Main Street, Placerville, early 1860s, from the third floor of the Cary House, looking east. The passing freight wagon was typical of the period. (Society of California Pioneers: Lawrence & Houseworth stereo album, number 608)

Figure 6.   Main Street, Placerville, 1996. This picture was taken from the second floor of the Cary House, which still functions as a hotel in downtown Placerville. (photograph by author)

Figure 7. Sportsman's Hall, early 1860s. This establishment, near the 12-mile marker east of Placerville, figures prominently in many travel accounts of the pre-railroad period. The first changing point for eastbound Pony Express riders was here. (Society of California Pioneers: Lawrence & Houseworth stereo album number 611)

Figure 8. Sportsman's Hall, 1996. The present incarnation of Sportsman's Hall, a restaurant, is said to include some interior foundations from the building shown in figure 7, which burned long ago. With that possible exception only the name remains. (photograph by author)

Figure 9. Sugar Loaf Mountain and Webster's Station, early 1860s. The view is east, uphill. Webster's, with a bar on the ground floor and sleeping rooms upstairs, was one of many road-houses along the Lake Tahoe Wagon Road. High-sided double freight wagons like this one plied the road by the hundreds during the Comstock Boom. (Society of California Pioneers: Lawrence & Houseworth stereo album number 615)

Figure 10. Sugar Loaf Mountain and Chevron station, 1996. The site is very near, if not directly on, Webster's Station as shown in figure 9. (photograph by author)

Figure 11. Feeding the Teams. Scene on the Placerville Route, early 1860s. These would appear to be loads of mining equipment bound for the silver mines of Virginia City. All the mining equipment used in the vast Comstock Lode had to be brought up from California in this fashion. The exact site of this equivalent of a truck stop is not specified, but from the numbering of Houseworth's stereo pairs, it was probably not too far from present-day Kyburz. (Society of California Pioneers: Lawrence & Houseworth stereo album number 621)

Figure 12.   Strawberry Valley Station, early 1860s. This was another important stopping point along the Lake Tahoe Wagon Road, much remarked upon by writers of the period. J. Ross Browne's account, in *A Peep at Washoe,* of dinner and lodging at Strawberry in March 1860, during the Comstock silver rush, rivals anything in Mark Twain's *Roughing It.* (Society of California Pioneers: Lawrence & Houseworth stereo album number 623)

Figure 13.   Strawberry Lodge, 1996. Strawberry Lodge today retains many of the functions and even some of the appearance of its predecessor, shown in figure 12. (photograph by author)

Figure 16.   Dutch Flat and Donner Lake Wagon Road, 1860s. The setting is near Donner Pass, and the time would appear to be spring, judging from the appearance of the snow and the fact that the man in the foreground is in shirtsleeves. The wagons are mostly empty, suggesting that they are returning from the Comstock Lode. Tolls on eastbound wagons were commonly higher than on westbound, because their heavy loads caused more wear and tear on the road. (Bancroft Library)

FACING PAGE;

TOP: Figure 14.   Pyramid Peak, from the top of the Grade at Slippery Ford, early 1860s. Evident here is the excellent quality of the Lake Tahoe Wagon Road, shown here in one of its steepest and most easily eroded stretches. Tolls generated by freight traffic to the silver mines paid for the work. (Society of California Pioneers: Lawrence & Houseworth stereo album number 632)

BOTTOM: Figure 15.   Pyramid Peak from grade on US 50, 1996. This must be fairly close to the site of figure 14, though alterations in topography caused by blasting and earth-moving equipment over the years can make it hard to find the exact camera sites used by Thomas Houseworth. (photograph by author)

Figure 17.   Loading Wells Fargo Coaches at Cisco. The beginning of the end of an era. By the summer of 1867 the Central Pacific RR was running trains as far up into the Sierra as Cisco (5,710 feet), where they were met by stagecoaches for the onward trip to Virginia City on the Dutch Flat and Donner Lake Wagon Road. The photograph is from a series of stereo pairs made by Alfred A. Hart to document the Central Pacific's construction. (Wells Fargo Bank)

Figure 18.   Donner Pass from the east, 1996. The arch bridge of old US 40 can be seen to the right of center, and snowsheds on the now-abandoned Southern Pacific are faintly visible as a horizontal line against the rock face near the left edge of the picture. (photograph by author)

Figure 21. The Truckee Turnpike from Jackson Meadows, 1996. This once-important stagecoach route to Virginia City faltered when the Central Pacific Railroad was finished in 1869, and survives today as a gravel-and-dirt forest service road running along the ridge in the background. The tops of the Sierra Buttes appear in the distance. (photograph by author)

FACING PAGE;
TOP: Figure 19.   Carson Pass from Red Lake, 1996. Today's highway 88 rises to the pass from the right, blasted out of the rock face. Thousands of pioneers in covered wagons toiled up a much steeper route through the trees at left. (photograph by author)

BOTTOM: Figure 20.   West Pass from Caples Lake, 1996. This gateway to California, as it was regarded by many travelers, is the small notch on the skyline in the center of the picture. At 9,500 feet it was the highest point on any of the main wagon routes into California. Travelers ascended from the far shore of the lake through pine woods to the "perpetual snowbank" visible just below the skyline toward the right side of the picture. Here they turned to the left and scrambled across a treeless slope to the pass. (photograph by author)

Figure 22.   The Hawley Grade, 1996. This stretch of toll road, forming a shortcut between Echo Summit and Luther Pass, is a fairly well preserved example of an improved road from the stagecoach era, now part of the National Historic Trails system. (photograph by author)

The Washoes led the Powers party to Charity Valley and then Hope Valley, where they came out on what Powers called the Old Hangtown and Carson Road, that is, the Carson Pass emigrant road pioneered by the eastbound Mormons in 1848. The Big Trees route thus was not a completely new route all the way through between the gold country and Carson Valley but only as far east as Hope Valley, where it merged with the established emigrant route. Big Trees route promoters hoped that emigrants could be diverted at this point by the prospect of avoiding the stiff climbs over Carson Pass and West Pass. Instead they might travel around this area on the south, over a stretch of elevated but somewhat less rugged mountain country, to Hermit Valley and then on down to the diggings around Murphys, Angels Camp, Columbia, and Sonora, or perhaps go all the way to Stockton.

The Big Trees route was not one of the other five routes Ryland considered, and so it had not been publicized in state documents. Powers sent in a five-page report to Marlette, who included it in his annual report.[36] This was the first officially published description.

Powers and his Calaveras County and Stockton backers evidently had high hopes for the Big Trees route. The distance from Murphys to Cary's Mill (Woodfords), the entrance to Carson Valley, was 65 miles, only 10 of which would require much money or labor. The distance from Placerville to Cary's Mill on the Carson Pass route was only a half dozen miles less, not an enormous difference. Probably for many westbound gold seekers the choice hinged not so much on the difficulty of the road as on the anticipated richness of the diggings around Murphys and Angels Camp versus those around Placerville.

Stockton businessmen subscribed $5,000 to open the new road and divert traffic to it in Hope Valley. The roadwork took place in the summer of 1856. On August 16 the *Calaveras Chronicle* was able to report that the heavy work had been completed, including eight bridges, the largest being 75 feet long and 14 feet wide. On August 23, 1856, the *Chronicle* stated that the road was ready for travel. And not a moment too soon. There were seven hundred teams on the trail west of Humboldt Sink, and runners had been sent out to lure them to competing northern routes. To counteract these blandishments, Calaveras County was having large posters printed and put up along the trail to attract traffic down the Big Trees route.[37]

These early billboards evidently had some effect. On October 9, 1856, a *Sacramento Daily Union* editorial commented enviously on the success of the new road. Most emigrants who reached Carson Valley had chosen the Big Trees route, it lamented, and then gone on to Stockton or the San Joaquin Valley instead of coming to Sacramento. This was the result of a good road and vigorous promotion, plus the fact that the previous winter rains had eroded the "old Johnson trail" so badly it was difficult even for mules. Sacramento should take note and improve its connections through Placerville to Carson Valley.[38]

The Big Trees promoters, however, failed to distinguish between the requirements of a summer-only emigrant road and those of a year-round wagon and coach road (or perhaps they were interested primarily in the emigrants). Sherman Day, who was out surveying the Carson route in the summer of 1855 and almost encountered the Powers party in Hope Valley, had a more realistic view from the beginning:

> I made, however, a short excursion up the upper and southernmost head of Hope Valley, some five or six miles above where the Carson road joins it, and on my return I have learned that this forms a part of their route. We crossed the summit between the head of Hope Valley fork of the Carson River, and a tributary of the Mokelumne. The ascent on the north side was not difficult, nor excessively steep or rocky. A wagon might ascend it in its natural state. . . . In summer I have no doubt a good road could be made over the portion which I could see; but the earth had the appearance of being much covered with deep snows in winter. My principal objection to this route is that it traverses the mountains too much in a line parallel with the main ridge, and it must consequently be much obstructed in winter. I have no doubt it would be an excellent route for stock in summer.[39]

Day turned out to be right. There was too much snow at higher elevations for the Big Trees route ever to become a year-round road. Emigrants used it extensively in 1856 and 1857, but traffic dropped off thereafter, as improvements to the Day route proceeded. The Big Trees route became little more than a summer shortcut between the southern mines and Carson Valley. A May 1860 newspaper item describes the arrival of travelers announcing that the snow was almost gone and the road could be considered open for the season.[40]

That portion of the Big Trees route between Hermit Valley and Hope Valley eventually went out of use. The northern two-thirds survives as the Blue Lakes Road, a gravel road used for summer recreation and not kept open in winter. It may be possible to get through the rest of the way, from the Blue Lakes area to Hermit Valley, in a high-clearance vehicle, but there is no road worthy of the name. A historical monument along Highway 4 in Hermit Valley marks the point where the Big Trees route turned to the north, but it takes some effort to see any traces of a road on the floor of the pine forest that occupies the site now.

A Setback for the State Road

Whether it emanated from Stockton or elsewhere, opposition to the first state-backed road across the Sierra was successful for a time. In the change of administration in Sacramento in January 1856, Neely Johnson replaced John Bigler as governor, and John A. Brewster succeeded Seneca Hunt Marlette as surveyor general. Brewster had his own agenda for road construction in the Sierra.

The Emigrant Wagon Road Act was declared unconstitutional by the California Supreme Court on December 8, 1856. The fatal flaw was article 8 of the state constitution, which set the state debt limit at $300,000. The $100,000 appropriated by the act pushed total debt over this limit. The appropriation would have been legal, the justices said, only if put to popular vote, which had not been done. This seems fair enough, but then the justices went on to say that the debt limit had been ignored before, and that now was a good time to crack down. Such arbitrary enforcement of the law suggests that the supreme court was part of the political attack on the Day route.

Sherman Day, back in Sacramento in his capacity of state senator, had anticipated a constitutional attack on the Emigrant Wagon Road Act. Apparently trying to soothe local rivalries, he introduced another road bill into the California senate in March 1856, which provided for the survey and improvement of no less than five wagon roads, as follows: Nobles Pass, $20,000; Henness Pass, $60,000; a road up the South Fork of the American thence via Luther's Pass to Carson Valley, $100,000; Big Trees, $40,000; and Cajon Pass, $20,000. The total of $240,000 was to be paid for with state bonds, the measure to be placed on the ballot as a referendum measure at the next election.

Day's measure never came to a vote, because of dissatisfaction over amounts allotted to various roads and opposition by railroad advocates who said that the railroad would make road expenditure unnecessary.[41] State activity in encouraging road links was thus brought to a halt for a time, but that did not stop a variety of local measures from going forward. In the Lake Tahoe area, for example, another survey was carried out by the official surveyor of Placer County, Thomas A. Young. His party went up the Forest Hill Divide and crossed to Squaw Valley, ascended the Truckee to Lake Tahoe, followed the north shore of the lake, and crossed the Carson Range to Washoe Valley. This survey blazed a trail that was promoted as the Placer County Emigrant Road, which may have attracted emigrant parties for a season or two but does not seem to have become more than a trail.

Father north somewhat more serious results were achieved. James Birch's California Stage Company had moved its headquarters to Marysville and dominated northern California land transportation. In 1855 the *Marysville Herald* began a vigorous editorial promotion of the Henness Pass route, presenting it as a way for Marysville to compete successfully with such rivals as Sacramento, Stockton, and Placerville in attracting emigrants.[42] In his 1856 Annual Report, Surveyor General Marlette included a two-page report by D. B. Scott of Marysville on the Henness route, recommending improvements that Scott thought could be done for less than $50,000. Scott also had a plan, somewhat chimerical, to run the road from Henness Pass through Dog Valley to Pyramid Lake and the Humboldt, bypassing Truckee Meadows.[43]

State-funded improvements were not forthcoming for the Henness Pass route, however. Scott's report was but two pages, while reports by Day, Goddard, and Marlette himself on routes via Placerville took up some ninety-seven pages of the Annual Report. The *Marysville Herald* editor was probably right when he fumed that the fix was already in for state aid to a Placerville route across the mountains.

Management of the California Stage Company evidently took a pragmatic view of things, though. When on June 28, 1856, the citizens of Placerville voted to spend $5,500 for an improved wagon road to Carson Valley along Day's route, the company announced it would run stagecoaches on it as soon as it was completed.

In August 1856 Surveyor General Brewster responded to a request from Downieville, county seat of Sierra County, and led a survey party up the North Fork of the Yuba River. They crossed over into Sierra Valley by way of Chapman Pass, somewhat to the north of Yuba Pass. From Sierra Valley they crossed Beckwourth Pass and then went southeast to Truckee Meadows (Reno). From here they made an excursion down the Truckee River to Pyramid Lake and back. Returning to California, the Brewster party followed the Henness Pass route part way, turned off to Sierra Valley, and retraced their steps to Downieville.

Brewster's conclusion from these rambles was that a good road could be made up the North Fork of the Yuba River through Sierra Valley to Beckwourth Pass, with some work. He admitted that he was not sure how much of a snow problem there would be. Such a road would have been the ancestor of today's Highway 49. Was it built? According to Stewart Mitchell there was a pack trail across Yuba Pass to Downieville, but the first wagon road from the east into the upper valley of the North Fork of the Yuba was via Henness Pass and Goodyears Bar.[44] Evidently Highway 49 came later.

At the same time that Brewster was reconnoitering the Downieville route, William Gamble and Job T. Taylor were exploring a route from Marysville north along the ridge between Butte Creek and the west branch of the Feather River. This proposed road would have passed through the vicinity of today's Lake Almanor and intersected the Nobles road near Susanville. The *Sacramento Daily Union* reported optimistically that the roughest portions could be improved by Butte County for $300 and that there was good grass and water all along the way.[45]

It is clear from all this that trans-Sierra roads were the subject of great popular interest, and controversy, in the mid-1850s, as cities and counties competed with each other to have such roads pass their way. In the background there remained interests opposed to *any* trans-Sierra road. The Pacific Mail Steamship Company and other shipping companies were receiving a $1.2 million annual subsidy for carrying mail and might lose it if overland mail transportation became established. And railroad enthusiasts maintained that road construction would be a waste of money since it was just a matter of time until the railroad would be built.

Though the first state efforts at road building had bogged down in political and judicial conflict, the halt was only temporary. Much had been achieved. A number of routes across the Sierra had been reconnoitered and publicized in state documents. A transect across the Sierra from the vicinity of Placerville south of Lake Tahoe to Carson Valley had emerged as the leading contender, and variant routes within that general corridor had been surveyed in detail.

CHAPTER 6

The Distant Prospect of Railroads

Even before California became part of the United States, a rail line between the Mississippi Valley and Oregon had been widely discussed in the East. Many Americans saw it as a way to unify a huge national territory and to bring the trade opportunities of the Pacific closer. The great expectation was that such a line would become not only a means of domestic transport but also a great avenue of world commerce, linking Asia and Europe across North America. This may have been an echo of the notion of the "Northwest Passage," so important in the geographic thinking of the sixteenth century, but it was a new kind of northwest passage that was proposed this time, of steel rather than water.

Railroad enthusiasts proposed a transcontinental line almost as soon as the first few miles of track were laid in the Atlantic states in the 1830s. The first person to work out the details was Asa Whitney, a New York businessman who had spent two years in China. In 1845 he proposed to Congress that he be granted a strip of land 60 miles wide from Lake Michigan to the Pacific Coast. By selling the land to settlers he would raise money to build the railroad. It is interesting to see the language Whitney thought would persuade Congress to his point of view.

Nature seems to have ordained here an empire of the East and one of the West; but this great work of man's art and labor would, by a moral certainty, nullify this decree and naturally maintain an indissoluble union between them. . . .

> ... [I]t will create the same commercial relations between the United States and Asia, over the bosom of the Pacific, and across this continent, between Europe and Asia; thus making a belt running over and through the heart of our country the great channel of the commerce of the world. And yet another object, dearer and more precious to every good mind than all this, is, that this great and common interest of nations would naturally tend to secure the peace of the world, while the greatest benefit would be ours—this country being the pivot on which these vast interests would turn.[1]

Whitney memorialized Congress at least three times in the late 1840s, but he was ahead of his time. Not that Whitney's "Pacific Railroad" completely failed to find support; Thomas Hart Benton, of Missouri, introduced a Pacific railroad bill in the Senate in 1849. But it was to be twenty years before the railroad became a reality, and in the meantime transport entrepreneurs used the much cheaper and ready-to-hand technology of wagons and pack animals to satisfy demand.

Yet the assumed railroad was in the background of every discussion of roads, which were thought to be expedients of a more or less temporary nature. Because the inevitable rail connection to the East was in every Californian's mind from the very beginning of the American period, an understanding of the course of road development in the Sierra requires some consideration of the political struggle for the Pacific railroad. By reviewing some of the railroad debates, we can better understand the geopolitical thinking that underlay road proposals.

Less than two months into the first session of the California legislature (1849–50), John Bigler, assembly speaker, and John McDougal, president of the senate, introduced "Joint Resolutions in Relation to a National Railroad from the Pacific Ocean to the Mississippi River." California's congressional delegation was instructed to urge on Congress the importance of such a railroad. The resolutions called for the organization of "an efficient Engineer Corps, to make complete surveys and exploration of the several routes which have been recommended to public notice as practicable for the line of said road."[2] Nothing came of this measure, but it did make the new state's ambitions clear from the beginning.

In 1853 Chicago and New York were connected by rail. That year the Pacific railroad was the subject of prolonged debate in Congress, as a project that was already technologically feasible and awaited only the mustering of political will. But there were two serious political obstacles in the way of the railroad.

The first was "sectional rivalry," that is, the conflict between North and South. Congressional delegations from the northern states were afraid that a southern route to the Pacific would stimulate a flow of population into the land recently acquired from Mexico and so lead to the creation of more slave states. Those from the southern states were equally sure that a northern route would lead to more free states. The conflict of interest proved to be an insuperable problem as long as the United States was divided into these "sections." Congress was unable to pass a transcontinental railroad bill until 1862, after the Civil War had begun and opposition from southern legislators had vanished along with the legislators themselves, leaving those remaining free to choose a northern route unhindered. (It was actually a central route geographically, but northern politically). Then the war itself delayed construction a few more years, and it was not until 1869 that the famous golden spike was driven at Promontory.

The second obstacle had to do with interpretation of the U.S. Constitution. Quaint as the notion may seem in an era when commuters jam local freeways built mostly with federal funds, many Americans in the 1850s thought that federal financing of internal improvements such as roads and railroads was unconstitutional. Proponents of railroads and wagon roads were forced to rely on creative argumentation based on article 1, section 8, which provides that "Congress shall have power . . . to establish post offices and post roads," or else on the military necessity of roads to protect borders or pacify Indians. Without sectional rivalry the constitutional objection probably would have atrophied as successive elections brought a more railroad-oriented generation to Washington, D.C., but avid sectional rivalry kept it alive.

Senator Benton's Efforts

Despite the obstacles, many members of the House and Senate continued to press for a Pacific railroad. Not surprisingly, a strong center of support was the West, which in those days included what we now call the Middle West. One of the strongest western railroad enthusiasts was Senator Benton. In a speech on February 7, 1849, Benton introduced his bill for "a national central highway from the Mississippi River to the Pacific Ocean." Warming up with a review of attempts by France, Spain, and Britain to find a northwest passage across America and an assertion of the vital importance of "Asiatic commerce" to Western civilization since the days of the Phoenicians, Benton then recapitulated the exploring career of his son-in-law, John C. Frémont, with long extracts from Frémont's reports, all conducing to show that the obvious choice of routes for a Pacific railroad lay generally along the thirty-eighth parallel between St. Louis and San Francisco.

Benton had no confidence in private entrepreneurs like Asa Whitney: they were inappropriate agents to negotiate with the Indians for the right-of-way, were incompetent to carry out the job, and would inevitably "make it a great stock-jobbing business, to be sold in the markets of Europe and America" (which is not far off the mark of what happened twenty years later with the Union Pacific). Instead Benton proposed a "national central road, a highway not merely for ourselves, but for our posterity, for all time to come."

What Benton envisioned would today be called a transportation corridor: a right-of-way one mile wide within which several technologies could be put in service alongside each other—railroad, plank road, macadamized road, even what sounds like an early version of magnetic levitation—with the proviso that a 100-foot strip would be forever reserved for local farm traffic, toll free. There were to be military posts along the road at appropriate intervals, and the whole project was to be financed by the sale of public lands. The federal government would own this corridor and license individuals and companies to provide transport services along it. This would be "the American road to India" and would ensure that "the rich commerce of Asia will flow through our center." It was a great vision, but the bill died in the Committee on Public Affairs.[3]

On December 16, 1850, Senator Benton reintroduced his transportation corridor bill, with the added feature of 160-acre grants to encourage settlement along the right-of-way. Benton emphasized the centrality of a thirty-eighth parallel route, its multiuse nature allowing many kinds of travel and communication, its ownership by the federal government, and self-financing through public land sales. He disparaged the idea that only men of science could lay out the road.

> There is a class of topographical engineers older than the schools, and more unerring than the mathematics. They are the wild animals—buffalo, elk, deer, antelope, bears—which traverse the forest, not by compass, but by an instinct which leads them always the right way—to the lowest passes in the mountains, the shallowest fords in the rivers, the richest pastures in the forests, the best salt springs, and the shortest practicable lines between remote points. . . . [T]he Indians follow them, and hence a buffalo road becomes a war-path. The first white hunters follow the same trails in pursuing their game; and after that the buffalo road becomes the wagon road of the white man, and finally the macadamized or railroad of the scientific man.

After reviewing examples of how some important thoroughfares in the eastern United States had been established in this way, Benton went on to promote his own favorite route, which he projected in fairly exact geographic detail across the Plains and central Rockies, only to trail off somewhat vaguely in the Far West: "and through the Great Basin, crossing the Sierra Nevada near its middle, or turning it on the south." Benton then returned to his fundamental theme: "When finished it will be the American road to Asia, and will turn the Asiatic commerce of Europe through the heart of our America. It will make us the mistress of that trade—rich at home and powerful abroad—and reviving a line of oriental and almost fabulous cities to stretch across our continent— Tyres, Sidons, Palmyras, Balbecs." Not to be confined to the Old World for his inspiration, he pointed out another great road system for Americans to emulate, that of the Incas, which he described with extracts from William H. Prescott and Alexander von Humboldt.[4]

This was Benton's swan song, however. After five terms in the Senate, he had been defeated in the election of 1850, and his long career there was in its final days. (He later served one term in the House of Representatives, 1853–55.)

Senator Gwin's Efforts

California's Senator William Gwin, it is surprising to learn, was opposed to Benton's proposal. Evidently unimpressed with the surveying powers of buffalo and Indians, Gwin noted (accurately) that animals, and men on foot or horseback, often cross mountains on grades far too steep for railroads. Gwin was concerned that Benton's plan would mean a premature commitment to a particular route. On December 30, 1850, he presented resolutions from the California legislature calling for "the organization of an efficient engineer corps to make complete surveys and explorations of the several routes which have been recommended to public notice as practicable for the line of said road."[5]

No federal action followed from Gwin's efforts at first. A public meeting in San Francisco on November 28, 1851, pressed the legislature on the need for a Pacific railroad. The meeting's fourteen-page statement pointed out the benefits of a railroad between the Pacific and the Mississippi Valley in enthusiastic if somewhat general terms. Such a line would bind the nation together, become a great thoroughfare uniting Europe and Asia, serve for the defense of California in case of invasion,

and so forth. The statement mentions the Whitney and Benton proposals without favoring either or proposing an alternative and ends up
asking to have "a competent corps of engineers employed to obtain
prompt surveys of all known or probable routes for such a road."[6]

Gwin offered his own railroad proposal in the next Congress, on August 30, 1852. It came in the form of an amendment tacked onto a bill
to grant 10 million acres of land to the states for the support of indigent
insane persons, a bill being promoted by Dorothea Dix. The only connection Gwin's amendment seems to have had to the main bill was that
the railroad too would involve grants of public land.

Gwin proposed constructing not one but two and a half railroads connecting the Mississippi with the Pacific Ocean. One would run from a
point on the Red River near the southwestern corner of Arkansas via El
Paso to a point near the junction of the Gila and Colorado rivers, and
the other from a point on the western boundary of Missouri or Iowa on
the most direct route to the eastern boundary of California, with a
branch to some tidewater harbor in Oregon.

When two senators objected to making the indigent insane bill a vehicle for something quite different, Gwin replied, somewhat undiplo-
matically perhaps, that "its [the indigent insane bill's] importance sinks
into insignificance when compared to the great national measure em-
bodied in my amendment." (The transcripts of the 1853 debates on the
Pacific railroad make it easy to see how Gwin might have seemed a pushy
upstart to senators from the eastern states and that this may not have
helped speed action on the railroad.) Gwin went on to assert that national unity vitally depended on strengthening the precarious connections between the Atlantic states and the Pacific Coast. He failed to persuade a majority of his fellow senators, however, and his amendment
was rejected 31 to 21.[7]

Early in the following year, on January 13, 1853, Illinois's Senator
Stephen Douglas introduced a "bill for the protection of the emigrant
route and a telegraphic line, and for an overland mail between the Missouri River and the settlements of California and Oregon."[8] Gwin immediately introduced a substitute measure, distinctly more ambitious
than his August 1852 bill: nothing less than a western railroad *system*.
It came in the form of an amendment to Douglas's bill, which despite its
name continued to serve in the record as the vehicle for proposals regarding the railroad.

Gwin proposed a federal subsidy for a railroad to run as follows (in
the language of his bill):

From San Francisco, via Fulton, in Arkansas to Memphis. . . . 2000 miles.

The St. Louis branch from a point on the main trunk, thirty-five miles south of Santa Fé, to St. Louis. . . . 915 miles.

The Dubuque branch from a point on the St. Louis branch, where it intersects the Arkansas river, to Dubuque. . . . 610 miles.

The Texas branch from the source of Red river, or the southern bend of the main trunk, to the source of the Colorado river, and thence to Matagorda bay, on the Gulf. . . . 535 miles.

The New Orleans route from Fulton to New Orleans. . . . 405 miles.

And the Oregon branch from San Francisco, in California, to Fort Nisqually, in Oregon. . . . 650 miles.

total 5,115 miles

The main line from San Francisco to Fulton was to be south through the San Joaquin Valley, across the Mojave Desert to the Colorado River near Needles (thus with a great deal of mileage within the state of California), thence across New Mexico Territory to Albuquerque. In introducing his bill Gwin set the appropriate historical context for his plan by invoking Roman roads, the public works of Napoleon, and British projects to bring India closer to Europe by overland rail links. His peroration tried to entice easterners with the boundless possibilities that a closer connection with California offered and subtly threatened them with the consequences of losing that connection.

> Look at the commercial position she occupies in respect to the other members of the Union, and to Asia, the Japanese Islands, soon to be unsealed and opened to our trade, to Central and South America, and to the Sandwich Islands, (which 600 whaling ships visited in a single year,) besides other islands of Oceanica. With auriferous regions that defy exhaustion, with agricultural wealth, (the foundation of manufactures,) more valuable even than her mountain ridges of glittering gold, with harbors unsurpassed in the world, with a population full of enterprise, energy, skill, and activity in every department of the business of life, California, by the laws of her geographical and commercial position, is destined to draw within her golden gates the trade of Central and South America, with the rich traffic of the East; to hold the supremacy there, and be the great seat of commercial wealth and power on the Pacific ocean.[9]

Funding for the 4,400 miles outside Texas was to come through grants of public land totaling 97,536,000 acres, which, at $1.25 per acre, would raise about $27,700 per mile. (At this time, according to Gwin, railroads were being built east of the Mississippi for an average of $27,300 per mile.) Texas had come into the Union without federal public land, so equivalent payments would have to be made from the U.S. Treasury for the 715 miles to be built in that state. Gwin insisted that there were no constitutional problems with his proposal: such a railroad would be a post road within the spirit of the Constitution.

John Bell of Tennessee rose immediately to speak in support of the Gwin plan. There was a danger of losing the West Coast to England or France. It would be better to spend $100 million on the railroad to defend the coast than $500 million or $600 million later to recover it. If public land sales were insufficient, the Senate should vote to spend however much would be needed. The exact route did not matter.

Seven other senators were not so supportive. All except one claimed to support the Pacific railroad on principle as a grand national goal, but they had their doubts about this particular proposal. Hannibal Hamlin of Maine thought the Senate was being rushed; there were many other railroad proposals, and it was necessary to pick the best. Jacob Miller of New Jersey wanted to wait until more was known about the route. John Davis of Massachusetts thought it was unfortunate that Gwin had even mentioned the route, which should be decided by experts. He was also worried that the measure would be enough to build the track but not provide rolling stock. William Seward of New York was sure the project would cost far more than $27,000 per mile. Lewis Cass of Michigan wanted to lop off the branches and build a single direct trunk from the ocean to the Mississippi. Andrew Butler of South Carolina thought it was altogether too grand a scheme, and besides, there were constitutional objections. Thomas Rusk of Texas thought it should be left to private enterprise to find the cheapest route, but then the nation would have to guard against monopoly.

There followed many days of debate. The Pacific railroad proved to be the main issue of that session of Congress, and everyone had something to say about it. This material is of interest to historians of the Pacific railroad but must be skipped over here, except to note a few remarks that have a directly geographic bearing and indicate something about the nature of public opinion at that time.

Of particular interest is the question of crossing the Sierra Nevada. Gwin's partiality to a southern route led him to promote Walker Pass, though as a result of Frémont's error this was actually Tehachapi Pass. Gwin introduced a letter from Richard Kern, topographer on Frémont's disastrous expedition to the Colorado Rockies in December 1848.[10] The Kern letter outlined a route between Albuquerque and Walker Pass and asserted that it was "useless to imagine that a pass can be found north of Kern River for a railroad, into either the San Joaquin or Sacramento Valleys."[11]

Gwin's thoughts on a route through the Sierra, buttressed with references to Joseph Walker, came in a speech on January 19, 1853.

> We know that we can get through the Sierra Nevada at Walker's Pass, which is only at a latitude of about thirty-five degrees. We do not know any pass north of that through which we can go. The object of this bill is to get through that pass. Mr. President, I have no local partiality at all in regard to this matter. If we could get a road to run nearer to the center of California, it would suit me, and it would suit my constituents better. . . . I am prepared to show that one of the most celebrated trappers on the Pacific Coast (Mr. Walker) has passed five times over this route, and he says it is the best route between the Rio Grande and the Pacific. He would never go over any but the best route. That is the best evidence that is practicable.[12]

The next day, January 20, Salmon Chase of Ohio asserted that it was by no means clear that there was no pass north of Walker's and that he rather thought that the Sierra would be pierced at several points, just like the Alleghenies. Striking a sectional note, he opined that a central route from Independence to San Francisco would probably be best. On January 27, Thomas Rusk of Texas, a strong supporter of the railroad, made an impassioned speech to the effect that building the railroad would be the greatest possible service senators could do for the country. It would be an enormous stimulus to industry, he said, and would preserve international peace by connecting California firmly to the rest of the country and thus remove it as a temptation for foreign naval powers.

As the whole Senate was debating the Pacific railroad in general terms, a select committee of five senators was working on a proposal that would be less grandiose than Gwin's, and more passable. On February 2, 1853, they returned with a considerably altered bill. The president was to select the route by naming the principal mountain passes, leaving the detailed location work to the builders. The president was to be advised in this matter by the Corps of Topographical Engineers and up to ten civilian engineers. The railroad would be financed by grants of odd-numbered sections of public land for 6 miles on either side of the track in states and 12 miles in territories, 80 percent to be turned over in installments on completion of 50-mile increments and the remaining 20 percent on completion of the whole line. The contractors would form a corporation to be known as the Pacific Railroad and Telegraph Company.

In a February 5, 1853, debate on this matter, Bell, a member of the select committee, defended the committee's work. The Constitution gave the federal government the right to make military roads through the territories of the United States, he asserted, and a modern military road would be a railroad. There was too much delaying talk about more surveys. The country already had the findings of Pike, Long, Frémont, Emory, Stansbury, Abert, Simpson, Marcy, Sitgreaves, Johnson, and others. Traders and trappers had frequented the region for thirty years, and about fifty thousand immigrants were wending their way west every year. The possible routes were therefore already quite well known. In the Sierra Nevada, Walker Pass was known to be good, and possibly there was one at the head of the Sacramento Valley as well. The select committee had realized that Congress would never agree on the end points of the route and therefore wanted the president to do it, since he was less likely to be controlled by sectional or local interest. But having the president oversee the actual construction of the railroad would put too much patronage in his hands, so the committee had left that to private individuals or companies, with land grants and the $20 million as inducements. This $20 million was quite moderate; it would be worth even $200 million to secure the West Coast against the designs of Britain and France.[13]

Bell pressed on when the bill was next taken up, on February 17. He again heaped scorn on the notion that extensive new surveys were needed.

> The proposition . . . is now, in 1853, to commence the explorations and examinations of the route for this great work, as if during four years, I may say five years, since this new and last accession to our territory has been made, these examinations had not been going on with more or less assiduity, and more or less success; as if report after report had not been made to Congress, communicating observations and explorations; as if you had not, by your order, printed numerous reports of explorations and reconnoissances, with expensive charts and maps, of a large portion of the country intervening between the Mississippi valley and the Pacific ocean.

The only necessary surveys would be local ones, in Bell's opinion, as for example in the Sierra Nevada to see if there was anything better than Walker Pass. The great objects of the project were to provide a daily mail between the Mississippi and the Pacific, to assure the free transportation of troops and munitions, and to pacify the Indians. The railroad would democratize access to the gold and other wealth of California. It would contend against the interests of steamship companies and capitalists building railroads across the Isthmus of Panama. Eventually we could

look forward to two, three, perhaps even four Pacific railroads. Bell concluded with a long warning about how war with Britain or France remained a possibility, even if not now likely. It was extremely important
to bind the United States together militarily with a railroad.[14]

Truman Smith of Connecticut spoke after Bell. He paid more than the
usual amount of attention to potential problems in the Sierra Nevada
and emphasized the importance of securing the $5 million a month in
gold that California was sending east: "Every one admits that we can
build a railroad from the Missouri to the Sierra Nevada, but whether we
can get over that mountain is a matter of doubt. The Sierra would have
to be explored through several degrees of latitude and all the passes carefully examined. This would be the only point on that route of serious
difficulty."

Even after prolonged debate, the Senate was unable to come to an
agreement. On February 23, 1853, the members finally turned to other
business, the army appropriations bill. To keep the Pacific railroad issue
alive Gwin proposed an amendment to that bill authorizing the secretary of war to have the Corps of Topographic Engineers carry out surveys "to ascertain the most practicable and most economical route from
the Mississippi to the Pacific coast" and to appropriate $150,000 for the
job.[15] This was the beginning of the Pacific Railroad Surveys.

The Pacific Railroad Surveys

Thwarted in attempts to pass his grand Pacific railroad bill, Gwin had
settled for a scientific assessment of the various routes. Secretary of War
Jefferson Davis was to order the Corps of Topographic Engineers to organize as many survey parties as there were routes to be surveyed.

Actually, "survey" is a misnomer. There was neither time nor sufficient money appropriated for proper surveys. These were more in the
nature of reconnaissances. Six parties were sent out, covering the West
from just south of the Canadian border to just north of the Mexican one.
Ironically, the route along which the railroad was eventually built was
not included. Davis decided that Frémont and Howard Stansbury had
already sufficiently covered the central route as far as Salt Lake City, and
in any case it led to the middle of the Sierra Nevada, over which there
was thought to be no practicable pass.

Later, by a revision of plans, one of the surveys did pass the northern
edge of the Sierra, in that indeterminate zone where the Sierra and the

Cascades meet. This was the thirty-eighth parallel survey, leaving from Fort Leavenworth and led at first by Captain J. W. Gunnison, with Lieutenant E. G. Beckwith as chief assistant. The Gunnison party was to cross the Rockies by Cochetope Pass at the headwaters of the Arkansas, following the route long promoted by Thomas Hart Benton. Gunnison had already had some experience in the Rockies in 1849–50, when he served as chief assistant in Captain Stansbury's survey of the Great Salt Lake and a strip across what is now southern Wyoming.

Jefferson Davis did not at first plan to send the Gunnison party to the Sierra, explaining his reasons as follows:

> Reliable information, furnished by persons who had been extensively connected with the western explorations of the government, gave such assurance that no railway pass could be found north of Kern river, into either the Sacramento or San Joaquin valley, that it was not deemed proper to expend any part of the limited means appropriated in such a search; and having learned that the Mormons of the Great Salt Lake were making a survey for a railroad from their settlement to Walker's Pass, Captain Gunnison, whose former intercourse with their engineer would enable him to obtain whatever information he possessed, was directed to procure a report of that survey, thus connecting his line with the survey ordered to be made near the 35th parallel.[16]

After reaching Salt Lake Valley and interviewing the Mormons, Gunnison was to explore back in an easterly direction to look for a route through the Wasatch via the Weber or Bear River Valley.

As it turned out, Gunnison's chief accomplishment on this trip was to document the hopelessness of the Cochetope Pass route for a railroad. He did not live to see the attainment of other ends of the survey. On October 21, 1853, the party got into a fight with Paiute Indians near the Sevier River. Gunnison and seven others were killed. Beckwith took over, and after wintering in Utah he led the party the following spring in exploring possible routes through the Wasatch and Uintah ranges between Fort Bridger and Salt Lake, as planned. He then successfully petitioned Jefferson Davis to let him extend the forty-first parallel survey west from Salt Lake to San Francisco.

Beckwith took his party around south of the lake to the headwaters of the Humboldt and followed the river downstream along the emigrant trail. Instead of going all the way to the Truckee or Carson River, however, he left the Humboldt at Lassen's Meadows (vicinity of present Winnemucca) and explored two less-frequented entrances to California. One was the Nobles route near Honey Lake, already in use by wagons. The other went through a remote area known as the Madeline Plains, about 45 miles north of Honey Lake, thence to the Pit River, which it descended through two difficult canyons to the vicinity of what later became Redding. Beckwith favored this northern route, which seems strange, since the area was, and remains today, so far off the beaten track. The Pacific Railroad Surveys thus explored the northernmost fringe of the Sierra almost by accident.[17] (The army officer E. G. Beckwith was quite a different person from James Beckwourth, the trapper and mountain man who tried to promote a road through the north end of the Sierra two years earlier.)

In addition to the east-west routes, a survey was to be carried out within California. On May 6, 1853, Jefferson Davis ordered Lieutenant Robert Stockton Williamson, of the Corps of Topographical Engineers, to explore "the passes of the Sierra Nevada leading from the San Joaquin and Tulare valleys, and subsequently explore the country to the southeast of the Tulare lakes, to ascertain the most direct practicable railroad route between Walker's Pass, or such other pass as may be found preferable, and the mouth of the Gila."[18] Accordingly, Williamson proceeded to the south end of the San Joaquin Valley to explore Walker Pass and the crest of the Tehachapi Range to its junction with the Coast Ranges. (The Tehachapis are now not usually considered part of the Sierra Nevada.) Williamson concluded that the best gateway to the San Joaquin Valley was Tehachapi Pass, Walker Pass being "badly situated and impracticable." This honest assessment forced him to publicize an error in the popular account by Frémont, his famous senior in the Corps of Topographic Engineers. Frémont had mistaken Tehachapi Pass for Walker Pass in 1844. Williamson was diplomatic: "Colonel Fremont, in April [of 1844] had crossed the Sierra about half a degree south of this pass [Walker], and he may subsequently have concluded that the place he crossed was Walker's Pass, though I am not aware that he ever so concluded."[19] Williamson was too kind: the Pathfinder clearly thought that he had come through Walker Pass even after traveling a while with Walker himself later in the same expedition.

Williamson believed a practicable pass across the Sierra could be found farther north, and he prevailed on Jefferson Davis to let him try. On May 1, 1855, Davis instructed Williamson to carry out two supplemental surveys in California and Oregon. Williamson was first to find a route from the Sacramento Valley to the Columbia River, either via the Willamette Valley or the Deschutes Valley east of the Cascades. Davis's instructions continued:

> Make the necessary examinations and surveys to determine if a route practicable for a railroad exists crossing the Sierra Nevada, at or near the source of the Carson River. This may furnish the most direct railroad route from San Francisco to the Great Salt Lake. The duty first assigned you having been completed, you will ascertain from the commanding officer, Lt. Col. Steptoe, and others of the troops that may have crossed the Great Basin from Great Salt Lake and the Sierra Nevada, by the route near the sources of the Carson River, all the details necessary to a knowledge of the character of the route traversed by them and should the information which you may have gathered lead to the opinion that the route is practicable for a railroad, or that such a route may be found in that region, you will proceed to make the examinations and surveys necessary to ascertain if such be the case. It will not, probably, be necessary to extend this examination beyond the eastern foot of the Sierra Nevada.[20]

The results of such a survey, had it been carried out, would have formed an interesting episode in the history of western exploration at the very least, and possibly would have had an impact on the railroad project when it finally was undertaken, but the survey was called off. In an introductory letter in the published report Second Lieutenant Henry L. Abbot noted,

> At the completion of the survey for the railroad route from the Sacramento valley to the Columbia river, the season was so far advanced and the animals were in so jaded condition, that Lt. Williamson considered it impracticable to make any examination of the Sierra Nevada until the ensuing spring. Before that time, orders were received from the War Department, directing him to return at once to Washington to prepare the maps, profiles and reports of the exploration already made. The second survey contemplated in his original instructions was consequently omitted.[21]

In this way, the Pacific Railroad Surveys, a twelve-volume set with the full title of *Reports of the Explorations and Surveys to Ascertain the Most Practicable and Economical Route for a Railroad from the Mississippi River to the Pacific Ocean,* a great treasure trove of geographic information about the West, had little to say about the Sierra Nevada.[22]

Anyone who thought that the surveys would remove the question of a railroad route from the realm of sectional politics was in for a disappointment. Jefferson Davis concluded, "A comparison of the results stated above . . . conclusively shows that the route of the 32d parallel is of those surveyed, the most practical and economical route for a railroad from the Mississippi river to the Pacific ocean."[23] Davis's conclusion expressed some geographically valid concerns about distance and climate but was perceived in the north as thoroughly sectional. His choice of a thirty-second parallel route, the southernmost of the five, was assured of meeting a hostile response in the northern states.

Nor had the constitutional opposition to internal improvements evaporated. Indeed, the arrival of Franklin Pierce in the White House in March 1853 strengthened the opposition. In his first annual message to Congress, on December 5, 1853, Pierce showed a cautious approval of the Pacific Railroad Surveys, then under way, but insisted on "the obligation strictly to adhere to the Constitution and faithfully execute the powers it confers." To Pierce this meant that

> although the power to construct or aid in the construction of a road within the limits of a Territory is not embarrassed by the question of jurisdiction which would arise within the limits of a State, it is, nevertheless, held to be of doubtful power and more than doubtful propriety, even within the limits of a Territory, for the General Government to undertake to administer the affairs of a railroad, a canal, or other similar construction, and therefore that its connection with a work of this character should be incidental rather than primary.[24]

Pierce does not cite the Constitution or any judicial authority for his conclusion, which by opposing transportation projects even in the territories put him in the ranks of the strictest of strict constructionists.

Californians kept up the pressure for a Pacific railroad through the early 1850s, but as time went by no results were forthcoming, and it began to be the accepted political wisdom that nothing could be accomplished on the Pacific railroad until the sectional issue was somehow resolved. Overland transport advocates shifted their efforts to wagon and stagecoach roads.

CHAPTER 7

The Federal Government Builds West to California

The first proposal for a federal overland road came in 1850 from one William Bayard, who outlined a post road from Fort Smith (Arkansas) to San Diego, with the necessary stations and supply points and with mail coaches to be run on a weekly schedule. Bayard proposed that in addition to the right of using government timber and stone along the way, charging tolls to maintain the road, and preempting four sections at 10¢ per acre for every 30 miles of road, he would receive $750,000 from the federal government every year for fifteen years. After this time the road and improvements would revert to the government. The House Committee on Post Offices and Post Roads reported favorably on a bill to this end on March 3, 1851.

The influential oceanographer Matthew Fontaine Maury testified in favor of the measure.

> Practically—not designedly, but nevertheless practically and in effect—the isthmus route is almost exclusively for the benefit of the people of the seaboard. Let them have it, but do justice to the West; and the West, I have maintained often, has never yet received its fair share of public expenditure.
>
> California had been scarcely annexed before the coast survey was on its way there to point out shoals and dangers, and to make the way smooth, safe, and easy to the people of the seaboard, for the people of the seaboard are those "who go down to the sea in ships," and who reap the first benefits and profits of commerce. For the safety of that commerce and the people who are engaged in it light-houses are maintained, the coast survey is carried on, and the navy is supported, at a cost, all told, of some eight or ten millions a year.

None of this money is expended among the western people. They are left to battle the watch with snags in the rivers—with the forest, with wild beasts, and savages on the land; and there are but few ways in which the government finds it expedient or practicable so to shape its disbursements as to give them their fair share.[1]

Maury, a naval officer, is remembered for a sea-based program of empire building, so it is interesting to see him argue so strongly for the landsman's point of view. Despite Maury's support, Bayard's proposal seems to have died without further action.

The notion of a transcontinental federal road had been mooted, however, and even taken to the point of proposed legislation, in the first year of California statehood. The idea faded for a while in the early 1850s, probably because of premature optimism about prospects for the railroad. But with the Pacific railroad stalled year after year, Californians began to think anew about roads. Along with their local- and state-level efforts, they turned their attention to the federal government as well. Political strife within California over the routes of trans-Sierra roads did not prevent Californians from crying with one voice for federal assistance in improving overland transportation between the Missouri frontier and the east side of the Sierra Nevada.

In early 1856, mass meetings in San Francisco, Sacramento, Marysville, Placerville, and elsewhere around the state accumulated 75,000 signatures on a petition asking for a military wagon road to be created along the central overland route. The text of this petition reminded Congress that California had produced some $300 million worth of gold and then went on to claim that the state's great necessity was increased population, "an immigration of the working and producing classes." The language is typical of political and journalistic expression at that time.

Our petition to Congress is for the immediate construction of a wagon-road between the frontier of the States of Missouri and California, following the general route of the old emigrant road, passing through the valley of the Great Salt Lake, and reaching California at a point on the eastern slope of the Sierra Nevada, where the Carson Valley leaves the mountains, and where now is established a flourishing village, known as Carson Valley Settlement [Genoa]. This is the route of the great immigration of 1849 and 1850. It is mostly a level plain, requiring a few small bridges, the establishment of ferries, occasional excavations, and the sinking of a few wells. It is central; already have 300,000 people crossed it, thus satisfactorily demonstrating the practicability of the route.

> Our petition is also for the establishment of military posts at such conve-
> nient posts along the line of said route as shall effectually contribute to the
> protection and safety, the construction of workshops, blacksmith shops, and
> such other aid as may be necessary for the public.
>
> We are now, as it were, a distant colony.[2]

Even as the signatures accumulated in California, Senator John Weller
was busy in Washington, D.C., preparing a bill "to provide for an overland mail from some point on the Mississippi river to San Francisco in
California." Introduced on February 14, 1856, the bill was referred to
the House Committee on Post Offices and Post Roads.[3] Weller wanted
a post *road,* not merely the establishment of postal *service* over such
tracks as might already be available. The committee struck the road out,
however, when it reported back. Weller was unfazed and turned to a
new and more ambitious proposal: a bill for an overland military road.
The petition and its signatures, said to be the largest number ever brought
before Congress, would not go to waste.

Sentiments for improved overland transport, and the number of signatures on the petition as well, doubtless were increased by a sensational
riot in Panama City on April 6, 1856, between California-bound Americans and Europeans on one side and local residents on the other. The affair began as a dispute between an Irish emigrant and a Panamanian fruit
vendor over the price of a melon and escalated into a street fight. Others joined in on both sides, and when it was over at least sixty-three
"Americans" (evidently this included some Europeans) and an unknown
number of Panamanians had died.[4] There were calls in California for a
retaliatory expedition, but no ships were willing to provide free passage
to the avengers, and nothing further happened. The affair fueled the argument that relying on passage through a foreign country to connect
California with the rest of the United States was asking for trouble and
that only an internal overland route would ever be truly secure.

The 75,000 California signatures, bound in leather volumes, were sent
to Washington. Weller took them to the floor of the Senate on May 26,
1856, to provide a dramatic display for his new bill, which aimed "to
provide for the construction of a military road from some point in the
state of Missouri via Great Salt Lake to Carson Valley settlement, on the
eastern frontier of the State of California, and for the establishment of
military posts, and the sinking of wells thereupon."[5]

Weller told the Senate that federal action would be met with match-
ing action in California. The legislature there had appropriated $100,000

for a road across the Sierra Nevada to Carson Valley and then made a further appropriation of $140,000. Under the state constitution this would have to go to popular vote, but Weller was confident that the people of California would support it: "I have no doubt but that just as soon as you have made this road through your own Territories, you will find the people of California prepared to intersect it from as many points as the commerce and business of that country may demand."

Weller was bluffing, as we have seen. The first appropriation of $100,000 for a road to Carson Valley was being challenged in the state courts, and soon would be ruled unconstitutional. The additional $140,000 is apparently a reference to Sherman Day's bill (actually authorizing expenditures of $240,000), which had not passed the legislature and was not going to pass.

Weller proposed to appropriate $300,000 for a line of bridges, ferries, assured water supply points, protective military outposts, and blacksmithing facilities along the existing California Trail. His aim was to make the passage easier for people who came in their own wagons, the much-desired "working and producing classes." Consistent with his strict constructionist position in the Pacific railroad debate in early 1853, he did not request road assistance within California but only in the territories that separated California from the other states.

It was no surprise that the Committee of Military Affairs, of which Weller was chairman, reported back favorably on the bill. Debate on June 26, 1856, further clarified what was being proposed. The project would be under the direction of the secretary of war, though the starting point in Missouri and the locations of military posts were to be chosen by the president. Senator Seward began to make a speech in the bill's favor, but the impatient Weller interrupted him. Weller wanted to bring the matter to a vote and told Seward to save his speech for the El Paso to Yuma road bill, which Weller would introduce soon. Senator Richard Brodhead of Pennsylvania asked if $300,000 would be enough to do the job. Weller said it would, that he was confident that he would never have to come back and ask for more. Senator John Crittenden of Kentucky said there should be more discussion of such an expensive measure. Weller replied that the matter had been sufficiently considered by the Committee on Military Affairs. And without further debate, the bill was passed, apparently by voice vote.[6]

Weller had originally wanted the Interior Department to undertake this project, rather than the War Department, which was the agency that usually built roads in the territories. The War Department's Corps of

Topographic Engineers, Weller claimed, spent too much time on natural history research, as evidenced in the Pacific Railroad Surveys, and not enough on the practicalities of transportation. He had to back down on this point, however, to get the votes of those senators who would support federal expenditures on roads only when they were alleged to be of military value. This concession helped the bill pass the Senate but caused trouble in the House of Representatives, where northern members were loath to see Jefferson Davis in charge of any project that might have sectional import. In the House Weller's bill was first read on July 10, 1856, and was referred to the Committee on Military Affairs.[7] On August 18 it was reported back favorably from committee, but then it was "referred to the Committee of the Whole on the state of the Union." This was apparently a parliamentary tactic for burying the bill for the session.[8]

Weller's proposal was not dead, though, only dormant. Eighteen fifty-six was a presidential election year, and improved communication with the Pacific Coast had become a campaign issue. The new Republican party, running none other than John C. Frémont for president, declared in its platform that "a railroad to the Pacific Ocean by the most central and practicable route is imperatively demanded by the interests of the whole country, and . . . the Federal Goverment ought to render immediate and efficient aid in its construction, and, as auxiliary thereto, the immediate construction of an emigrant road on the line of the railroad."[9] In California especially the Republicans emphasized their positive position on federal aid to transportation. Their slogan there was "Freedom, Frémont, and the Railroad," and the party could claim that their candidate had personally explored much of the route.[10]

The Democrats modified their long tradition of opposing internal improvements, and James Buchanan campaigned on a platform that included the following:

> That the Democratic party recognizes the great importance, in a political and commercial point of view, of a safe and speedy communication, by military and postal roads, through our own territory between the Atlantic and Pacific coasts of this Union, and that it is the duty of the Federal Government to exercise promptly all its constitutional power to the attainment of that object, thereby binding the Union of these States in indissoluble bonds, and opening to the rich commerce of Asia an overland transit from the Pacific to the Mississippi River, and the great lakes of the North.[11]

After Buchanan won the 1856 election (including California), a revived version of Weller's road bill was brought back for consideration in the postelection session of the House of Representatives. It was now called "a bill for the construction of a wagon road from the South Pass of the Rocky Mountains, in Nebraska Territory, via Great Salt Lake Valley, to Honey Lake Valley, in the eastern portion of the State of California." (Nebraska Territory in 1856 extended much farther west than the later state.)

In this new road bill construction contracts were in charge of the secretary of the interior instead of the secretary of war. Amendments extended the eastern starting point of the proposed road from South Pass to Fort Kearney and raised the total appropriation to $300,000. Another amendment eliminated the military outposts along the way, presumably because this was now a Department of the Interior project. On Saturday, February 7, California representative Philemon T. Herbert made a brief but impassioned speech in favor of the bill.

The House was in a road-building mood, up to a point. Virginia representative William Smith offered an amendment that appropriated $200,000 for a road between El Paso and Fort Yuma, and it was approved. The delegate from New Mexico Territory, Miguel Otero, proposed an amendment that appropriated $50,000 for a road from Fort Defiance (on today's Arizona/New Mexico border a little north of Zuñi) to the "mouth of the Mojava [sic] River on the Colorado River," and it too was approved. (This is a curious bit of geographic misunderstanding. Jedediah Smith discovered in the 1820s and Frémont publicized in the 1840s the fact that the Mojave River sinks into the desert far short of the Colorado River.) Michigan representative David Walbridge then tried an amendment appropriating $300,000 for a road from Lake Superior to Puget Sound, but this was defeated. Tennessee representative George Jones claimed that all such projects were without constitutional validity, which prompted Solomon Haven of New York to point out that even President-elect Buchanan, of Jones's own party, had changed his mind on that hoary issue. The House adjourned before coming to a vote, but on Monday, February 9, the road bill was almost the first order of business and passed handily 119 to 48.[12]

The Senate took the bill up on February 14, 1857, and passed it with no debate, except for an exchange between Weller and Brodhead. Brodhead raised the question of why these road projects were now being given to the Department of the Interior, when such roads had always been regarded as military affairs, to be undertaken by the outstanding topographic and engineering corps that was already on the payroll of the War Department. Weller replied by repeating his criticism of the War Department: too slow and too much given to "sketching topography." This apparently satisfied Brodhead. The bill was read a third time and passed without a roll call vote.[13] Outgoing President Pierce signed it on February 17, 1857.

The federal goverment was now committed to building a road from Fort Kearney in the middle of Nebraska to the border of California. This must have been good news to Californians, although it still left them with the task of building connecting roads over the Sierra Nevada.

It had been much easier for Congress to pass a road bill than a railroad bill, because the sectional issue could be sidestepped. There would be only one Pacific railroad, almost everyone thought, due to the enormous expense. The South would be benefited, or the North, but not both, and therefore sectional rivalry was intense. Wagon roads, in contrast, were much less expensive undertakings, and both southern and northern interests could be satisfied. As one senator put it during the brief debate, it would involve "less expenditure to make these wagon roads than it has been to make surveys of railroads, and publish them with the drawings and engravings connected with them, as we have done during a Congress that has passed."[14]

The Wagon Road Act as passed was not entirely the same as Weller's original, which called for a road to "Carson Valley settlement." The act stipulated that the western terminus would be the boundary of California near Honey Lake. The change is somewhat mysterious. Carson Valley had been for well over a decade the main emigrant destination and rest stop east of the Sierra. Honey Lake was almost 100 miles to the north, well off the beaten track. Some emigrants were going that way on the Nobles route, but it was not much of a draw compared to Carson Valley.

Honey Lake seems to have been first proposed as part of a long-distance transportation route in Lieutenant Beckwith's report to the Pacific Railroad Surveys. The *Sacramento Daily Union* editorialized that the change in the Weller bill was "accomplished through the influence of W. H. Nobles, who now resides in Minnesota. He naturally preferred the Pass named after himself to all others, and it is not likely that he ever crossed the Sierra Nevada by any other."[15] How Nobles came to have such influence the *Daily Union* did not explain. The change must have originated with California's House delegation, or at least been approved by it, perhaps as the result of lobbying by Shasta City and Weaverville interests. In addition, the bill was passed during the hectic last month of the session, which was also the last month of the outgoing Fillmore administration, and the change may have been slipped into the bill's language at the last minute without leaving a trace in the written record.

The projected federal road was divided into three sections between Fort Kearney and Honey Lake, with a superintendent for each section. The western section between Honey Lake and City of Rocks in southern Idaho was so sparsely settled that much, if not most, of the labor force and equipment would have to come from California. This meant that the Democratic party, then in power in California, would control some attractive roadwork contracts. California Democrats split on the question of who was to get the superintendent's job. Weller and others supported Dr. Wozencraft, but a significant number supported a rival candidate, John Kirk, an engineering contractor in Placerville.

Secretary of the Interior Jacob Thompson selected Kirk and instructed him to find a route between Honey Lake and City of Rocks that would pass north of the Humboldt River, avoiding it as much as possible, because of the alleged "deleterious character of the waters of this river, and its destructive effect upon cattle and horses." On June 27, 1857, the Kirk party left Placerville for Honey Lake and spent the next two months exploring northern Nevada (then still Utah Territory). Kirk concluded that there was no feasible new route between City of Rocks and Honey Lake; the valley of the Humboldt was the only practicable one as far west as the "Great Bend" of the Humboldt (vicinity of present Winnemucca).[16]

West of the Great Bend, the best course was less obvious. Kirk was constrained by the language of the act to bring the road to a western terminus at Honey Lake, but he tried to bend the law, and the road, a bit, by sticking to the Humboldt as far downstream as Big Meadows (near present Lovelock) and then going around the south end of Pyramid Lake. Honey Lake could easily be reached from this point, after all, and the inevitable side road to Carson Valley would be much shorter.

Wozencraft, perhaps still angling for Kirk's job, complained to the Interior Department that Kirk had disregarded his instructions by taking a circuitous route. Kirk, he claimed, owned property in El Dorado County and was seeking to increase its value. The dispute was settled by Kirk's boss, Frederick West Lander, appointed to oversee the entire Fort Kearney, South Pass, and Honey Lake Road project.

Lander was an energetic explorer with a mind of his own. Four years earlier he had worked for the Pacific Railroad Surveys as a civilian engineer with the Isaac L. Stevens party on the far northern route. He had grave doubts that the Stevens route was practical and persuaded the Washington territorial legislature to back him in surveying an alternate one between Puget Sound and South Pass. Lander's argument was that California had become so important to the Union that it would draw the

Pacific railroad to itself regardless of the fact that a forty-ninth parallel route was a shorter way to Asia, and that therefore Puget Sound would get railroad connections sooner through a branch line taking off from the main line near South Pass or Salt Lake. Lander's expedition was arduous almost to the point of disaster, but he did locate a route, and his report attracted favorable notice in Washington, D.C. When the Interior Department needed an engineer for the Fort Kearney, South Pass, and Honey Lake Road, Lander got the job.

In the fall of 1857 Lander fired Kirk and so put official support behind a more direct route to Honey Lake. Lander did not pay much attention to the western division at first, however. His main concern seems to have been creating a new road from South Pass through the Bear River country north of Great Salt Lake to the headwaters of the Humboldt.

At the same time that Lander was busying himself north of Great Salt Lake, the War Department took an interest in the Great Basin. In 1859 Captain James Simpson of the Corps of Topographic Engineers surveyed a road across central Nevada between Carson Valley and Camp Floyd in Salt Lake Valley. Simpson's *Report of Explorations Across the Great Basin of the Territory of Utah for a Direct Wagon-Route from Camp Floyd to Genoa, in Carson Valley* is an important document of western exploration geography, though only a small and incidental part of the report (which is examined more closely later) dealt with the Sierra Nevada.

Simpson's exploration, linked to Topographic Engineers' surveys made farther east earlier in the decade by Captain Howard Stansbury and Lieutenant Francis T. Bryan, enabled the secretary of war to claim that the War Department had its own central overland route and that it was shorter than the one being laid out by Lander for the Department of the Interior. The question was still being debated as late as November 23, 1859, when the *Sacramento Daily Union* ran a long editorial reviewing California's repeated attempts to get good overland connections and balancing the two alternatives that now seemed to be available. The writer noted that Lander's new route north of Salt Lake was intended to benefit emigrants during the summer, when the high elevation would ensure more grass and water. But the other side of the coin was the cold and deep snow of winter, which would make the road unsuitable for year-round freighting and stagecoaching.

As for the western end, the *Daily Union* had been given to understand that there was still $75,000 left from the federal appropriation and that Lander was proposing to use it to build a line of water tanks across the desert from the Humboldt to Honey Lake. But if Simpson's more direct and more snow-free route was in fact better, the money would be better spent on his route. The editorial went on to urge Lander and Simpson to meet and consult with each other and compare their knowlede; neither had seen the other's route. Perhaps it would be useful to have two routes, for use at different seasons.[17]

Lander was thus under some pressure to prove the superiority of the Interior Department's route. The most questionable link was the difficult desert crossing between the Humboldt River and Honey Lake. Just as the *Daily Union* had intimated, Lander decided to spend the money left in his appropriation to improve the water supply for emigrants in this stretch. Part of the money went for building a large water-holding tank at Rabbit Hole Springs, an important water source just east of the Black Rock Desert. This decision firmly committed the Interior Department to a route north of Pyramid Lake, negating Kirk's attempt to go south around Pyramid Lake with connections for Carson Valley.

Lander directed operations on the road until the Civil War took him away into the army as a brigadier general. He was killed in action in 1862.[18] Despite his improvements the west end of the Fort Kearney, South Pass, and Honey Lake Road never became the main entryway into California. Like the Nobles route on which it was superimposed, it offered an easier way into California than any of those around Lake Tahoe, but it brought emigrants into a part of California, the northern end of the Sacramento Valley, that was of relatively little interest to most of them. Gold mining districts there, such as Shasta and Weaverville, were only sideshows to the Mother Lode. Nor did major population centers like San Francisco, Sacramento, Marysville, and Stockton lie near the end of this trail.

The Nobles/Honey Lake route did get some use in the 1850s and 1860s, but it never replaced the more central routes. Commercial ventures like the Pony Express and the central overland mail adopted the rival Simpson route and crossed the Sierra Nevada on Johnson's Cut-off and its successors via Placerville. After the railroad was completed in 1869, the Honey Lake Road faded into obscurity. Only some segments of it ever became paved highways. Between Redding and Susanville its course is followed today by California 44 and various local roads. In Nevada it is approximated only by unpaved county and ranch roads.

Mail Contracts and Stagecoach Service

California senators Gwin and Weller, once they had secured funding for the Fort Kearney, South Pass, and Honey Lake Road, followed up with a measure that would authorize the postmaster general to contract for an overland mail coach service between San Francisco and some point on the Mississippi River. This appeared as an amendment in the annual post office appropriations bill. The amendment provoked a lively debate, with opponents claiming that the overland service would be a money-losing extravagance, but the measure eventually passed on March 3, 1857, two weeks after outgoing President Pierce had signed the road bill.

The legislation was fairly specific about many aspects of the new service. Conveyance had to be in four-horse coaches or spring wagons suitable for passengers as well as mail. Stations were to be built at intervals of 10 miles, and contractors could claim 320 acres of public land for each station. A maximum of twenty-five days was allowed for a one-way trip. Maximum amounts of annual payment were set: $300,000 for semi-monthly trips, $450,000 for weekly, $600,000 for twice weekly. In one highly important aspect, the measure was silent; it did not specify a route.

It would be reasonable to expect that since Congress had just passed a measure to develop a wagon road along the central route, the mail coach would go that way. But the new postmaster general in the incoming Buchanan administration was a southerner, Aaron V. Brown, former governor of Tennessee and former law partner of James K. Polk, and this overrode reasonable expectations.

Bidders who aspired to operate the new service were to specify a starting point on the Mississippi River and intermediate points on the way to San Francisco; in other words, to propose a route. Nine bids were received: six for a southern route, one for a central route, one for the far north, and one nonspecific.[1] Brown favored a southern route with branches from St. Louis and Memphis converging at Fort Smith. The line would then run across Indian Territory and Texas to El Paso, Phoenix, Yuma, Los Angeles, and finally San Francisco. Brown awarded a contract on this route to Butterfield & Company, which was a consortium of the leading express companies of the day—American Express, National, Wells Fargo, and Adams (i.e., the East Coast Adams & Company, which survived the 1855 bankruptcy of its San Francisco affiliate). John Butterfield, a friend of President Buchanan, lent his name to the whole. It is interesting to note that although the Butterfield route was a southern one, all the members of this consortium were from the urban Northeast.

Brown's support for a far southern route might have been sectionalism, but it was not unreasoning sectionalism; he discoursed in some detail on the motives for his choice. He ruled out the central route via Salt Lake and Tahoe by citing the difficulties Chorpenning had had with snow and the resulting long delays. He ruled out a midsouthern route via Albuquerque, Zuñi, and the Navajo and Hopi country also on account of winter weather, though not so much snow in this case as extreme cold (evidenced in voluminous temperature records collected at army posts), which might make the trip fatal for coach passengers. He then described the openness of terrain and salubrity of climate along the far southern route, relying especially on extracts from the reports of Captain Randolph B. Marcy and John R. Bartlette of the post–Mexican War Boundary Commission.[2]

The most serious competitor of the Butterfield consortium in the bidding on the overland mail contract was James Birch, the grand mogul of the California Stage Company; in fact, he was the only serious competitor, according to one historian of the stagecoach era.[3] Birch, who had moved his headquarters from Sacramento to Marysville and was showing interest in establishing service across the Sierra via Henness or Beckwourth Pass, had also agreed to run coaches along Day's route when it was finished. Any of these three routes could have formed the west end of a central overland route. Though Birch lost out to the Butterfield group on the big contract, he did get the twice-monthly service between

San Diego and San Antonio. This became known as the "Jackass Mail," apparently because of its reliance on mules rather than horses.[4]

The creation and operation of the Butterfield Overland Mail was a major undertaking and forms a justly famous chapter in the story of western transportation. Despite its achievements, however, the Butterfield line received an unrelenting hail of criticism as the "oxbow route," accused of favoring the South by going far out of the way to reach "California," which to most people meant the San Francisco Bay region, the gold country, and intervening parts of the Central Valley. The Butterfield line was a reasonably direct route to *southern* California, but that part of the state was of relatively little interest in the 1850s.

Critics clamored for a central route to be added, one that would run more directly between Missouri and northern California. Brown acquiesced rather easily to these demands, now that his southern route was established as the primary one, and authorized a secondary central overland route from St. Joseph via Salt Lake to Placerville. There was after all a strong federal interest in more frequent and reliable links, both from San Francisco and from the Missouri frontier, to Mormon country, where the army now had a substantial presence as a result of the "Mormon War." In addition, Brown was an adherent of the view that the post office should be more than a business, that it had a civilizing mission, and this helped justify a central route, which he thought would be difficult and unprofitable from a strict business point of view.

There was no direct service from Salt Lake City to northern California at the time Brown authorized this central route. The closest thing to it was George Chorpenning's monthly run between Salt Lake and San Diego. As we have seen, Chorpenning was an old hand at the transport business on the California end. He had the mail contract to Salt Lake via Carson Valley in the early 1850s, and then made a number of route changes before the summer of 1854, when he signed a four-year contract to carry mail between San Diego and Salt Lake City monthly, on a twenty-eight-day schedule, for $12,500 per year. In 1856, citing Indian trouble, he got Congress to increase his remuneration to $30,000 per year.

Chorpenning apparently had been performing satisfactorily, because Brown wanted to keep him on. With the new Butterfield route already providing service to southern California, however, there was no point in paying Chorpenning to go to San Diego. Accordingly, on March 22, 1858, the post office discontinued service between Salt Lake City and San Diego and put Chorpenning back on the road between Salt Lake City and Placerville, carrying the mails once a week in each direction on a sixteen-day schedule for $130,000 per year. Chorpenning was evidently ambitious to achieve a high level of service. In June 1858 he was reported as having a Placerville stock dealer buying mules and preparing to establish and stock stations along the Humboldt, where he was to meet a consignment of Concord coaches being driven overland.[5]

On the eastern portion of the central overland route, between Independence and Salt Lake City, S. B. Miles had been providing monthly service using four-horse coaches from April to December and pack mules in winter, at $32,000 per year. The Miles contract was now annulled and the Independence–Salt Lake run given to John Hockaday: four-horse coaches to run weekly on a twenty-two-day schedule for $190,000.[6]

The result of these measures was a weekly mail coach service between Independence and Placerville. Travel time was thirty-eight days one way. This central overland route actually got into operation before the better-known Butterfield line did; the first arrival in Placerville was on July 19, 1858, whereas the Butterfield line was not running until October.[7] In December 1858 the two lines competed to carry a presidential message to San Francisco. Butterfield got it there first, but only because of official finagling that gave the firm an unfair early start. In actual elapsed time on the road, the central route proved itself faster.[8]

On the west end, Chorpenning maintained service through the winter of 1858–59, though sometimes he was unable to run a coach across the Sierra and had to fall back on packhorses or ski messengers like Snowshoe Thompson. His accomplishment was hailed in San Francisco: "The Sierra Nevada, which at Washington has been considered utterly impassable during winter, on account of the deep snow, has been crossed so far this season without inconvenience. . . . [T]he Postmaster-general . . . has been imposed upon in reference to the impassable depth of snow which falls upon the snowy mountains."[9] This was written three days before Christmas, with much winter weather still ahead, but one way or another Chorpenning evidently managed to keep going through that winter.

Chorpenning used the Humboldt River route at first. By the end of 1858, though, he had moved operations somewhat to the south, passing south of Great Salt Lake and crossing what is now the middle of Nevada. Chorpenning seems to have gotten the idea from a Utah pioneer named Howard Egan, who won a bet in 1855 by crossing from Salt Lake to Sacramento on a mule in ten days. Chorpenning found Egan's route shorter and easier in winter than the Humboldt River route. But both routes across the Great Basin converged in Carson Valley, so the shift had no effect on the route across the Sierra Nevada. From Carson Valley west Chorpenning would have used the most expeditious route, which by this time was the Lake Tahoe Wagon Road. In general the central overland service, provided by Chorpenning on the western half and by Hockaday on the eastern half, was a success. The coaches ran very close to schedule, and for a time at least both firms made money.

On March 8, 1859, Aaron Brown died. The next postmaster general, Joseph Holt of Kentucky, was not interested in the civilizing mission of the post office, inclining rather to the view that the post office was a business and should be self-supporting. He was thus less friendly to federal subsidies of the Pacific mails and cut service to keep costs down. Weekly service on the central route was reduced to semimonthly.

Both interpretations of the post office's mission had strong advocates in Congress. If Brown had lived, the more liberal view probably would have prevailed. But Holt had his backers too, and attempts to reverse the service cuts failed.[10] Yet even weekly service was not enough for Californians who had long clamored for a *daily* mail. As far back as March 2, 1855, California representative James McDougal had introduced an amendment to the post office route bill for a daily overland mail, but it was defeated 78 to 49.[11]

Doubtless there would have been continuing struggles over the frequency of service. Then another gold discovery, this one in Colorado, changed the situation. In the summer of 1858 gold was found near what was to become Denver. Even as Holt was cutting service, the "Pike's Peak rush" was on, creating new markets for transport and communications services across the plains along the central overland route.

Russell, Majors & Waddell

The business concern most capable of fulfilling the demands of the Pike's Peak rush was the giant Missouri freighting firm of Russell, Majors & Waddell. Throughout its existence, this firm's main field of operations was the Plains and the Rockies, but because it created the Pony Express, which ran all the way to Sacramento, Russell, Majors & Waddell became part of Sierra transportation geography as well, so a bit of background history is in order.

Up until 1854 the army had been buying transport services in the West through many small short-term contracts. Then, in response to enlarged responsibilities caused by an increase in civilian travel and settlement, army planners decided to purchase all their transport needs west of the

Missouri River through one giant contract. Since no existing firm seemed capable of bidding on such a large operation, three businessmen in Lexington, Missouri, formed a partnership on January 1, 1855, to consolidate their resources and secure the contract. Alexander Majors had made many trips to Santa Fe and was thoroughly conversant with the practicalities of long-distance transport by ox team. William Bradford Waddell was involved in a variety of retailing and wholesaling activities and had the skills and connections to assemble large orders for shipment. William Easton Russell, an energetic entrepreneur and speculator in many lines of business, became chief financier and lobbyist for the concern. For a time they thrived.

In the winter of 1858–59 Russell was in Washington, D.C., and happened to meet John S. Jones, who had a freighting business in western Missouri and was advertising in northeastern newspapers to carry freight between Missouri River towns in Kansas and the new mining districts in the Rockies. Russell transformed Jones's idea into the notion of running Concord coaches—top-quality vehicles—daily from Leavenworth across Kansas to the new goldfields. (The area up to and including the Front Range of the Rockies was part of Kansas Territory from 1854 until 1861, when Colorado Territory was created. This accounts for the odd-sounding references in the newspapers of the day to "the mountains of Kansas" and "the Kansas goldfields.")

In February 1859 Russell and Jones announced plans to launch a stagecoach service to be called the Leavenworth and Pike's Peak Express. In this venture Russell was operating on his own account; Majors and Waddell were not involved, at first. Russell had wanted them to come in on the scheme, but Majors refused to have anything to do with it, saying it was premature.[12] Waddell was even more opposed and wrote angry letters to Russell, berating him for spending too much time away from the affairs of Russell, Majors & Waddell.[13]

Russell and Jones wanted to get their coaches on the road before someone else beat them to this new mining bonanza. In March and April 1859 they had a survey party in the field laying out the route and stations every 10 or 15 miles up the valley of the Republican River across Kansas. With notes payable in ninety days, they bought one thousand mules and enough Concord coaches for daily service over this distance.[14]

The first westbound coach reached Denver on May 7, 1859, after nineteen days on the road; the first eastbound coach reached Leavenworth on May 20, after only ten days. Soon the average travel time shook down to six or seven days.[15] Their new service had hardly begun when Russell and Jones bought out J. M. Hockaday & Company's mail contract between St. Joseph and Salt Lake City, together with the company's equipment. Hockaday had gone into this as a weekly venture, and he now was in financial trouble because Holt's budget cuts had reduced him to twice-monthly service. The price of $144,000 was to be paid over a year, and Russell and Jones borrowed whatever was necessary.

After a month or so of running parallel operations, Russell and Jones abandoned their own Republican River route and consolidated the Leavenworth and Pike's Peak Express with Hockaday's service along the Platte. The last run on the original route, leaving on May 25, 1859, carried Horace Greeley on the first leg of a trip that would be widely publicized, first as a series in the *New York Tribune* and then in book form as *An Overland Journey*.

Russell and Jones now had a line of daily coaches along the old Oregon/California Trail route to the forks of the Platte River and then up the South Platte to Denver, as well as the weekly mail coach to Salt Lake via South Pass. They had borrowed heavily to accomplish this, and not enough money was coming in to make the payments on time. By the middle of October 1859, after five months of operation, the Leavenworth and Pike's Peak Express was $525,532 in debt.[16]

Russell was doing all this in his partnership with Jones. Meanwhile, the firm of Russell, Majors & Waddell had become involved in retailing and other businesses in booming Denver through a subsidiary, R. B. Bradford & Company.[17] The firm's success in Denver apparently induced Majors and Waddell to change their minds about Russell's staging venture, despite its mounting debts. On October 28, 1859, the firm of Russell, Majors & Waddell took over the Leavenworth and Pike's Peak Express, along with its debts, and reorganized it.

His earlier reluctance overcome, Majors now took a hand in the stagecoach venture. Looking back many years later he seemed rather pleased with what Russell, Majors & Waddell had been able to do with the Leavenworth and Pike's Peak Express. Indeed, the way he described it, one would think it had been a Russell, Majors & Waddell undertaking from the very first.

> I made a trip in the fall of 1858 in their [Hockaday & Liggett's] coaches. It was 21 days from the time I left St. Joseph until I reached Salt Lake, traveling at short intervals day and night. As soon as we bought them out we built good stations and stables every 10 or 15 miles all the way from Missouri to

Salt Lake, and supplied them with hay and grain for the horses and provisions for the men, so they would have to drive a team from one station to the
next, changing at every station.

Instead of our schedule time being 22 days, as it was with Hockaday &
Liggett, and running two per month, we ran a stage each way every day and
made the schedule time ten days, a distance of 1200 miles.[18]

But Russell, Majors & Waddell had incurred debts in rescuing Russell
and Jones, and the gold rush around Denver turned out to be only a faint
echo of the California boom of a decade earlier. It did not generate nearly
enough business to pay off these debts.

To the ever-optimistic Russell, the best way out of trouble was to
plunge in further and get beyond it: perhaps the future was not in serv-
ing a shaky mining district like Denver but in a full-scale overland mail,
freight, and passenger business all the way to California. What the firm
needed was something spectacular that would demonstrate the practi-
cality of the central route as an alternative to the much-criticized Butterfield oxbow route and also attract federal financial support in the form
of a lucrative mail contract all the way to the coast and not just to Salt
Lake.

The Pony Express

Russell wanted the firm to take a decisive step on its own, one that would
generate favorable publicity and then garner a federal subsidy. To that
end he now proposed a daily overland mail to be carried on horseback
with unprecedented speed. Such an operation would be a sensational
demonstration of the viability of the central route and might help wrest
the overland mail contract away from Butterfield & Company.

The basic idea of relays of mounted messengers had been around at
least since the Persian Empire in the sixth century B.C. Russell himself
seems to have been thinking about a horseback message service as early
as January 1858, when the firm of Russell, Majors & Waddell was
freighting supplies for the army in the Mormon War of 1857–58. Russell was impressed with the ease with which two employees had returned
to Missouri from Fort Bridger on horseback. He brought the two to
Washington, D.C., and discussed the possibility of an express contract
with Secretary of War John B. Floyd. High-level support came from California's Senator William Gwin. In the fall of 1854 Gwin had ridden from
California to Washington (or at least to the railhead in Missouri) with

B. F. Ficklin, later to be Russell, Majors & Waddell's superintendent, and along the way the two discussed a horseback express service.[19]

Senator Gwin led Russell to believe that he (Gwin) would be able to push legislation through for a federal subsidy once Russell showed that the Pony Express was feasible. Majors later suggested that the Pony Express was more Gwin's idea than anyone else's.

> Knowing that Russell, Majors & Waddell were running a daily stage between the Missouri River and Salt Lake City, and that they were also heavily engaged in the transportation of Government stores on the same line, he [Gwin] asked Mr. Russell if his company could not be induced to start a pony express, to run over its stage lines to Salt Lake City, and from there to Sacramento; his object being to test the practicability of crossing the Sierra Nevadas, as well as the Rocky Mountains, with a daily line of communication.
>
> After various consultations between these gentlemen, from time to time, the Senator urging the great necessity of such an experiment, Mr. Russell consented to take hold of the enterprise, provided he could get his partners, Mr. Waddell and myself, to join him.[20]

Another story is that some Russell, Majors & Waddell employees in Salt Lake City in the winter of 1859 became interested in trying to beat the Butterfield southern route in carrying the mail. They came up with a plan and map, proposing to cover the distance from St. Joseph to Sacramento in twelve days, and sent them to Russell.[21]

Whatever the origins of the Pony Express, the idea seems to have been in the air by late 1859, and it is not surprising that it attracted a risk taker like Russell. Waddell and Majors, on the contrary, decided it would never make a profit. Russell argued with them, saying that Gwin had worked hard for the overland route for years but was stymied by objections regarding the alleged impassability of the route during winter. He had faith in Gwin:

> [I believed] that as soon as we demonstrated the feasibility of such a scheme he [Senator Gwin] would use all his influence with Congress to get a subsidy to help pay the expenses of such a line on the 39th to 41st parallel of latitude; . . . that he could not ask for the subsidy at the start with any hope of success, as the public mind had already accepted the idea that such a route open at all seasons of the year was an impossibility; that as soon as we proved to the contrary, he would come to our aid with a subsidy.[22]

In the end, Russell sold his partners, Majors and Waddell, on the idea. On January 27, 1860, he sent the following telegram from Washington to his son John in Leavenworth: "Have determined to establish a Pony Express to Sacramento, California, commencing the 3rd of April. Time ten days."[23] In February 1860 the Leavenworth and Pike's Peak Express, as though to proclaim its ambitions, changed its name to the Central Overland California & Pike's Peak Express (COC&PP).

The Pony Express did in fact begin service on April 3, 1860, just as Russell had said. Stations east of Salt Lake City were already in use or were being built for the stagecoach service of the Central Overland California & Pike's Peak Express, so most of the additional work of equipping the line and setting up the organization would be west of Salt Lake City. Over the Sierra Nevada the Pony Express could use the Lake Tahoe Wagon Road.

Though William Hamilton is commemorated as the first eastbound rider from Sacramento, the first rider to cross the Sierra was Warren Upson, who came from a more urban background than most of the riders; his father, Lauren Upson, was the editor of the *Sacramento Daily Union* and a friend and supporter of Theodore Judah in his attempts to interest California capitalists in a railroad over the Sierra Nevada. Upson was waiting for Hamilton at Sportsman's Hall, about 9 miles east of Placerville on the morning of April 4, 1860. By 8 o'clock he was on his way.

The Sierra was a challenge to the Pony Express from the first. Heavy snow in the previous few days had halted stagecoach operations over the summit. Snow was again coming down fast at higher elevations when Upson came through on that first day of service, obscuring wagon tracks and forcing him to dismount and lead his horse. Snow was an impediment over Luther Pass and in Hope Valley as well. But once Upson was down through the canyon into Carson Valley he could move faster, and he arrived safely at the end of his run, Carson City, late that night, having covered 85 miles. It was a promising start for the Pony Express: despite terrible snow conditions the mail had not been deterred.

Upson waited at Carson City for the first westbound Pony Express, which had left St. Joe at 7:15 on the evening of April 3 (about an hour after the Sacramento steamboat had pulled away from the dock in faraway San Francisco). He left Carson City on the first westbound trip at 3:30 on the afternoon of April 12. This was rather late in the day compared to his early departure from Sportsman's Hall, and Upson might reasonably have worried about crossing the lonely snowbound heights in darkness. His problem this time, however, was quite the reverse: the heights were not lonely at all. The storm had passed, and the Lake Tahoe Wagon Road was full of wagons and pack trains bound for the Comstock, forcing Upson to run an obstacle course and sometimes plunge through deep snow at the side of the road to get around and keep his schedule.

When the Pony Express was launched, Chorpenning was still carrying the mail on twice-monthly trips between Placerville and Salt Lake. On May 10, 1860, Postmaster General Holt annulled his contract, on the grounds of irregular and imperfect service resulting from failure to provide an adequate supply of draft animals.[24] Holt then gave the contract to the firm of Russell, Majors & Waddell. In this way Russell, Majors & Waddell acquired the entire central overland mail route. This contract was only for the regular mail, however, going by way of the stagecoaches of the Central Overland California & Pike's Peak Express. The Pony Express remained a private venture—very fast, very unprofitable. Exactly how unprofitable is hard to say, because it used the same facilities as the company's stagecoach and freight operations. We might ask why Russell, Majors & Waddell kept the Pony Express going, since they now had the central overland mail route contract. The answer would seem to be that the existing contract was only for service every two weeks, and the firm wanted to establish something much more frequent. Futhermore, they still expected a federal subsidy for the Pony Express.

The expected subsidy never materialized, however, and the Pony Express was a slow financial disaster for Russell, Majors & Waddell, contributing to the firm's eventual collapse. Even so, it operated on schedule through the winter of 1860–61 and thus did much to promote the central overland route in the public mind.

The Pony Express was not the only source of financial difficulty for Russell, Majors & Waddell. In April 1860, through a different series of events, the firm lost the Utah part of its army freighting business to other carriers. In July Russell, desperate for money, went to a clerk in the Interior Department who was in charge of bonds being held in trust for Indian tribes. In a complicated series of steps, all quite illegal, Russell first borrowed the bonds to serve as security on loans and then, when this failed to bring in enough money, began to sell the bonds. On Christmas Eve 1860 Russell was arrested in New York and charged with fraud and receiving stolen property. There was a congressional investigation, and Russell confessed in detail.

Russell's lawyer got the criminal charges thrown out because Russell had already testified for Congress, and Russell avoided going to prison. But the timing of these events could not have been worse. The secession of a half dozen southern states made improved communications with California imperative for the federal government. The Butterfield route, with its hundreds of miles in secessionist territory, was no longer useful. On March 2, 1861, Congress passed a Post Office appropriations bill that provided for a daily overland mail on the central route. The COC&PP should have been perfectly situated to get the contract. They already had a daily coach service between Leavenworth and Salt Lake, a twice-monthly coach service from Salt Lake to Sacramento, plus the twice-weekly Pony Express, now world famous, running over the entire distance from St. Joe to Placerville. But now the firm was tainted by the bond scandal, and the Post Office reconfirmed the Butterfield consortium in the new daily mail contract, on condition that they would relocate men, draft animals, and movable property to a central route between Missouri and Placerville by July 1, 1861.[25]

By this time, however, Butterfield & Company had gone through financial convulsions itself. The Post Office was way behind in its payments for services rendered, because Congress failed to pass the annual appropriations bill before adjourning on March 4, 1859. The company continued service but was paid in federal IOUs, which were heavily discounted by the market. Passenger revenues were not enough to make up the difference, and the firm borrowed heavily from Wells, Fargo & Company. In March 1860 Wells Fargo, which had a controlling presence on the board of directors, ousted John Butterfield as president and reorganized operations as the Overland Mail Company, with William B. Dinsmore of Adams Express Company as president. So when the Butterfield Overland Mail (as it was still commonly called) did provide the first daily stagecoach service along the central route, it did so only as a subsidiary of Wells, Fargo & Company.[26]

The COC&PP hung on a little longer. In a business-sharing arrangement with the Overland Mail Company it continued to operate the Pony Express and daily coaches on the eastern end of the overland route, between the Missouri River and Salt Lake, while the Overland Mail Company operated west of Salt Lake.[27] The Overland Mail Company subcontracted the Sacramento–Carson Valley portion of the route to the Pioneer Stage. The first Overland Mail Company coach under this new arrangement left St. Joseph on July 1 and reached San Francisco July 18, 1861.[28]

By this time the colorful Jared Crandall was no longer in control of the Pioneer Stage. Loûis McLane (California manager for Wells Fargo) and his brother had bought the firm in 1860. McLane did not give up his position in Wells Fargo but operated the Pioneer Stage on the side. Wells Fargo used the Pioneer Stage for express shipping for some years and then quietly bought it from the McLanes, keeping it intact as a subsidiary.

Russell, Majors & Waddell continued to lose money and slide farther into debt. Much of their loss can be attributed to the Pony Express. Their Central Overland California & Pike's Peak Express had been borrowing money from Ben Holladay, a freighting and coaching magnate with his own routes on the Plains and in the Rockies. As indebtedness to Holladay mounted, he acquired more and more power over the firm. On April 26, 1861, the board of directors of the COC&PP forced Russell to resign and replaced him with Bela Hughes, a cousin of Ben Holladay.

Completion of the transcontinental telegraph on October 24, 1861, put the Pony Express out of business. Holladay finally demanded a mortgage as security on further loans, and when the COC&PP continued to lose money, Holladay got a court order to have the bankrupt company sold at auction. He bought it for $100,000 on March 21, 1862. He assumed the debts of the COC&PP, about a half million dollars, and paid them off. This event marked the end of the Russell, Majors & Waddell era and the advent of the supremacy of Ben Holladay, the "Stagecoach King."[29]

Holladay was able to enjoy his prominence undisturbed for only two years, however. All these transportation activities of the late 1850s and early 1860s were a threat to the Plains Indians, who, despite Hollywood imagery, had taken a relatively benign attitude to the emigrant wagon trains in earlier years. Emigrants were, after all, simply passing through in the summer on their way somewhere else, whereas freighting and stagecoaching, operating all year and building way stations every few miles along the line, looked suspiciously like the beginning of a permanent occupation. With the recall of army troops occasioned by the looming Civil War, the Indians had an opportunity to fight back. The Indian wars began in earnest in 1864 and continued intermittently along the Platte for several years, until the return of the army and vastly increased troop mobility along the new railroad pushed the Indians far to the north and south. Holladay did not last that long, however. After suffering major losses of employees, stock, and stations, and being forced to move his line over a several-hundred-mile stretch in southern Wyoming, Holladay in late 1866 sold out to Wells Fargo, which thus dominated road transport in the entire West.

With regard to road traffic across the Sierra Nevada, it is important to keep federal contracts and subsidies (and expectations of contracts and subsidies) in some perspective. Though they played an important role in strengthening transportation links across the Sierra—mail service helped get roads built and improved—they generated a rather small proportion of the total traffic across the mountains. When Aaron Brown was postmaster general there was only one mail coach per week, and with Holt that dropped to one every two weeks. The increase to daily service in 1861, though a dramatic upgrading, still meant only one coach a day in each direction, while the road between Placerville and Virginia City was crowded with other vehicles. Most movement on roads over the Sierra was stimulated by the silver that had been discovered in prodigious amounts in the Virginia Range just to the northeast of Carson Valley. The most practical source of men, capital, and equipment for extracting it was across the Sierra in California.

CHAPTER 9

A Revival of Interest in Road Construction in California

The federal Wagon Road Act of 1857, along with the activities of Lander and Simpson during the following two years, gave Californians a larger context in which to view their own efforts to build roads across the Sierra Nevada. It would no longer be simply a matter of smoothing the entryway for emigrants but rather of linking California with large-scale, well-funded federal activities east of the mountains. An editorial in the *Sacramento Daily Union* exemplified the new mood that was in evidence as early as the spring of 1857.

> The recent action of Congress in relation to the construction of National Roads through the Territories of the United States, with a view to the more intimate connection of the Atlantic with the Pacific, has to some extent diverted the attention of the people of our State from the sea coast to the Sierras. We are beginning to contemplate the time when the order of things will be reversed, or rather restored to a natural channel, when we may all look for news from our old homes in the East—to the eastward rather than to the westward—to the transit of our mails across our own territory, rather than from a remote quarter of the globe, by sea. The first movement in this great change is now going on, and along the whole base of the Sierra Nevada, from the Oregon line far to the south, all is activity and bustle, and the desire prevails everywhere in connection with the contemplated national roads. Numerous local meetings have been held, roads discussed, and delegates appointed to assemble in Convention.[1]

California road activists, who had been thrown into some disarray when the state supreme court ruled against the 1855 *Act to Construct a*

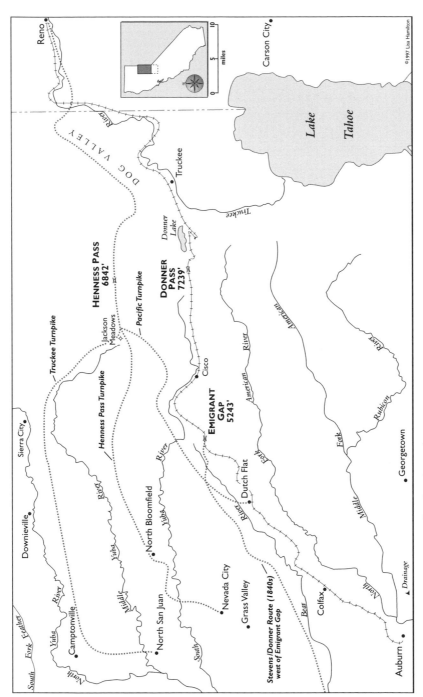

Map 3. Trans-Sierra routes north of Lake Tahoe.

Wagon Road over the Sierra Nevada Mountains, went back to work with renewed vigor. They avoided another attempt to have the state fund a trans-Sierra road directly and instead concentrated on ways to make it easier for counties to raise the money. On April 27, 1857, two months after President Pierce signed the Weller road bill, Governor Johnson signed an act allowing Sacramento and El Dorado counties to assess themselves, by popular vote, $25,000 each to build a road to Carson Valley.[2]

Organizing Efforts

California newspapers in the spring of 1857 reported dozens of local meetings intended to drum up political and financial support for favorite road projects. Many of these meetings were preliminary affairs intended to select delegates for larger regional meetings, usually called "conventions" in the newspapers.

The Mokelumne Hill Convention

A local meeting in Carson Valley on April 25, 1857, picked its delegation for a convention to be held in Mokelumne Hill on May 2 and instructed the delegates to push for a route between Carson Valley and Big Trees, with "houses at suitable points on the route, supplied with fire wood to facilitate and insure safe and expeditious travel through the winter."[3] Why did Carson Valley favor the Big Trees route over a Placerville road? Perhaps the project seemed farther along. In addition, one possible east-end variant of the rival Placerville road, skirting the shore of Lake Tahoe and crossing the Carson Range via Eagle Pass, would cut off most of Carson Valley, whereas the Big Trees route, coming up from a southwesterly direction, was more likely to pass right through it. A similar meeting in Stockton on April 28 selected delegates for Mokelumne Hill and resolved that the proposed road should not have as its western terminus any point north or south of the Big Trees or Murphys—in other words, should be pointed directly at Stockton.

An editorial in the *Sacramento Daily Union* on the Mokelumne Convention's opening day applauded the event and took an unusually broad view of things, saying that if the Big Trees route turned out to be the best way to cross the mountains, a road from Sacramento could be built to connect with it. The more roads there were across the mountains, the better it would be for the whole state.[4] On May 3, the *Daily Union* reported the Mokelumne Hill Convention in detail at the top of the front page.

It is not clear why a meeting to promote the Big Trees route should have been held at Mokelumne Hill, which is actually closer to Volcano and other Amador County towns that were pressing for improvement of the Carson Pass trail, branching off at Corral Flat west of Tragedy Spring (along the line of today's Highway 88). Perhaps the steep route down into the canyon of the Mokelumne River and back up discouraged the residents of Mokelumne Hill from seeking road connections via Amador County and made them look to the Big Trees route instead. Yet Amador County itself sent delegates to the Mokelumne Hill meeting. Perhaps road advocates there felt that the Big Trees route movement had picked up enough momentum that Amador should try to connect with it, despite having to cross the Mokelumne canyon. Or it may have been common strategy for towns to send delegates to any road convention that seemed to have any chance of benefiting them.

In addition to those from Amador County, delegates showed up in Mokelumne Hill from San Joaquin, Contra Costa, Alameda, Santa Clara, and Calaveras counties and from Carson Valley. They resolved to work for the construction of a road along the Big Trees route and also to cooperate with El Dorado, Placer, and Sacramento counties in road-work through Carson Canyon, which they were all likely to share.

The surveyor general of California, John Brewster, addressed the Mokelumne Hill Convention, and his speech was reproduced in the next day's *Daily Union*. After reviewing the alignment of the Big Trees route, Brewster discussed the necessary work, which he did not expect to be too difficult. He thought most of it would be in Carson Canyon and near the western summit (Pacific Grade Summit on today's Highway 4) where the ascending road crossed from the upper Stanislaus valley to the upper-most part of the Mokelumne Valley. Even this could be accomplished largely by rolling rocks out of the way and doing a small amount of excavating. No blasting would be required, Brewster claimed, and the grade would nowhere exceed 5 percent. He was enthusiastic about the abundance of water and grass, the good camping places, and the business opportunities:

> The mineral resources of the country to be opened by this road are greater in variety and extent than many persons imagine, and only await means of convenient communication to attract the attention of miners. The people on the eastern side have grain, cattle, and other matters to dispose of, which will find a ready market in the mines in exchange for manufactured goods which they desire of you, and they will readily co-operate in the undertaking. Of the

character of the snow lines, Mr. Noyes and Mr. Thompson, who are present, can inform you more readily than myself.[5]

Brewster skimmed over the snow question rather cavalierly. As we saw earlier, Sherman Day examined the high-elevation portion of the Big Trees route, between Hope Valley and Hermit Valley, in August 1855 and predicted serious snow problems. Day's opinion has appeared in the official report of Surveyor General Marlette for 1856, and it seems likely that Brewster, Marlette's successor in office, would have read it, but if so he ignored this sobering information in his speech.

The Mokelumne Hill Convention voted to raise $30,000 to improve the Big Trees route and appointed a committee to oversee the project. Delegates discussed the necessity of multiple western endings for the road. The idea was to join forces in building a trunk road across the Sierra crest and leave the western, lower-elevation branches to local initiative. There was already at least one such local branch: a 22-mile track from West Point to Big Trees, opened in October 1856 by the people of West Point to rescue an emigrant train caught in an early snowstorm.[6]

Other Conventions

On May 4, two days after the Mokelumne Hill Convention, the Marysville Wagon Road Convention drew five hundred delegates from the counties of Butte, Sierra, Yuba, Plumas, Colusa, and Sutter. They discussed a route from Honey Lake to American Valley (Quincy and environs). West of American Valley branch routes were "to be left to the sense, enterprise, and liberality of the counties and people through which such routes shall pass."[7] There had already been a mass meeting in Shasta on April 27 to consider measures for improving the emigrant road to Honey Lake via Nobles Pass.[8]

On May 6 there was a Placer County Wagon Road Convention at Yankee Jim's, then a populous gold camp on the Forest Hill divide between the North and Middle forks of the American River. In attendance were delegates from eleven other town or camps in addition to Yankee Jim's. The assembled delegates at Yankee Jim's were full of the confidence and optimism that seemed to characterize these road conventions. As usual the claim was made that a passable road already existed much of the way and there were really only a few rough spots that needed a little work. According to a speaker from Iowa Hill, loaded teams could climb the Forest Hill divide as far east as the Forks House already, though

8 miles farther on, at Secret Springs, there was a bad hill that would need work. But then there was a gradual ascent along a dividing ridge past Robinson's Flat and on to the west summit without impediment. After descending into Squaw Valley, the road would go up the valley of the Truckee to Lake Tahoe and follow the shore around to a point whence it would cross the Carson Range and come down in Washoe Valley (between Carson Valley and Truckee Meadows). The distance was claimed to be 32 miles shorter than the proposed El Dorado road. The meeting appointed a committee of management to pursue the work.[9]

The Yankee Jim's delegates were clear about the topography of their proposed route and confident it would be built, but this particular connection across the Sierra crest was never completed, or was so little used that it vanished long ago. The western summit area above Squaw Valley is today the Granite Chief Wilderness and will presumably remain forever roadless. This shows that the road meetings of 1857 were not simply assemblies to ratify the obvious and inevitable. Despite their optimism road promoters were not sure at this time what the successful routes across the mountains would be. Some road ventures, including this one, were destined to fail.

The El Dorado Wagon Road Convention met at Placerville on the same day as the Yankee Jim's meeting, May 6. The Placerville meeting resolved that as the expense of the transmountain road would be borne by the taxpayers of the whole county it should be planned as a common trunk over the mountains, to which various locally funded western branches might then connect. The convention resolved to form alliances with Sacramento and Yolo counties and nominated no fewer than 120 delegates to the May 11 convention in Sacramento.[10]

On May 11, 1857, county representatives from Yolo, Sacramento, and El Dorado began a two-day convention in Sacramento to discuss the road question. The committee on routes, with George Goddard as its chairman, recommended the route selected by the state commissioners in September 1855. This was Sherman Day's route, which Goddard too had carefully explored. The committee identified it as the shortest, lowest, and least snowbound, as evidenced by the fact that it, or its forerunner, Johnson's Cut-off, was the only traveled route across the mountains in winter. In addition it had the advantage of having already been surveyed.

In answer to a question from the floor Goddard made some remarks, reviewing his explorations with the Ebbets party in 1852–53, that show how anecdotal and partial the knowledge of winter snow conditions at high elevations was in those days before snow surveys. The elusive

Ebbets Pass seems to have owed most of its allure to John Ebbets's claim that he found it free of snow during one transit in April 1851. Goddard for his part was prepared to advocate Johnson Pass after a single trip, during the 1852–53 expedition, when he found no more than three feet of snow on the ground.

In an editorial on the day of the Sacramento meeting, the *Daily Union* reviewed and commended all these local meetings. The paper noted that "the subject of wagon roads still engrosses almost entirely the attention of the people of the midland counties of our State." An adjoining column addressed the question in detail:

> A suitable stage road, with a line of stages carrying the mail over it twice a week, when once located and built, will bring after them the telegraph line, an active population, a series of settlements, on the line of travel, and in a few years the Pacific Railroad will be laid down over the same general route.
>
> As to where the road ought to cross the mountains, and as to which is the best and most favorable route, it is natural that a diversity of opinion should exist. It is reasonable and right that the people of the several counties, through which immigrant roads cross the Sierra, should strive to show that their pass is to be preferred. The result of this diversity will be an increased interest among the people generally, as well as the opening of several good roads into the valleys east of the Sierra, over either of which immigrants, traders, and stage coaches may enter the state at all seasons of the year without difficulty.
>
> Already Conventions have been held, at which the preliminary steps were taken to raise money to push forward the several routes under consideration.[11]

The Sacramento meeting voted to raise $50,000 from three counties ($20,000 each from El Dorado and Sacramento and $10,000 from Yolo) to build a road along Day's route.[12] It was to be called the Sacramento and Carson Valley Wagon Road. A board of directors was created.

Building the Day Route

On June 8, 1857, the board of directors of the newly formed Sacramento and Carson Valley Wagon Road met in Placerville. The directors heard an encouraging report from the collection committee and voted to authorize some construction work near Slippery Ford, high up on the South Fork of the American River a few miles below the western summit.

The directors planned to leave the next morning to go over the entire route. The *Sacramento Daily Union*'s correspondent reported that "the Pioneer Stage Company have generously tendered to the Board of Directors an extra four-horse coach, which has been accepted; and it is understood that Crandall, the indefatigable friend of pioneers, and general agent of the company will drive the *car* in person."[13] This would be a historic occasion: the first stagecoach trip over the Sierra, an expedition evidently intended to show these interested parties which sections of the road were most in need of improvement while at the same time demonstrating that the trip as a whole was already possible for stagecoaches.

It is not surprising that the Pioneer Stage Company was so accommodating: an improved road would allow it to extend its service area. The state's biggest stagecoach operation, James Birch's California Stage Company, had moved its headquarters from Sacramento to Marysville. The California Stage seemed to be more interested in Henness or Beckwourth Pass and did not follow up on its promise to start service over Johnson Pass. This left the way clear for the Pioneer, which took the first step that would make it the leading stagecoach service to the Comstock Lode and the westernmost link in the daily overland mail, both still a few years in the future.

The passengers on this historic trip included a reporter from the *Sacramento Daily Union,* who sent in a lengthy three-part report. (San Francisco's *Daily Alta California,* in contrast, reported Crandall's accomplishment in one paragraph, below an item about the 92-degree heat experienced in the city the previous day.)[14] The 15 miles from Placerville up to Brockliss Bridge (where the road crossed the South Fork to Peavine Ridge, north of the river) was, in the reporter's opinion, already as good a road as the one from Folsom to Placerville. Plans for a greatly improved road east of this point were evidently already known. The reporter wrote, "The proposition is, as I suppose you are well aware, to construct a good substantial road from Brockliss Bridge to Crandall's Camp—a distance of 15 miles—which is three or four miles from Strawberry's Valley, or five miles west of Slippery Ford."[15] But the "substantial road" was still in the planning stage, and on this trip Crandall followed the old Johnson's Cut-off from Brockliss Bridge up onto Peavine Ridge, where there were still patches of snow under the trees.

Despite dire predictions about the perils of Slippery Ford, located near the upper end of the moderately inclining portion of the South Fork canyon where the steep climb to the summit began, Crandall had no great trouble getting the coach across it, or on up to the summit at Johnson Pass. The ride down from Johnson Pass to Lake Valley, back up through Luther Pass, and down again through Hope Valley and Carson Canyon was so uneventful that the reporter scarcely mentioned it, though this might have been because he was saving space for lengthy descriptions of Carson Valley and its inhabitants, especially the Mormons and their fascinating polygamous ways. (Three months after the Pioneer Stage trip, the Mormons were to leave Carson Valley for Salt Lake, as part of Brigham Young's strategic withdrawal from a "greater Deseret" in the face of federal government troop movements in the Mormon War.)

The *Daily Union* reporter mentioned evidence of activity on the Big Trees route, in an attempt to rouse the attention of complacent Placerville businessmen who might lose the overland trade if that route succeeded in becoming the main road. On the whole, the reporter was optimistic about the road up from Placerville and pleased with his trip over it. Even without the pending improvements, it had been possible to make the stagecoach trip from Placerville to Carson Valley in 27 hours and 15 minutes of travel time, including dinner and lunch stops.

A considerable amount of roadwork was done during the summer of 1857 by private subscription,[16] and apparently this work continued under the direction of the board for the rest of 1857. The superintendent of the road was John Kirk, who the previous summer had been superintendent of the western division of the Fort Kearney, South Pass, and Honey Lake Road, until Lander fired him.[17]

It was clear that more money would be needed to complete the job. On January 8, 1858, the supervisors of Sacramento and El Dorado counties met and discussed ways of implementing the $25,000 assessment allowed to each county by the law of April 27, 1857, for road construction along the Sherman Day route. Referring to this meeting, the *Daily Union* editorialized that since money raised through individual subscriptions had been spent on work near the summit, grading the eastern approach to Johnson Pass and the hill above Slippery Ford, this new source of funds—the tax assessment—should be used farther west to get the road down off Peavine Ridge, specifically to grade the 16-mile stretch from Brockliss Bridge to Slippery Ford.

On March 8, 1858, the legislature amended the law to create the Board of Wagon Road Commissioners of El Dorado and Sacramento Counties. This body consisted of three members, one from each county named in the act[18] and a third to be selected by the first two. The board was directed to receive bids and contract for roadwork.[19]

In late May the commissioners made a trip into the mountains from Placerville to view and approve the proposed route.[20] The *Daily Union* noted on June 26, 1858, that Crandall & Company was running stages between Placerville and Mormon Station—the name Genoa had not yet taken hold—each way in one day, and would make the trip in even less time when the Board of Wagon Road Commissioners finished its work.

On June 28, 1858, the construction contract was awarded to William
M. Cary, who had been on board for Crandall's first trip, and A. M. Johnson, for $24,800. (One of the seven losing bids was from John Kirk, for
$35,400.) The contract provided for a road from Sacramento to Carson
Valley twelve feet wide, cleared of all obstructions, with elaborate speci-
fications for slope and camber, to be completed by September 30, 1858.[21]

The road between Sacramento and Placerville, being heavily traveled,
needed relatively little attention, so the bulk of the work was east of
Placerville. In late July Cary and Johnson were reported to have one hundred men on the job and several miles of road completed. It would appear that Cary and Johnson's work was on the difficult side-hill portion
on the lower slopes of Peavine Ridge.[22]

George Chorpenning was quoted as saying that the work was so good
that stagecoaches could go uphill or down at a trot. The new grade from
the western summit down to Lake Valley, which as we have seen was
built by private subscription in the first stage of the work, was the best
road for the money he had ever seen, considering the difficulties of the
location. Even so there were plans to widen this stretch by four feet; Cary
and Johnson could do it for $2,000, and the mail contractors (i.e., Chor-
penning) were ready to subscribe $500 for the work. J. A. (Snowshoe)
Thompson was sure the road could be kept open in the winter and offered to take on the job for $1,500. Everything, in short, seemed to be
going well.[23]

Three months was not a great deal of time, though, and Cary and
Johnson realized in early September that they would not be able to finish within budget. They stopped work, and the contract was reassigned
to one J. C. Plummer, along with a provision to build a new bridge near
Brockliss Bridge, for an additional $11,300. The board inspected the
work in the last days of November and rendered a favorable report.[24]
For some reason El Dorado County objected, finding fault with some
part of its section of road, but after a second favorable inspection by the
board on December 10, the county acquiesced.[25]

Johnson's Cut-off versus Day's Route

Crandall had been running the Pioneer Stage all this time, first along
Johnson's Cut-off and then on the new road as portions of it were completed. The proximity of the Day route and Johnson's Cut-off in the vast
landscape of the Sierra Nevada makes it hard to distinguish the two.

Confusion was apparently rife in the 1850s as well, so much so that Day was motivated to write a long letter to the *Sacramento Daily Union* on May 13, 1857, from New Almaden, where he had become an engineer in the famous quicksilver mines. Day was concerned about press accounts confusing his route and Johnson's Cut-off. He wanted people who were familiar with the hardships of the Cut-off to appreciate the improvements he had made, so he set out the difference in some detail. Day's route, crossing the western summit eastbound about 1 mile south of Johnson's, descended 1,000 feet to Lake Valley in 2 miles with a uniform grade of 5 degrees, while Johnson's made the same descent in three-quarters of a mile with slopes as steep as 23 degrees.

From Lake Valley east the two routes were completely different. Johnson's inefficient track around Lake Tahoe climbed and descended several lofty spurs of the Carson Range, some actually higher than the final pass over the range. Day's route through Luther Pass and Carson Canyon allowed a steady ascent and descent, with slopes nowhere more than 5 degrees. Finally, Day noted, his route, as far as the mouth of the Carson Canyon, was inside California, whereas the Johnson route left the state as it rounded Lake Tahoe.

West of the western summit, Day conceded, "the two roads touch or approach each other somewhat as two crooked sticks laid side by side might do," but there were important differences. Johnson's road climbed almost 1,400 feet up Peavine Ridge and then followed the crest of the ridge west, to come down again at Bartlett's Bridge. Day's route kept going downhill.

> My route westwards from the point of divergence, instead of *ascending* Peavine Hill, continues descending by means of side-hill grades along the southern slope of that ridge. It maintains generally an altitude of 100 to 500 feet above the bed of the South Fork, thus insuring an early melting of the snow from the road on the warm side of the hill. The line, after passing the southern slope of the Peavine ridge, crosses the South Fork near Brockliss' bridge, about one and a half miles above where Johnson's route crosses, and then ascends the Placerville ridge by a uniform grade of five degrees.

One reason his route was not as well known as it should be, Day said, was that without culverts and bridges it could not be used by wagons and therefore was familiar only to the few people who had traveled it on horseback.[26]

Day's other important "side-hill grade," the alignment down the steep face of the western summit ridge toward Lake Tahoe from Johnson Pass, soon had competition. Day's route made a sharp turn at the bottom of this grade, on the floor of Lake Valley, and turned south along the Upper Truckee River toward Luther Pass. In 1858 Asa Hershel Hawley built a more direct side-hill grade down from the summit ridge, in a southeast direction, bringing traffic directly to the point where the road up Luther Pass began to climb. This shortcut provided a savings of about 5 miles. According to Mitchell, Hawley built his "Hawley Grade" for El Dorado County and not as a toll road venture.[27]

In the fall of 1860 the Day route was reconstructed under the name Meyers Grade and became the main road until realignment in the 1940s. The Meyers Grade project was related to the opening of the Kingsbury toll road over Daggett Pass, between Lake Valley and Carson Valley, in the summer of 1860. These two summit crossings, Meyers Grade on the west and the Kingsbury road on the east, defined a third route between Johnson Pass/Echo Summit and Carson Valley, between the old Johnson route on the north and the Day route on the south.

Captain James Simpson of the Corps of Topographic Engineers left an interesting report on the state of the road as he found it in the summer of 1859. In June the Simpson party completed a westbound traverse of the Great Basin from Camp Floyd, near Salt Lake, to the eastern base of the Sierra, where they were welcomed with a certain amount of fanfare at Genoa. Simpson left his men and pack animals in Carson Valley to rest and recuperate while he made a quick trip to San Francisco to check in with army authorities. He crossed over to Lake Valley by way of Daggett Pass, on a trail he found to be steep and dangerous in places but which he thought might possibly be improved into a satisfactory road. (This was a year before the toll road was opened.) Simpson reached Lake Valley by midday, where he was joined for the rest of the trip by the famous expressman Snowshoe Thompson.

On the 2-mile climb to Johnson Pass, Simpson found that the grade was good except for the top portion, which in his opinion was overly steep. Simpson noted that this grade marked the beginning (i.e., for someone going west, as he was) of the work for which Sacramento and El Dorado counties had paid $50,000 and that the "supervising engineer" on the job had been Sherman Day. He was greatly impressed with the grandeur of the landscape near Slippery Ford and went on to spend the night at "Barry's" (probably Strawberry). Resuming the trip early the next morning, he soon came to the new road built along Day's survey.

> Two miles from Barry's a side cut of excellent grade commences, which continues for 25 miles, and is a piece of road which would do credit to any of our older States. Its defects are in not being sufficiently wide for teams of more

than two draft animals to turn (except with the greatest care), its sometimes steep angles, and in places it does not admit of teams passing each other.

At the lower end of this new side cut Simpson crossed the South Fork.

> To this point (the bridge) we have been traveling from summit of Johnson's Pass along north side of this river, which at times we could see as much as 1000 feet below us, and always raging, rushing, and making a din. . . . As soon as we crossed the American Fork, we emerged from the mountainous region, and the country became more open and rolling. Farms, farm-houses, and improvements generally increase as you approach Placerville.[28]

Simpson exaggerated the elevation of the road above the river. The whole point of the new road was to get through the canyon below the zone of heavy snow. According to Day, the road ranged from 100 to 500 feet above the river.

Simpson reached Placerville by sundown on June 14 and visited Frederick A. Bee, president of the Placerville and St. Joseph Overland Telegraph. Bee was interested in the suitability of Simpson's route across the Great Basin for a proposed telegraph line to Salt Lake City. Simpson must have had encouraging words, because the line was later built approximately along the route of his expedition.

After a brief stay in San Francisco, Simpson returned east. He left Placerville on June 21, retracing his route to Carson Valley in an "ambulance," a light covered wagon, with Snowshoe Thompson as driver. They reached Yankee's, the mail station in Lake Valley, on the night of June 22, but Simpson was off again at 3:00 A.M. on the mail stage, anxious to get to Genoa as soon as possible. Simpson's desire for speed was foiled, however. The driver was drunk, leading to various mishaps and the loss of any time advantage, but even worse was the condition of the road.

> The road from Lake Valley to mouth of Carson Cañon, . . . a distance of 12 or 13 miles, *is the worst portion of the whole road over the Sierra Nevada.* The ascent from Lake Valley to summit of Luther's Pass is very steep, and the road is filled with tremendous rocks, which should have been removed. It is astonishing, considering this is a portion of the great emigration road over the continent, that Congress has not done something toward ameliorating it. . . . At least $30,000 should be appropriated for the portion between Carson Valley and Johnson's Pass and $10,000 for the portion to the west. . . . Several bridges to be built across fork of Carson River in cañon.[29]

Simpson's remarks suggest that the joint road project of Sacramento and El Dorado counties extended only as far east as Lake Valley. Evidently the beaten track over Luther Pass and down Carson Canyon, now almost ten years old, was not thought to be so bad as to need government assistance, despite the outrage to Captain Simpson's engineering sensibilities. And also, perhaps, plans for a toll road across Daggett Pass were already known, reducing pressure on the counties to do anything further.

The Washoe Silver Rush

Within a few weeks of the time Simpson made his trip, silver was discovered in what had until then been only a third-rate gold mining district in the mountains at the north end of Carson Valley. The story of how gold prospectors there finally realized that the "blue mud" they had been shoveling out of the way was really high-grade silver ore is a classic of western mining lore but must be passed over here. The important point is that the silver rush to Washoe, as the district centered on Virginia City was known, was a great stimulus to the pace of road development in the central Sierra. The Washoe rush began in the late fall of 1859, as the first hopefuls tried to cross the mountains before the snow got too deep, and resumed with greater force in the spring of 1860.

Conditions of travel on the Lake Tahoe Wagon Road that spring were vividly described by J. Ross Browne in *A Peep at Washoe*.[30] Brown left San Francisco "toward the latter part of March" and thus undertook his trip over the Sierra at a time when the weather was moderating somewhat, but there was still much snow on the ground and new storms were possible. He reached Placerville by stagecoach from Sacramento and found that "the streets were blocked up with crowds of adventurers all bound for Washoe." Stagecoach service to Strawberry had been suspended because of bad road conditions, and there were no more horses and mules at affordable prices. Browne therefore walked across the mountains, in company with hundreds of others.

> The road from Placerville to Strawberry Flat is for the most part graded, and no doubt it is a very good road in summer; but it would be a violation of conscience to recommend it in the month of April. The melting of the accumulated snows of the past winter had partially washed it away, and what remained was deeply furrowed by the innumerable streams that sought an outlet in the ravines. . . . [T]he road was literally lined with broken-down stages, wagons, and carts, presenting every variety of aspect, from the general smash-up to the ordinary capsize.[31]

The effort of this long walk did nothing to discourage Browne's powers of description.

In the course of this day's tramp we passed parties of every description and color: Irishmen, wheeling their blankets, provisions, and mining implements on wheel-barrows; American, French, and German foot-passengers, leading heavily-laden horses, or carrying their packs on their backs, and their picks and shovels slung across their shoulders; Mexicans, driving long trains of pack-mules, and swearing fearfully, as usual, to keep them in order; dapper-looking gentlemen, apparently from San Francisco, mounted on fancy horses; women, in men's clothes, mounted on mules or "burros"; Pike County specimens, seated on piles of furniture and goods in great lumbering wagons; whisky-peddlers, with their bar-fixtures and whisky on mule-back, stopping now and then to quench the thirst of the toiling multitude; organ-grinders, carrying their organs; drovers, riding, raving, and tearing away frantically through the brush after droves of self-willed cattle designed for the shambles; in short, every imaginable class, and every possible species of industry, was represented in this moving pageant. It was a striking and impressive spectacle to see, in full competition with youth and strength, the most pitiable specimens of age and decay—white-haired old men, gasping for breath as they dragged their palsied limbs after them in the exciting race of avarice; cripples and hunchbacks; even sick men from their beds—all stark mad for silver.[32]

Browne was an energetic hiker; on the evening of the second day he reached Strawberry, some 44 miles uphill from Placerville.

The winter road for wheel-vehicles here ended; and indeed it may be said to have ended some distance below, or the last twelve miles of the road seemed utterly impracticable for wagons. At least, most of those I saw were fast in the mud, and likely to remain there till the beginning of summer.[33]

Browne's description of dinner and lodging at Strawberry is a masterpiece, but would have to be quoted in full, and takes us too far from our immediate subject, the road itself.

After a false start and another night at Strawberry, on the second morning Browne toiled up and over Johnson Pass through a morass of melting snow and mud, with occasional blasts of sleet. He did not spend the night at the Lake House, "a tolerably good-sized shanty at the foot of the grade," but went on, through more deep mud and melting snow, over Luther Pass to Hope Valley. The solitary inhabitant of Hope Valley was unwilling to put him and his traveling companions up for the night, so they pushed on another 6 miles, down through Carson Canyon, to Woodfords. Several hundred other people were already there.

We must leave aside Browne's acerbic descriptions of Carson City and Virginia City and jump ahead to his return trip to California. Though it is hard to say from his account just when this was, it would seem to have been several weeks later, though there was still plenty of snow on the ground. Browne got a ride in an oxcart south through Carson Valley to

Woodfords, where he found several hundred travelers already and learned that "there was a line of pedestrians all the way over to Strawberry."[34] His boots were stolen during the night, and he was forced to spend $30 to ride an unoccupied horse in a saddle train. Despite being able to ride, Browne's second trip over the Sierra was as perilous as his first one. The worst problem was with the many mule trains going in the opposite direction, freighting supplies to Washoe.

> It was considered perilous to stop on any part of the Grade. The trail was not over a foot wide, being heavily banked up on each side by the accumulated snow. . . . The Spanish mules are so well aware of their privileges when laden, that they push on in defiance of all obstacles, often oversetting the unwary traveler by main force. . . .
>
> "Now, boys," said the captain, "keep together. Your lives depend on it! Watch out for the pack trains, and when you see them coming hang on to a wide place! Don't come in contact with the pack-mules, or you'll go over the Grade certain."
>
> There was no need of caution. Every nerve was strained to make the summit as soon as possible. It should be mentioned that the "Grade" is the Placerville state road, cut in the eastern slope of the Sierra Nevadas, and winding upward around each rib of the mountain for a distance of two miles. It was now washed away in many places by the melting of the snow, and some of the bridges across the ravines were in a very bad condition. From the first main elevation there is still another rise of two or three miles to the top of the divide, but this part is open and the ascent is comparatively easy. In meeting the pack trains the only hope of safety is to make for a point where the road widens. These places of security occur only three or four times in the entire ascent of the Grade. To be caught between them on a stubborn or unruly horse is almost certain destruction at this season of the year. The only alternative is to dismount with all speed, wheel your horse round, and, if possible get back to some place of security.[35]

After two desperate dashes and one riotous encounter with a mule train, Browne's party reached the summit. They made their descent to Strawberry in the dark, on a road that Browne describes as "a running stream of mud, obstructed by slippery rocks, ruts, stumps, and dead animals."[36] At Strawberry the Washoe-bound crowds were thicker than ever.

Browne's account gives the impression that the vast majority of travelers over the Lake Tahoe Wagon Road in the spring of 1860 went on foot or horseback. Though stagecoach service had been started, it had temporarily broken down due to road conditions. There is no indication of the enormous freight wagon traffic that later observers were to mention; instead everything moved by mule train. Even allowing for humorous exaggeration, the road Browne experienced in the spring of 1860 was clearly in much worse condition than the one Simpson traveled over in June 1859, when it was good enough for regular stagecoach service. Maintenance in this area of steep slopes and heavy weather was clearly less than satisfactory.

In May 1860 the *Sacramento Daily Union,* as if to confirm Browne's account, reported serious erosion of the roadbed by runoff from the heavy snows of that winter, which in fact had scarcely yet stopped falling. Repairs had been made, but many travelers expressed doubts about how adequate these were. The report concluded that "the travel has become so great on this mountain route that at any of the bad points on it toll roads, it is believed, would prove profitable." But conditions were expected to improve rapidly. McDonald and Kingsbury's toll road from Lake Valley to Carson Valley over Daggett Pass was nearing completion and was expected to open by the end of June. Two road entrepreneurs named Reese and Trumbo were said to be building bridges in Carson Canyon and preparing to charge tolls. There was also talk of building a toll road around a difficult stretch at Slippery Ford.[37]

Toll Roads

The greatly increased traffic across the Sierra stimulated road entrepreneurs to supplement the efforts of state and local government. California adopted a policy of allowing private toll roads to be built along the line of the Day route. One early historian of El Dorado County, writing a couple of decades later, suggested that the Lake Tahoe Wagon Road would never have been finished if the Washoe boom had not created a profitable situation for toll road entrepreneurs.[38]

The concept of toll roads seems to have been somewhat different then. These were not thoroughfares connecting distant end points but short improved segments along difficult parts of an existing road. The road as a whole was in effect a transportation corridor (through public land) in which entrepreneurs might construct bridges and shortcuts in the expectation that the public would pay to avoid at least some of the toils and tribulations of travel that Browne so vividly described.

These toll road ventures can be considered conveniently in two groups: those between Placerville and Johnson Pass and those between Johnson Pass and Carson Valley. There were at least three toll roads on the western slope between Placerville and Johnson Pass: (1) Oglesby Road ran along the south side of the river for about a dozen miles in the middle of the stretch between Placerville and the western summit. Although it was located on a north-facing slope, it was evidently below the elevation of heavy snowfall. Stagecoaches used this road from 1861 to 1864.[39] (2) Pearson and McDonald operated a toll road along the present Highway 50 from 14-Mile House (east side of present Pollock Pines), passing through Riverton, to the junction with the Oglesby road where it crossed the river. (3) Farther up the South Fork valley, Slippery Ford Grade was in operation as a toll road by a man named Swan. This stretch of road became part of the state highway and remained so until 1931, when the highway was rerouted between Strawberry and Sayles Flat.[40]

East of Johnson Pass there were also various toll roads, but these were not closely parallel alternatives to each other, as in the South Fork canyon, but widely splayed east ends of the trunk road. There were at least two toll roads from Lake Tahoe Valley over the Carson Range to Carson Valley. The one over Daggett Pass (7,334 ft.) was known as the Kingsbury Grade. Sherman Day had noted a potential route over the mountains here during his explorations in the summer of 1855; he mentioned "a pass in the rear of Dr. Daggett's, about three miles south of the Mormon Station, leading over to the south-east corner of Lake Bigler, but it is used only for horses and mules, having never been graded for wagons."[41] In 1859 Simpson came to a similar conclusion, saying that considerable work would be needed to make it fit for wagons, as related above. In 1860 two entrepreneurs named Kingsbury and McDonald took the gamble on improving the track into a toll road suitable for wagons. They were successful and attracted much of the traffic that had been taking the Day route through Luther Pass and Hope Valley. Today the Daggett Pass Road is Nevada 207, and at the pass there is a busy intersection formed by an entrance to the Heavenly Valley ski resort.

After a time, however, the Kingsbury Grade faced competition from Walton's Road (later U.S. 50) and, in 1863, Kings Canyon Road, both of which seem to have been improvements in Johnson's Cut-off. They crossed the Carson Range from about midway along the east shore of Lake Tahoe to Carson City.[42]

The Lake Tahoe Wagon Road

By the early 1860s the various road segments had merged into what was generally known as the Lake Tahoe Wagon Road, famous for the high quality both of the road itself and the stagecoach service available on it. For evidence of the improvements we can refer again to the writings of

J. Ross Browne, who returned to Virginia City in the summer of 1864.[43] This time he rode the Pioneer Stage instead of walking. Browne's description of the animated scene at the Folsom railroad station, with stagecoaches meeting the train from Sacramento to take on passengers for various destinations in the Sierra, and his colloquy with Charlie the driver once they were under way have been mined (not always with attribution) more than once by later writers.

For the first 10 miles east of Placerville, maintenance was not keeping up with wear and tear caused by heavy use, but when they reached "the grade," bad road was at an end and they were on a "smooth broad highway." Browne was not precise about where and why the transition occurred, but it seems likely that they had entered onto one of the various segments of toll road that followed the South Fork valley. A few miles farther on, he described the road as "a magnificent piece of engineering—smooth, broad, and beautifully regular."[44] And still farther along: "The road over the mountain from Strawberry has been greatly improved. It is now a magnificent highway. Formerly the ascent to the summit was difficult and dangerous. The rise is now so beautifully graded as to be scarcely appreciable. Our horses trotted along briskly nearly the whole way."[45]

Watching from his perch next to Charlie, Browne was struck by the changes in the character of the traffic.

> From the first hour after leaving Placerville we passed along the road-side numerous teams and trains of wagons, most of which were grouped together under the trees, or in front of the station-houses, in the old-fashioned camp style. I commenced a rough calculation of the number of wagons, but soon gave it up as a hopeless task. It seemed to me that there were enough of them, big and little, to reach all the way over the mountain. At the least calculation we must have passed two or three hundred. Every wagon was heavily freighted—some with merchandise, others with iron castings for the mills, and quite a goodly number with families, fruit, whisky, and furniture. There were horse-teams, and mule-teams, and ox-teams. I never before saw so many teams on one road.[46]

In the midst of these remarkable developments, Browne found cause for regret.

> Yet I must confess the trip to Washoe has, to me at least, lost much of its original charm. No longer is the way variegated by long strings of pedestrians, carrying their picks, shovels, and blankets upon their backs; no longer are the stopping-places crowded every night with two or three hundred

adventurers inspired by visionary thoughts of the future; no longer are the wild mountain passes enlivened by grotesque scenes of saddle-trains and passengers struggling through the mud and snow; it is all now a regular and established line of travel; too civilized to be interesting in any great degree, and too convenient to admit of those charming discomforts which formerly afforded us so much amusement. Only think how the emigrants who crossed these mountains in 1848 would have stared at the bare suggestion of a Pioneer stage-line.[47]

The Lake Tahoe Wagon Road had become one of the great thoroughfares of the West. Hubert H. Bancroft left a description of stagecoach service over the road:

There was never any stage service in the world more complete than that between Placerville and Virginia City. A sprinkled road, over which dashed six fine, sleek horses, before an elegant Concord coach, the lines in the hands of an expert driver, whose light hat, linen duster, and lemon-colored gloves betokened a good salary and an exacting company, and who timed his grooms and his passengers by a heavy gold chronometer watch, held carelessly, if conspicuously, on the tips of his fingers—these were some of its conspicuous features. This service continued until it was supplanted by the Central Pacific railroad from Sacramento.[48]

This was not merely California boosterism. Samuel Bowles, editor of the Springfield (Massachusetts) *Republican,* reported similarly about a trip he made in the summer of 1865 with Schuyler Colfax, speaker of the House of Representatives, and William Brook, lieutenant governor of Illinois.

Our journey now,—be it borne in mind,—was before the Railroad, which has destroyed this, the finest bit of stage travel in all our continental journey. There were two well-graded toll roads over the mountains, from Sacramento in California to Virginia City in Nevada; one by Placerville and Lake Tahoe, the other by Dutch Flat and Donner Lake,[49] and each about one hundred and sixty miles long. The Railroad takes substantially the route of the latter; but in the days of staging and teaming, the Placerville road was the favorite. The amount of traffic upon it was immense. Two or three stage loads of passengers passed each way daily. Merchandise and machinery were carried in huge freight wagons, holding from five to ten tons each, and drawn by ten or twelve large, strong horses or mules, moving to the music of bells attached to their harnesses. . . . To keep the road hard and in repair, as well as to allay the fearful dust that would otherwise have made the ride a trial rather than a pleasure, nearly the whole line was artificially watered during the long, dry summer. Luxurious as this seems,—the daily sprinkling of one hundred and fifty miles of mountain road,—and expensive as it was, it was found to be the simplest and cheapest mode of keeping the road in good repair. The stages were drawn by six fleet, gay horses, changed every ten miles, without the driver's even leaving his seat.

Thus munificently prepared, and amid the finest mountain scenery in the world, we swept up the hills at a round trot, and rolled again at the sharpest gallop, turning abrupt corners without a pull-up, twisting among and past the loaded teams of freight toiling over into Nevada, and running along the edge of high precipices, all as deftly as the skater flies or the steam car runs; though for many a moment we held our fainting breath at what seemed great risks or dare-devil performances. A full day's ride was made at a rate exceeding ten miles an hour; and a continuous seven miles over the rolling hills along the crest of the range was driven within twenty-six minutes. The loss of such exhilarating experience is enough to put the traveler out of conceit with superseding railroads.[50]

The very success of the Lake Tahoe Wagon Road helped speed its decline. The fledgling Central Pacific Railroad, which aimed to capture much of the trans-Sierra business, carried out a detailed census of the amount of traffic on the road. Theodore Judah stationed an agent at Strawberry for fifty-six days in 1862 (August 16–October 10) and had him count the traffic going by. Some of the results are as follows (numbers are for traffic in both directions): stagecoaches, 340; buggies, 107; freight wagons, 8,606. Judah made a few calculations.

A four horse or mule team, which makes the trip in about 16 days, pays for tolls $22.75; a six horse or mule team pays $30 tolls. Average the time at 18 days, the tolls at $25 per trip, and we find that the enormous sum of $693,000 per year is paid for tolls by freight teams.

The returns show that the stage averages 37 passengers per day, which, at $30 per passenger, amounts to $405,150. It is believed, however, that the total receipts of this stage line exceeds this sum.[51]

The Henness Pass Routes

Although the Lake Tahoe Wagon Road was the leading road across the mountains in the decade before the Pacific railroad was finished, it did have rivals for commercial traffic. One, the Dutch Flat and Donner Lake Road, came into use in 1864 as a temporary subsidiary of the Central Pacific Railroad and is considered in the next chapter.

At the beginning of the 1860s the Lake Tahoe Wagon Road's chief rival was the Henness Pass system of roads. "System" seems the appropriate word here because a single road leading up to the pass from the east split into three branches descending the western slope. These spread out widely with additional subbranches to various gold camps.

As we saw in chapter 4, Henness Pass began to be used early in the 1850s by those emigrants and gold seekers on the Truckee route who

were looking for a shortcut to the diggings on the Yuba and Feather
rivers. Throughout the 1850s it remained a rough wagon road. Then
came the Washoe silver boom. "Cities like Marysville and Nevada City
realized that if they were to obtain their share of the rapidly increasing
Washoe trade they must build a good wagon road to tap the region."[52]
Acting independently, both Marysville and Nevada City moved to up-
grade the old emigrant route into an important stagecoach route. In each
town a company was organized to build roads through Henness Pass.

The Marysville concern was the Truckee Turnpike Company, started
in November 1859 to build up to the pass from North San Juan, which
was already connected to Marysville via Bridgeport. The company collapsed when one of the main shareholders withdrew, but it was revived
with new backers in time for the spring and summer construction season
of 1860. The road ran along the interfluve ridges between the North and
Middle forks of the Yuba River. On May 3, 1860, the *San Francisco Bulletin* reported that the directors expected to open it to wagons and stagecoaches very soon and to have the whole project finished by July 15.

The California Stage Company was to begin service on the Truckee
Turnpike, to Forest City by May 10 and all the way to Virginia City as
soon as the road was sufficiently ready. The distance of 136 miles would
be covered in two days. The *Bulletin* reported that the new road was
very straight, with easy grades, and ran through charming pasture valleys. The reporter did not think snow would be an insuperable obstacle:
many stations would stay open in the winter, and the narrow belt subject to deep snow would be crossed on sleighs.[53]

The other firm seeking to use Henness Pass to attract Virginia City
business traffic was the Henness Pass Turnpike Company, organized in
Nevada City in December 1859 to build along the San Juan Ridge, between the Middle and South forks of the Yuba River, to the pass. By late
May the company was reported to be stocking its stations with feed and
provisions and to be preparing an express service of twelve hours between Nevada City and Virginia City. Several shortenings of the route
had been achieved, making the total distance 89 miles, and others were
proposed which would decrease the distance to 81 miles.[54]

The Truckee Turnpike was described as being 15 to 18 feet wide,
banked, with ditches for drainage and a grade not steeper than 6 feet in
100. Presumably the Henness Pass Turnpike was similar. The two roads
met at Jackson Meadows, near the 6,000-foot level on the Middle Fork.
(The meadows are now inundated by Jackson Meadows Reservoir.)

There the companies joined forces to build through Henness Pass, which lay a half dozen miles to the east, and on to Virginia City.

In July 1860 the *Marysville Appeal* reported that the Truckee Turnpike was nearing completion and described it as even better than the existing road between Marysville and North San Juan. Tolls (presumably daily) were projected to be 75¢ for a two-horse wagon on the up trip, 50¢ on the down trip; for a four-horse wagon, $1.25 on the up trip and 75¢ on the down trip; for a six-horse wagon, $2 and $1; for an eight-horse wagon, $2.50 and $1.25. Various lesser tolls would be charged for horsemen and loose stock. The rationale for the price difference between up trips and down trips was that the former would usually carry heavy loads of mining equipment and other gear for Virginia City, causing increased wear and tear on the road, while the latter would carry lighter loads. Construction was said to have proceeded as far as Jackson Meadows, the junction point with the Henness Turnpike from Nevada City. Supervisors from each company would jointly let contracts for the remaining portion. Total cost for the joint road was not expected to exceed $24,000. The reporter reminded his readers that the route was already traversed by an imperfect road made by emigrants with wagons and later improved somewhat by hay ranchers.[55]

By the fall of 1860 the combined forces of the two companies had built as far east as Dog Valley Hill and were working hard to surmount that obstacle before snow began to fall. The California Stage Company was to provide coach service on the new road.[56] In May 1864 a third branch opened west of Jackson Meadows connecting with Dutch Flat via Bear Valley and Bowman's Ranch. Known as the Pacific Turnpike, or Culbertson's Road, it would thus appear to be the ancestor of the present Bowman's Lake Road.[57]

As a result of these ventures, Henness Pass provided an important gateway to California across the Sierra Nevada in the 1860s. By the early summer of 1864 the California Stage Company, operating from Marysville through Henness Pass, was described as the principal competitor of industry leader Pioneer Stage on the Placerville route.[58] Nevertheless, the Henness Pass route did not survive as a major road but fell into obscurity after the Central Pacific was completed on an approximately parallel line not far to the south. Businessmen in Marysville and the mining areas around Nevada City must have found it more convenient to connect with Virginia City along relatively short feeder roads to the Central Pacific at Colfax or Dutch Flat.

The Henness Pass routes did not survive into the automobile age as paved highways across the Sierra. On the east side there is a two-lane blacktop road between State Highway 89 and Jackson Meadows Reservoir, running through the pass itself, but west of the reservoir dam the old stage routes now survive only as gravel and dirt U.S. Forest Service roads, barely passable in an ordinary car. In 1955 businessmen in Nevada City tried to get the state highway department to modernize the Henness Pass route rather than widen U.S. 40 to four lanes, but the state apparently found their argument unpersuasive.[59] U.S. 40 was widened and later became Interstate 80. Yet if Californians ever should decide that another highway from the Sacramento Valley to the Reno area is desirable, a revived Henness Pass route seems the most likely candidate.

The Far Northern Sierra

There was a burst of toll road activity in the 1860s in the far northern Sierra, in connection with the rush to the Owyhee silver mines in what later became Idaho. This appeared to some optimists to be another Comstock Lode. John Bidwell, leader of the Bidwell party in 1841 and now, a quarter century later, a prosperous rancher in Chico, received a state franchise for a toll road between Chico and Honey Lake. With his partners, Bidwell began work in the spring of 1865 on the Chico and Humboldt Wagon Road Company. The road followed the course of today's State Highway 32 as far as Loma and thence Humboldt Road across Humboldt Summit (6,610 ft.) to the vicinity of Big Meadows, now Lake Almanor. At the same time, road entrepreneurs in Red Bluff opened another road from Red Bluff east along the line of today's Highway 36. The two roads met and went on via Fredonyer Pass (5,748 ft.) to Susanville. Traffic could then take the federally sponsored Honey Lake Road into Nevada and eventually across the southeast corner of Oregon into Idaho. The Owyhee rush soon fizzled out, and the road and its stage service lasted only a short time.[60]

CHAPTER 10

The Central Pacific Railroad

In Washington, D.C., the sectional impasse regarding the Pacific railroad continued right up to the Civil War. Only when southern members walked out of the Senate and House of Representatives was it possible for these bodies to act, and in 1862 they chose a central route, from Omaha to Sacramento. To congressmen who examined this route on a map it must have looked at first like the familiar California/Oregon Trail, but a closer look showed some changes, especially in what was to become southern Wyoming, where the proposed rail line passed well south of the wagon ruts that ran along the North Platte and Sweetwater rivers and then through South Pass. The geographer James E. Vance has discussed this route change in detail, making the distinction between economic and noneconomic transportation. The latter is exemplified by the Oregon Trail, where success was measured mainly by getting through once to the other end to start a new life; the former, by the Union Pacific Railroad, where success was measured by the profitable carriage of passengers and goods in both directions over a long period. In the case of the railroad, then, the selection of the most energy-efficient route and the reduction of operating costs became matters of great importance.[1] This same idea, a movement from noneconomic to economic forms of transportation, also sheds some light on the history of the development of roads over the Sierra Nevada.

As it turned out, the Pacific railroad was built without much direct reference to the Pacific Railroad Surveys. The eastern half, the Union

Pacific, did draw on earlier army surveys made by Frémont and Stansbury, but the surveys had ignored the Sierra Nevada, as a result of the marching orders given by Jefferson Davis, who was sure the range would be impassable in winter. It is true that as an afterthought to the main program Lieutenant E. G. Beckwith had surveyed a line from Lassen's Meadows to the north end of the Sacramento Valley, but this was too far north for the Central Pacific.

Surveys of the California portion of the Pacific railroad, then, were carried out locally. Despite years of pronouncements about the inevitable sequence of wagon road first and then railroad, the Central Pacific departed completely from the established routes south of Lake Tahoe and instead revived the original Truckee route, pioneered by the Stevens party in 1844 but largely forgotten a decade later.

The Beginning of Railroads in California

The chief engineer of the Central Pacific, Theodore D. Judah, first came to California in 1854 to be chief engineer of the Sacramento Valley Railroad. Only twenty-eight at the time, he had already achieved a brilliant engineering reputation in upstate New York, most notably for building the Niagara Gorge Railroad, said to be an impossible job by older and more-experienced engineers. Building a 22-mile line across the grassy plains from Sacramento to Negro Bar (later Folsom) was not much of a challenge after that, but it was Judah's ticket to California. Even before leaving New York he was looking ahead to building a railroad over the Sierra Nevada.

As it turned out, the Sacramento Valley Railroad was a good exercise for Judah. The line's promoters evidently had only a general idea of their project and left all the details to him. Seeing the railroad as a connector between tidewater port facilities in Sacramento and a vast hinterland of mining districts, Judah took a broad view of the traffic potential of interior California when he projected the economic possibilities of the line. He was always mindful of the fact that it might eventually become a link in the great Pacific railroad. Judah was not an undisciplined visionary, however; he kept an eye on the details as well. For example, to evaluate potential transmountain business he made a detailed count of vehicles, pedestrians, and livestock passing two points at the city limits of Sacramento during the course of a week.[2]

Much as Californians had clamored and petitioned for a railroad connection to the East, they were far from ready to undertake it themselves in February 1856, when the Sacramento Valley Railroad was finished to Folsom, at the base of the western slopes of the Sierra. Judah cherished schemes to push on into the mountains and/or extend the line to Marysville, but the owners were unwilling to invest any more money. For the next three years Judah was involved in several other railroad surveys, Benicia to Sacramento and San Francisco to San Jose, for example, but there was no actual construction even on these relatively unchallenging projects. Still, doing the surveys and writing the reports were stimulating for Judah. They allowed him to see more of California, and the productive potential of this new state continued to grow in his mind. He saw the Benicia-Sacramento line as "the beginning of the end of the great National Rail Road."[3]

Judah began to explore the Sierra in his spare time, scouting for railroad routes across the range. His wife, Anna, often accompanied him, and her sketches and paintings of Sierra scenery later decorated Central Pacific stock certificates. In late 1856 the couple went to Washington, D.C., by ship and the new railroad across the Isthmus of Panama. In the national capital Judah realized the depth of sectional feeling when he tried, unsuccessfully, to get California's Senator Gwin, a southerner by origin, to support a central route.

While in Washington, Judah published at his own expense the *Practical Plan for Building the Pacific Railroad.* In this pamphlet he advocated a scheme to finance and build the line by private capital, saying that sectional rivalry made federal assistance a vain hope. He pointed out that private capital had already built 25,000 miles of rail line in the eastern United States and asked, "Why is it, if this vast amount has been raised to build our Railroads, that the same course cannot be adopted to procure the money for construction of the Pacific Railroad? Simply because, as yet, no survey has been made upon which capitalists can base their calculations, they do not know that a line is wholly practicable upon any route."[4]

Judah proposed to fund the railroad by the sale of stock in small amounts to large numbers of people. The line was to be built from both ends. As a preliminary the government should build a wagon road along the proposed route. This would induce settlement and allow supplies to be brought in for the railroad (apparently Judah did not foresee the giant work trains of the Union Pacific). Farmers would settle along the wagon road and grow food for railroad workers.

Judah admitted that snow would be a problem at certain points along the line, but snow was being dealt with successfully on eastern railroads.

Where necessary, the railroad could establish work camps of men whose sole job would be to shovel snow. As for Indian hostilities, Judah held that they would soon subside when the Indians realized how quickly large bodies of troops could be mobilized against them on the railroad. Judah thought it would be possible to make the trip between San Francisco and St. Louis with existing engines in five days, though he expected to see improvements to hundred-mile-per-hour operating speeds. He made glowing predictions of the profitability and population-drawing capacity of the railroad.[5]

Judah promoted his Sierra railroad scheme in speeches and newspaper pieces and in personal conversation so vociferously that, it is said, people began to avoid him in the street. Back in San Francisco he helped organize a Pacific railroad convention in September 1859 and was one of the main speakers. The executive committee of the convention appointed him its official agent to carry resolutions to Washington, D.C. The resolutions called for a railroad to be constructed along the central route and asked the federal government to guarantee loans of 5 percent and grant both the right-of-way across the territories and alternate sections 30 miles deep on either side if the constructing contractor completed the job in five years (only 10 miles if the contractor took longer).

The railroad convention also called on the federal government to donate to California public lands within the state and two years' worth of customs collections from San Francisco to cover railroad construction within the state. Similar arrangements were made with Oregon and Washington to cover the costs of building connecting branches.

Judah sailed back east on October 20, 1859. On the same boat were J. C. Burch, congressman from California, and Joseph Lane, senator from Oregon. During the long trip via the isthmus, Judah got to know both men well, which stood him in good stead later in making contacts in the halls of Congress. Judah was so successful in this regard that he was given an office in the Capitol, which he filled with maps and other exhibits on the Pacific railroad, to use as his lobbying office. He made excursions from Washington, D.C., to study eastern railroads, especially those, like the Baltimore & Ohio, that had constructed lines over the steep slopes of the Appalachians.

In addition to concerns about topography, Judah was forced to consider the problem of snow. He knew this question would arise in the minds of potential backers in California, so on his eastern trips he made a point of examining the snow situation on some of the higher rail crossings of the Appalachians. He found enough track mileage being successfully operated in heavy snowfall areas to feel confident that Sierra snow problems could be overcome.

In July 1860 Judah was back in California, ready to take what he had learned about the construction and operation of mountain railroads into the Sierra. He was still not sure of the best route across the range, so incomplete was topographic knowledge. He must have investigated, and dismissed, the existing wagon and stagecoach routes early on. The requirements of a railroad were much stricter than those of a wagon road, as were the economic constraints. Efficiency of operation and conservation of effort were of little importance to people making a onetime trip across the mountains. Extravagant outlays of human and animal energy could be accepted as part of the task. Most emigrants were making the trip only once and could put up with anything. We have seen from accounts of wagon travel that wagons could be dismantled and pulled up over almost vertical rock faces and dragged around to make 180-degree turns. For a stagecoach enterprise, the requirements were somewhat stricter. Many repeat trips were contemplated, passenger comfort had to be taken into account to some degree, and operators wanted roads that would minimize wear and tear on coaches and horses. Still there was much flexibility in these matters. A stagecoach entrepreneur like Jared Crandall could use a bad road while waiting for a better one to open. He could detour around washouts or make temporary repairs. Passengers would put up with jolts and dust if there were no alternatives but horseback or walking.

Railroad technology was much less forgiving. The engine, cars, and track constituted after all a single, complex, highly expensive machine of many parts, stretched out over vast distances in a violently changeable environment. This machine had to run smoothly and efficiently for a long time to pay back the investment in it. Over a mountain range it was important to find a route that ran steadily uphill or downhill, but not too steeply, and without redundant grade, that is, undulations in the line's profile requiring trains to go downhill and then back up again. Creating such a proper grade was sure to require cuts, fills, and tunnels, although these had to be kept to a minimum because they were so expensive. By such exacting standards, the wagon roads in use when Judah began his search were hopelessly unsatisfactory.

In a progress report to the Central Pacific's board of directors dated July 1, 1863, Judah outlined five "barometrical reconnoisances" (i.e., lines of elevations determined with a barometer) across the Sierra: (1) via Folsom, Greenwood, and Georgetown; (2) via Auburn and

Illinoistown (Colfax), Dutch Flat and Donner Pass; (3) via Nevada City and Henness Pass; (4) via Downieville and Yuba Gap; and (5) via Oroville, Bidwell's Bar, Middle Feather River and Beckwourth Pass. These evaluations were perhaps intended to deflect objections from bypassed towns, by showing good topographic reasons why they could not be included. Judah had already proclaimed his choice—route number two.[6]

Revival of the Truckee Route

Famous as it had been, and was to be again, the Truckee route had fallen into oblivion when Judah began his search. California's overland traffic now crossed the mountains elsewhere, most important, just south of Lake Tahoe, with additional significant flow still farther south or else well north of the Truckee route.

Judah had no personal experience of overland travel; all his trips between California and the East were by ship via Panama. Perhaps this is why he did not consider the Truckee route until "Doctor" Strong in Dutch Flat called his attention to it. Daniel Strong was actually a druggist who had set up shop in the hydraulic mining boomtown of Dutch Flat, at the 3,200-foot level on the ridge between the Bear River and the North Fork of the American. He was ambitious for himself and his adopted town, and though not a surveyor, he evidently knew enough about allowable grades on railroads to appreciate the way the ridge Dutch Flat was on continued steadily up toward the Sierra crest. Strong had evidently met Judah once before, or at least knew from newspaper accounts what the engineer was interested in. He wrote to Judah and invited him to visit and examine the interesting ridge. In late October 1860 the two went up with mules as far as Donner Summit and got back down just ahead of the first big snowstorm of the season. Judah had found what he was looking for.

The seeming parallelism of Judah's railroad route to the main emigrant route pioneered by the Stevens party in 1844 and used until the Carson route supplanted it at the end of the 1840s may make it hard to see how this route could have fallen into such obscurity by 1860 that it had to be rediscovered. Actually, it was only partially the same route, and viewed from the Central Valley it was not the same route at all. West of Emigrant Gap (5,200 ft.) the emigrant trail did not come down the ridge where Dutch Flat was located but rather crossed over to Lowell Hill Ridge on the other side of the Bear River's deep valley. Lowell Hill Ridge had some steep slopes that made it unattractive for railroad construction, so to someone like Judah, looking uphill from the west end, the derelict Truckee wagon route would have had little to recommend it.

Judah set forth the advantages of the new route in an 1860 pamphlet:

> This line effects a saving in distance, over the northern line, of one hundred and fifty miles, and avoids the passage of two cañons on the Sacramento [Pit] river, twenty miles long, estimated by Lieutenant Beckwith to cost $4,200,000; while it affords a direct line to Washoe, across the narrowest portion of the State, and a local road for the business of Sacramento, Placer, and Nevada counties.

Judah's survey line rose from the Central Valley, just above sea level, to the 7,000-foot summit, with no redundant grade. Not only did the summit lie conveniently at the top of a natural ramp from the west, but it was also opposite the gorge cut by the Truckee River through the Carson Range. As we have seen, other routes across the mountains had double summits, imposing redundant grades of as much as a thousand feet. If a rail line could be laid through the Truckee gorge, then the Dutch Flat route would allow track to rise steadily from either side to a single summit, at a grade of no more than 105 feet to a mile.

It was obvious that the east side of Donner Pass, which had been almost too difficult even for wagons, was much too steep for a railroad. But a railroad company would have the resources to blast and tunnel a line along the granite mountainside south of Donner Lake and so stretch out the horizontal component of the slope between Truckee and the summit to a manageable grade.

Birth of the Central Pacific

On their return from the mountains Judah and Strong drew up the articles of incorporation for the Central Pacific Railroad. (According to Central Pacific lore, they did the writing on the counter of Strong's drugstore, and stayed up most of the night doing it.) They found some subscribers for the stock in Dutch Flat, but California law on railroad incorporation required that $1,000 actually be paid in for each mile of the projected road. Since their preliminary survey showed 110 miles from Sacramento to the state line, they needed $110,000, and this was more than they could raise in Dutch Flat alone. Judah went to San Francisco, where, he was confident, investors would be eager to subscribe for stock.

He was in for a great disappointment. Whether because there was more assured profit in mining investments, or because a railroad threatened established interests in shipping and stagecoaches, or perhaps because of simple lack of confidence, San Francisco's capitalists were unwilling to put $110,000 into the railroad. Disappointed but not discouraged, Judah returned to Sacramento and made the rounds of that city's moneyed men. At an evening meeting he attracted the attention of Collis P. Huntington, a dry goods merchant. Huntington came to see Judah the next day to learn more and was sold on the idea. He brought in his partner, Mark Hopkins, and fellow merchants Leland Stanford and Charles Crocker. These men became known to history as the Big Four.

In this way the Central Pacific became a Sacramento, as opposed to a San Francisco, company, provoking an intercity rivalry that might not have been as strong had the company been located in San Francisco. Three other towns especially felt a threat in Sacramento's becoming the western terminus of the railroad—Stockton, Placerville, and Marysville. As we have seen, similar rivalries had developed in connection with wagon roads.

Placerville businessmen in particular were put out. Placerville had been aligned with Sacramento on road issues for some years now, whether it was the Carson Pass route, Johnson's Cut-off, or the Lake Tahoe Wagon Road. And now the railroad was going way off to the north through Dutch Flat and cutting Placerville off! Placerville critics emphasized the snow hazard and harped on the Donner party as an example of the disasters that awaited a railroad along Judah's line. Carson Valley residents also attacked it, since the proposed line would have access to the Washoe silver mines from the north and leave Carson Valley isolated on the south. (Their fears were well founded; Truckee Meadows [later Reno] did overtake Carson Valley in population after the railroad was built through it.)

The Dutch Flat and Donner Lake Wagon Road

The Truckee route began to regain its importance as a transportation route even before the railroad was finished. To draw off traffic from the Lake Tahoe Wagon Road, the Big Four decided on a temporary wagon road of their own, from the end of track to Virginia City. The history of this road can be reconstructed from the pages of the *Sacramento Daily Union.*

In April 1861 the *Daily Union* carried a brief item saying that ground had been broken by the "officers of the road" and that the road itself was now under construction. There was no mention of the Central Pacific.[7] On June 5, 1862, the *Daily Union* announced that C. P. Huntington had returned from Placer County on business connected with this road. E. L. Bradley and Dr. Strong of Dutch Flat are described as having united with Huntington, Mark Hopkins, "and other capitalists of this city" to construct the wagon road. S. S. Montague was surveying the route, the expected cost of which would amount to $100,000.[8] S. S. Montague was an engineer who was later to preside over much of the construction of the railroad after Judah's death. So it could hardly have been a secret that the road was part of the greater Central Pacific project.

On October 6, 1862, the Dutch Flat and Donner Lake Wagon Road Company, C. Crocker, president, advertised in the *Daily Union* for sealed bids on constructing two sections of road.[9] Crocker was head of the nominally independent construction company that was building the railroad and evidently head of the road company as well. On August 6, 1863, the *Daily Union* reported two hundred men at work, half of the 40 miles from Dutch Flat to Truckee Valley completed, and 6 more miles nearly finished. The grade was said to be easier than any existing Sierra road. The California Stage Company had purchased the stage route from Lincoln to Dutch Flat, with the intent of putting on a line of coaches.[10]

On September 25, 1863, the *Daily Union* reported that the work was advancing rapidly but would not be completed that fall. There were 150 men at work from the summit to Truckee Valley, and they would work through the winter if necessary to be open by spring.[11]

On October 4, 1864, the *Daily Union* carried a first-person account of a trip over the new road, reprinted from the *San Francisco Bulletin* of September 27. The road had just opened and the reporter was delighted with his trip, which completed the 130 miles to Virginia City in only seventeen hours. There was "no part of the road you cannot trot a buggy right along." The only steep grade was between Donner Lake and the summit. The scenery at the summit was magnificent, and Donner Lake was even more beautiful than Lake Tahoe. The road was wide enough for two teams most of the way. Total cost of the road was $200,000. Most of the way the road ran close to the railroad survey, so the traveler could see how the Central Pacific was progressing.[12] By this time trains were running as far east as Dutch Flat.

On January 2, 1865, in what appears to be an annual business review section, the *Daily Union* reported some additional interesting facts about the road. It was 60 miles long, from Dutch Flat to its meeting point with the Henness Pass road in the vicinity of Dog Valley (about 20 miles from

Virginia City). It was 20 feet wide, and there was no slope of more than ten inches in a rod (16.5 ft.). It had cost $200,000, more than any other wagon road in the state; 350 men had worked on the project for ten months. It opened for travel on June 15, 1864. On July 15 the California Stage Company put on daily six-horse coaches between Virginia City and Newcastle. In the six months ending January 1, 1865, a total of 3,280 wagons (two to six horses each) had driven over it. Total travel time between Virginia City and Sacramento was eighteen hours in the summer, thirty in the winter.

Opponents of the Big Four charged that operating the Dutch Flat and Donner Lake Wagon Road was their real purpose, that the railroad was just a subterfuge for getting government money. The matter came to a head in May 1863 when the voters of San Francisco passed a measure to have the city subscribe for $600,000 of Central Pacific stock. Opponents called this "the Great Dutch Flat Swindle" and published a thick pamphlet against it with that title. The Central Pacific defended itself by pointing out that behind this attack were the Sacramento Valley Railroad, the "wagon road owners on the Placerville route," who, the railroad claimed, had collected over a million dollars in tolls in 1863, and the Pioneer Stage of Louis McLane & Company, who also made almost a million dollars on express, passengers, and treasure. The Big Four did indeed attempt to make as much money as possible out of the road, but they were sincere about building the railroad, from which they expected to make far more.

Since the eventual success of the Central Pacific has long been a fact of history, it is easy to forget that this success was by no means assured. The company faced opposition from shipping interests, stagecoach operators, and rival railroad promoters. One rival railroad group projected a San Francisco and Washoe railroad, to run through Placerville and up the South Fork of the American River to Carson Valley, that is, closely parallel to the Lake Tahoe Wagon Road but with a 2.75-mile tunnel under Johnson Pass. This was the project of Charles E. McLane, who owned the Placerville and Sacramento Valley Railroad, and L. L. Robinson, who owned an explosives company. McLane and Robinson carried out a vigorous attack on the Big Four in 1864, playing the "Dutch Flat Swindle" for all it was worth and attempting to have the Nevada legislature revoke guarantees to the Central Pacific and instead offer financial assistance to whichever railroad was the first to enter the state.

In the end, the opposition was unable to present an effective challenge to the Central Pacific, which had monopolized available investment capital for the western end of the Pacific railroad and carried it through to conclusion in 1869. There are still people in Placerville who argue that it would have been cheaper in the long run to have built the trans-Sierra railroad up the South Fork valley, tunneling under the western summit. Heavier initial outlays for construction would have been paid for by long-term savings on snowsheds and and snow removal, according to this view. This might have meant a main transcontinental rail line running along the shores of Lake Tahoe, however.

EPILOGUE

Trans-Sierra Roads after 1869

Theodore Judah's anticipation that the Central Pacific would capture most of California's business with Virginia City and points east proved to be correct. The railroad was able to haul passengers and goods faster and more cheaply across the mountains, and the glory days of main-line wagon and coach roads like the Lake Tahoe Wagon Road, the Dutch Flat and Donner Lake Wagon Road, and the various Henness Pass roads were over. Express, freight, and stagecoach operators on these roads had to scale down to being feeders for the railroad, or else move operations to areas as yet unreached by rail. The vehicles continued in operation for another half century in remoter areas, until they were finally replaced by the earliest motor trucks and buses.

The roads sank into decrepitude at varying rates, depending on how closely the railroad paralleled and outperformed them. Most did not completely disappear. In California the rail network was never as dense as in the Middle West, which was crisscrossed by tracks every few miles. This was especially true in the mountains. For forty years after 1869 only one line crossed the Sierra. Then in 1909 the Western Pacific built up through the canyon of the North Fork of the Feather River and out into the Great Basin through Beckwourth Pass. Even today there are only these two rail lines across the Sierra, though the Western Pacific has since been incorporated into the Union Pacific. Because of this extreme channelization of long-distance rail traffic, roads in the mountains necessarily retained some importance for local traffic and as feeders to the railroad.

The Lake Tahoe Wagon Road remained in business as a toll road until 1886. There must have been some break-even point along it above Placerville where it became cheaper to travel east over the summit than go west to connect with the rail network. In addition there would have been vehicles on local errands, as well as logging traffic from the vast forested areas along the road. In 1886 El Dorado County bought the road and declared it a public highway. When the state legislature created the Bureau of Highways in 1896, the new agency made the Lake Tahoe Wagon Road California's first state highway.

The state built a new stone arch bridge over the South Fork at Riverton in 1901 (a short distance upstream from the old Brockliss Bridge) and upgraded smaller bridges and culverts farther up the road. The road was unpaved at this time; in 1910 the state provided money to sprinkle it in summer to keep down the dust (thus bringing it back up to the standards of 1865, when Samuel Bowles made his breezy jaunt.)[1]

An era of systematic improvements began in 1917, with the creation of the California Highway Commission. The Lake Tahoe Wagon Road became Highway 11 in the new statewide numbering system.[2] By 1919 it was paved as far as Placerville, and there were plans to pave the 10 miles above Placerville with the proceeds of a bond issue of that year.[3] After the gasoline tax was enacted in 1923, the pace of widening and paving became steadier. The road became a segment of U.S. 50 after that system of federal highways was created in 1925.

The Dutch Flat and Donner Lake Wagon Road did not fare as well as the Lake Tahoe Wagon Road at first, though it later became the first road to be paved all the way across the mountains. Before the automobile age its location, parallel and close to the tracks, meant that it could do little for the traveler or shipper that the railroad could not do better. By 1909, when the legislature appropriated money for a state highway from Emigrant Gap over the summit to Donner Lake, the Dutch Flat and Donner Lake Wagon Road had deteriorated almost beyond use.[4] Repairs were made, though, and the road began to benefit from the growth of Reno as a destination. By 1920 it was "fairly well paved nearly up to the top of the Sierras on the western slope."[5] In 1923 a new alignment was graded up the east side of Donner Summit. In 1926 the road was incorporated into the new U.S. highway system as U.S. 40. In 1929 it was realigned between Emigrant Gap and Big Bend.[6] By 1934 Dutch Flat had been bypassed, and dangerous railroad crossings were being eliminated. In that year it was described as the "only year-round east-west trunk road leading out of Northern California, and . . . one of the main transportation highways between California and eastward points. Of the peak traffic (2000 units daily, expected to reach 4000 in a short time) a considerable portion consists, particularly in the summer, of interstate and transcontinental travel."[7]

Most of the through traffic now crosses the summit ridge on Interstate 80, built in the 1960s as a completely new road about 2 miles north of Donner Pass. Old U.S. 40, now called Donner Pass Road, is still maintained as a two-lane blacktop between Truckee and Soda Springs and gets heavy use today by skiers in winter and by hikers and rock climbers in summer. Apparently all traces of the original wagon route over the summit have been obliterated by the blasting and earthmoving that accompanied the construction and maintenance of the Central Pacific Railroad, subsequent automobile roads, and underground telephone and gas lines.

The railroad too has abandoned Donner Pass. In the early 1990s the Southern Pacific consolidated all traffic onto an auxiliary track running under Mount Judah, less than a mile to the south. Rails and ties have been removed from the historic alignment, leaving the roadbed as a gravel road, for conversion, one hopes, into a scenic trail high above Donner Lake. The original grades and tunnels of the Central Pacific are still there as an unlabeled monument to the army of Chinese laborers who constructed them.

The Henness Pass Turnpike, the Truckee Turnpike, and other roads converging on Henness Pass from the west were hard hit by the completion of the railroad, which passed parallel to them 10 or 15 miles south. Through traffic between Virginia City on the east and Nevada City and North San Juan on the west must have found it more convenient to access the railroad at Dutch Flat or Emigrant Gap. The old roads over Henness Pass were left with purely local traffic, primarily from hay ranches and logging operations, not enough to maintain them as anything more than rough gravel and dirt roads.

The Big Trees route, as we saw above, never did cross the mountains to Carson Valley on its own alignment. As laid out in 1856, it followed approximately the line of today's Highway 4 to Hermit Valley, a few miles west of Ebbetts Pass, and then veered off north to join the existing Carson Pass road in Hope Valley. At this time there was no good reason to build a road through Ebbetts Pass and down the steep eastern escarpment of the Sierra into the rough country of the East Fork of the Carson. The incentive appeared in the summer of 1863 in the form of a silver rush at Silver Mountain, a half dozen miles east of the pass.[8] Entrepreneurs then built a toll road from Hermit Valley over Ebbetts Pass to the mines. This road appears to have been maintained by private owners until 1911, when it was taken over by the state. It went on east to Markleeville, on the East Fork of the Carson River. (The Monitor Pass road, which turns off to the east 5 miles above Markleeville and connects it with U.S. 395, is much more recent, having been built through trackless territory in 1950.)[9]

The Sonora route, after its brief busy period in 1852–53 before road difficulties became notorious, was revived in 1859 as a result of gold strikes east of the Sierra in the Walker River area, especially at Mono Diggings, Bodie, and Aurora. At first these boomtowns were supplied via circuitous routes using passes farther north, but boosters in the town of Sonora quickly realized that their discredited emigrant route could now be promoted as a shortcut to the mines. A new road was begun in 1861, on a new alignment from Strawberry Flat, 30 miles east of Sonora, to Walker River at Pickel Meadows. This road followed approximately today's Highway 108 about halfway from Pinecrest to Sonora Pass, but then, instead of going along Deadman Creek, as the modern road does, the old road followed Clark Fork to Sonora Pass.

Known as the Sierra-Mono Wagon Road, this was a public project, funded by a local bond issue. Funds were exhausted on the summit portion, and in 1863 the state legislature authorized a franchise for a toll road. The toll road company abandoned the Clark Fork alignment for the present route up Deadman Creek. But the company had financial trouble in the summer of 1864 and forfeited its franchise. The towns of Bridgeport and Aurora contributed to the project, but financial shortages continued to delay completion of a satisfactory wagon road until 1870, by which time the mining districts were being served more cheaply by rail from the Nevada side, so the road was never a business success. In 1901 the state took it over from Long Barn to Bridgeport and declared it a state highway. At the time of the state takeover, the Department of Highways described 22 miles of the road as "nothing more than a creek bed" and noted that all the bridges were either rotten or already collapsed. The state made no improvements at first but began to appropriate small amounts in 1905, and by 1932 had made it into a reasonably passable automobile road over the mountains.[10]

The Carson Pass route had a complex later history, with major realignments. As described in detail in chapter 3, the original emigrant trail over Carson Pass crossed Caples Lake, traversed Carson Spur at West Pass, ran along Squaw Ridge past Tragedy Spring and Corral Flat, and then descended along Iron Mountain Ridge in the direction of Placerville.

Today's Carson Pass road, State Highway 88, goes around Carson Spur and then rejoins (approximately) the old route to go past Tragedy Spring to Corral Flat. At this point it departs decisively from the old emigrant route to run southwest down to Jackson. The modern highway thus leaves almost 20 miles of the old trail relatively undisturbed by later construction, though the presence of ski lift cable towers on the trail up from Caples Lake to West Pass may be distracting for hikers trying to recapture the feel of the emigrants' struggles.

West of Corral Flat the emigrant trail down to the Placerville area is approximated by a two-lane blacktop called Mormon Emigrant Trail Road, which turns off Highway 88 at Corral Flat and descends to Sly Park (now flooded by Jenkinson Lake Reservoir). From Corral Flat Highway 88 descends along the interfluve between the Cosumnes and the Mokelumne to the old mining districts around Jackson and Sutter Creek. The ancestor of this road was the Amador and Nevada Wagon Road, laid out in 1862 and financed partly through a bond issue by Amador County and partly through tolls. There was apparently a lively traffic in produce and lumber to the Comstock Lode on this road, though heavy snow put a stop to it for several months a year. At some point this road acquired the name Kit Carson Trail, though it diverges far to the south of the route down which Carson accompanied Frémont's party in late February and early March 1844. In 1932 the highest portions were being treated with oil for the first time, so it must have been much later that it was paved all the way across. The state did not begin to keep it open through the winter until the development of the ski resort complex at Kirkwood in the early 1970s.[11]

Wagon roads between Beckwourth Pass and the Central Valley date back to the promotional efforts of Jim Beckwourth in 1852. Most ran along ridges between the upper Feather River valley and the Central Valley, and some survive today as unpaved back roads maintained by the counties or the U.S. Forest Service. Early road builders avoided the deep and rugged canyons, and the main route traversing this area today, State Highway 70, through Feather River Canyon, was not built until 1937.[12]

Beckwourth Pass has been more significant to California as a railroad gateway. In 1909 the second Sierra railroad, the Western Pacific, constructed a line up Feather River Canyon to Sierra Valley, through Beckwourth Pass, and on across the Black Rock Desert to Winnemucca, Nevada, whence it ran approximately parallel to the Southern Pacific (originally Central Pacific) to Salt Lake. This Feather River route had been explored as a possible route by railroad promoters in the 1860s, including Collis Huntington. But the canyon would have required too much blasting and earthmoving for the technology available in the 1860s.

At one point the Union Pacific was considering building its own line to the Pacific, in competition with the Central Pacific. The Union Pacific's chief engineer, Grenville Dodge, had a falling out with the Central Pacific in 1870 over coordinating operations where the lines met in Utah. Dodge's survey of a line through Beckwourth Pass and down the Feather River to Sacramento was apparently enough to get the Central Pacific to cooperate, and nothing more came of it. More than a century later, the Union Pacific acquired the Western Pacific and merged this line into its system.

Any devotee of the Sierra Nevada will want to know something about the history of the Tioga Pass road, the highest (9,945 ft.) and most spectacular road across the range. Actually, its very altitude and steep grade on the eastern side are enough to suggest that this may not have been a significant artery of commerce in the wagon and stagecoach days. And in fact it was not. Joseph Walker and his party may have come through here in 1833, but there was apparently nothing more than a pack trail until 1882 when a wagon road was built by the Great Sierra Consolidated Silver Company to move machinery and supplies to mines in the Mono Lake area from the railhead at Copperopolis. (The name Tioga, Iroquois for "where it forks," was imported from the East in 1878 as the name of a mine.)

Maintenance on the Tioga Pass road ceased when the mines closed in 1884, and after a few years it was little more than a trail. In 1915 Stephen T. Mather, a businessman who had become wealthy in the borax business, bought the right-of-way and donated it to Yosemite National Park. The state of California built a connecting road up from Mono Lake via Lee Vining Canyon, and the scenic mountain highway was opened to summer traffic, though not paved until 1937. The road was closed to cars during World War II and used only for cattle drives. It was rebuilt by the National Park Service in 1961.[13]

NOTES

INTRODUCTION

1. Bidwell 1964: 33–37.

2. Some have called this the Bartleson-Bidwell party, because the elected captain at the outset was John Bartleson. Bidwell, however, became an important figure in the economic development of California and wrote the principal account of the trip (Bidwell 1964), and Bartleson returned to Missouri and disappeared from California history. For this reason, and because Bartleson and a few followers abandoned the rest of the party in the Great Basin, only to ignominiously rejoin it a few hungry days later, it seems more appropriate to speak of the Bidwell party.

3. The figure of 165,000 is given by Steward 1962: 319.

4. Bowles 1869: 309–11.

5. For a review of this research see Denevan 1992.

6. Norman Graebner's *Empire on the Pacific* provides an example of this common misconception: "Not until 1844 did Elisha Stevens blaze the Truckee route into the Sacramento Valley, a route which served thereafter as the great thoroughfare of migration into California" (1983: 12).

CHAPTER 1. MOUNTAIN WALL, SNOW, BASINS, AND RIVERS

1. A good introduction to these matters is Mary Hill's *Geology of the Sierra Nevada* (1975).

2. Two histories of the Humboldt River as a transportation corridor are Dale Morgan's *The Humboldt: Highroad of the West* ([1943] 1985) and Harold Curran's *Fearful Crossing: The Central Overland Trail through Nevada* (1982).

CHAPTER 2. TRANS-SIERRA TRANSPORT BEFORE
WHEELED VEHICLES

1. For a compendious review of items traded and routes traveled, see Davis [1961] 1974.

2. Frémont [1845] 1988: 235.

3. Farquhar 1965: chap. 3 covers the limited Spanish and Mexican activities in interior California. Expeditions into the interior are conveniently summarized in three maps, with commentary, in Beck and Haase 1974: maps 20–22.

4. For details on the Domínguez-Escalante expedition and more detailed cartographic history of the Buenaventura River, see Cline 1963: 43–49.

5. Morgan 1953: 85–87.

6. The exact route of Smith's eastbound journey has been the subject of some speculation and controversy, reviewed fairly dispassionately by Farquhar (1943). Cline (1963: 151–58) summarizes Smith's travels in the Great Basin. Alson J. Smith (1965) provides a good overall account of the expedition.

7. Irving 1961: 282.

8. Ogden's travels to and along the Humboldt are of great importance in the history of geographic discovery in the Great Basin and have been reviewed in detail by Cline (1963: 111–27).

9. Leonard 1959: 66.

10. Ibid., 67.

11. Ibid., 72.

12. Ibid., 79.

13. Ibid., 83. According to Leonard's editor, John C. Ewers, these could have been either the Merced Grove or the Tuolumne Grove.

14. Ibid., 122–23.

15. Ibid., 128.

16. Ibid., 130–31.

17. Ibid., 76, 129.

18. Ibid., 129.

19. Ibid., 129.

20. Bidwell 1890. This map seems to have shown not one but two Buenaventura Rivers.

21. Chiles 1970: 14. The colorful career of John Marsh had too many twists and turns to summarize conveniently here. It is sufficient to say that he came to California in 1836 and acquired a grant on the slopes of Mount Diablo. He sent word to Missouri to attract settlers for his lands, and that is how Bidwell knew about him.

22. Bidwell 1964: 22.

23. Ibid., 32–33.

24. Bidwell 1890: 128.

25. Ibid., 130.

26. Chiles 1970. Giffen 1969 is a good source on Chiles.

27. Hopper (1981) provides information on this trip.

28. Giffen 1969: 35.

29. Ibid., 36, 37.

30. Reading 1930: 176.

31. Bryant [1848] 1985: 269.

32. Carson 1935: 9–17.

33. The quote and Frémont's remarks on these three objectives are at Frémont [1845] 1988: 196.

34. Frémont [1845] 1988: 205.

35. Ibid., 214.

36. Benton 1883, 2: 580.

37. Simpson [1876] 1983: 19.

38. Preuss 1958: 105.

39. Ibid., 109.

40. The exact route of Frémont's 1844 crossing has been the subject of some debate. See Farquhar 1930 and Gianella 1959.

41. Frémont [1845] 1988: 270, 255–56.

42. See "Letter from Col. Benton to the People of Missouri," in Heap 1957: 51–52.

43. The map has been reprinted and placed in a pocket in the 1991 edition of Goetzmann's *Army Exploration in the American West, 1803–1863*.

CHAPTER 3. WAGON TRAINS ACROSS THE SIERRA

1. "Truckee" was the father of the Paiute chief Winnemucca and grandfather of Sarah Winnemucca Hopkins, who states in her autobiography (Hopkins 1883: 9) that this was not his real name. Truckee, his granddaughter noted, is "an Indian word, it means *all right* or *very well.*"

2. George Stewart republished Schallenberger's account, with much commentary, as *The Opening of the California Trail: The Story of the Stevens Party from the Reminiscences of Moses Schallenberger* (1953).

3. Stewart 1962: 103.

4. Frémont 1887: 439–40.

5. Graydon (1986) has traced the trail between Verdi and the neighborhood of Dutch Flat very clearly on a series of U.S. Geological Survey (USGS) 1:24,000 maps.

6. Greenwood's activities at Fort Hall are summarized in Kelly and Morgan 1965: 144–52.

7. Jackson 1967: 2–11 provides a detailed account of the history and geography of the Dog Valley route.

8. The text of the letter and the circumstances of its writing are given in Morgan 1963, 1: 18–20.

9. The account given here of the movements of the members of the disbanded Mormon Battalion is taken largely from the diary of Henry Bigler, as edited by Gudde (1962). The Mormon Battalion in general has been the subject of a number of specialist articles, but the most accessible account for the general reader is Bernard DeVoto's *The Year of Decision, 1846.*

10. Gudde 1962: 79.

11. Three diaries have been published: those of Bigler (Gudde 1962), Azariah Smith (1990), and Ephraim Green (Bagley 1991). Green is considerably more laconic than the other two.

12. Gudde 1962: 106.

13. Ibid., 114.

14. Frémont [1845] 1988: 237–45.

15. Gudde 1962: 116.

16. The chronology of this Mormon expedition and details of their route across the mountains have been researched in detail by George W. Peabody, a resident of Pleasant Valley, who mentions a local tradition that the murders were actually committed by white bandits (Peabody 1988: 370–72; 1989: 6–9).

17. Gudde 1962: 117.

18. Ibid.

19. Smith 1990: 137.

20. Clyman 1960: 238.

21. The editor of Clyman's journals goes into some detail to identify these four parties (ibid., 236–39).

22. Gudde 1962: 123–24.

23. May [1848] 1991: 29.

24. Ibid., 42–43.

25. Ibid.

26. Bruff 1944: 1207–8.

27. It is strange that this "western summit" has never acquired an official name. The contour lines on the USGS *Caples Lake* 1:24,000 quadrangle show it clearly enough in the middle of section 6 of township 9N, range 18E, but the map does not provide a name, although nearby are Covered Wagon Peak, Emigrant Creek, Emigrant Lake, and Scout Carson Lake. In July 1994 the 9,763-foot peak rising above the pass on the southeast was named after Melissa Coray, the only woman member of the 1848 Mormon party. The Nevada Emigrant Trail Marking Committee's *Guide to Trail Markers* calls the western summit Emigrant Pass. The Oregon-California Trails Association and trail signs today refer to it as West Pass, which seems more accurate and also avoids contributing to the overuse of "emigrant" in place-names.

28. Addison Crane, diary entry of August 23, 1852, in Eaton 1974: 297–98.

29. James A. Pritchard, August 4, 1849 (Pritchard [1849] 1959: 131).

30. Sarah Royce, October 17, 1849 (Royce 1932: 68–69).

31. John Hawkins Clark, August 27, 1852 (Clark 1852: 85–86).

32. James A. Pritchard, August 5, 1849 (Pritchard [1849] 1959: 132–33).

33. James A. Pritchard, August 6, 1849 (Pritchard [1849] 1959: 133).

34. John Hawkins Clark, August 27, 1852 (Clark 1852: 86).

35. James A. Pritchard, August 7, 1849 (Pritchard [1849] 1959: 134). The winters of 1848–49 and 1851–52 must have been wet ones, to judge from this and other references to large snowbanks on the trail in the following summers. Snow depth varies greatly from year to year. On July 8, 1992, there were only two patches remaining on the northeast side of the summit ridge, neither obstructing the trail, and only one very small one on the southwest side, also well off the trail. A year later, on July 8, 1993, after a wet winter, there was still a considerable amount of snow all over the northeast side of the summit ridge.

36. Richard Keen, July 21, 1852 (Eaton 1974: 307).

37. John Hawkins Clark, August 28, 1852 (Clark 1852: 86–87).

38. Sarah Royce, October 19, 1849 (Royce 1932: 72).

39. James A. Pritchard, August 8, 1849 (Pritchard [1849] 1959: 134).

40. John Hawkins Clark, August 28, 1852 (Clark 1852: 87). If Clark and company crossed West Pass at noon and reached Tragedy Spring at sundown, they were moving right along, as the distance is about 15 miles and includes some difficult rocky slopes.

41. Sioli 1883: 118.

CHAPTER 4. LOCAL INITIATIVES IN ROAD BUILDING

1. Day 1855: 4. In this casual anti-Chinese remark Day was the product of his times. Otherwise in his reports he comes across as a reasonably liberal-minded man.

2. Theodore Hittell (1897: bk. 9, chap. 6) described the role of tardy communications in some of the spectacular San Francisco business failures of 1855.

3. Unruh 1979: 281–83.

4. The isthmus route in its flourishing years, 1848–69, has been covered in great detail in Kemble 1943.

5. The wreck of the *Central America* was found on the ocean floor in 1992 and the gold salvaged by the Columbus-America Group of Columbus, Ohio. A federal court ruled that this firm must share a portion of the treasure with the companies (or their corporate successors) that insured the *Central America*, and the Supreme Court upheld this decision on appeal.

6. Kemble 1943: 142–43; Hafen 1926: 48.

7. Associated with Chorpenning in this venture was Ben Holladay, who was active in freighting and cattle drives between California and Salt Lake in the early 1850s and would later become nationally famous as the "stagecoach king" (Frederick 1940: 41).

8. Chorpenning 1889: 3, 4.

9. Hafen 1926: 56–70; Chorpenning 1889: 1–14.

10. Winther 1936: 23.

11. Winther (1936: 51–75) and Jackson (1966) are good sources on the history of Wells Fargo.

12. Winther [1945] 1968: 28–40.

13. The origins of the San Francisco panic of 1855 and its effect on express and stagecoach firms are given in detail in Winther 1936: 106–38. Another detailed account, with particular attention to the role of I. C. Woods, partner in the firm of Adams & Company, is given in Shumate 1986.

14. Banning and Banning 1930: 3–103.

15. Ibid., 20–21, 80–90. The Pioneer Stage will be covered in more detail in chapter 8.

16. Mitchell 1950: 55 has a photograph of the present Echo Summit road, so it was in existence at least as early as that year.

17. These figures are given in the *Sacramento Daily Union* of May 11, 1857.

18. From the diary of Thomas Turnbull, quoted in Eaton 1974: 297.

19. Eaton 1974: 308–9.

20. Maule 1938: 19.

21. Information on the lifting of tolls is from Sioli 1883: 119. But two pages earlier he mentions, in the present (1881) tense, a toll bridge that charges $1 per wagon. Perhaps the distinction here is between roads and bridges.

22. *Placerville Herald,* July 16, 1853, and August 6, 1853.

23. *Sacramento Daily Union,* September 15, 1852.

24. *Daily Alta California,* October 31, 1853.

25. *Placerville Herald,* August 6, 1853.

26. Farquhar (1965: 95) says this is identical with present Las Vegas, Nevada. Mitchell (1955) says it refers to Las Vegas de Santa Clara, a point just north of St. George, Utah. Either could have been on Benton's line.

27. Mitchell 1955: 211.

28. *San Francisco Daily Herald,* December 19, 1853.

29. Mitchell 1955: 218.

30. Goddard 1855: 217.

31. Shumate 1969 provides a good biographical sketch of Goddard (1817–1906).

32. Moore 1878.

33. The topography of this region has been described in detail in Durrell 1987.

34. Quoted in Wilson 1972: 135.

35. Here is the description of A. W. Keddie, engineer and promoter of the Western Pacific:

> Beginning at Beckwourth Pass, on the main summit of the Sierra Nevada Range, which is the divide between the waters of the Pacific and the Great Basin, the Beckwourth Trail went about due west through the northern edge of Beckwourth Valley—now called Sierra Valley—to its outlet at Beckwourth Ranch. Thence the trail turned to the left, and went down the hill to Spring Garden Valley; then followed Spring Garden Creek to American Valley; thence to the American Valley Ranch, now Quincy. From Quincy the trail turned to the right, and went in a northwesterly direction across the American Valley to Elizabethtown; thence westerly, up Emigrant Hill and on to Snake Lake Valley; thence southwesterly to Spanish Ranch and Meadow Valley. From Meadow Valley the trail followed about the line of the present wagon road to a point about a mile and a half beyond Meadow Valley, where it turned to the left, and reached the summit east of Buck's Ranch, by way of what is now known as Erdman Mine. From the Summit east of Buck's Ranch the trail—as near as I can determine—followed about the line of the present traveled wagon road through Buck's Ranch, Buckeye, Mountain House, and on to Oroville. (Quoted in Beckwourth [1856] 1972: 599)

36. Beckwourth [1856] 1972: 514–29.

37. Marlette 1856: 193–94.

38. *Sacramento Daily Union,* October 7, 1856.

39. Stewart 1962: 268–91 gives a good account of the 1849 Lassen route near-disaster.

CHAPTER 5. STATE GOVERNMENT ROAD MEASURES

1. Wozencraft developed these ideas more fully in his *Address Delivered Before the Mechanics' Institute on the Subject of the Atlantic and Pacific Rail-road,* published as a pamphlet.

2. All quotations are from a story in the *Daily Alta California,* December 13, 1854.

3. *Daily Alta California,* December 14, 1854.

4. Ibid., December 16, 1854.

5. Ibid., December 21, 1854.

6. A copy of the flyer exists in the Bancroft Library at call number Z 209 C25 E13 #144.

7. The report on the December 28 meeting and the editorial are in the *Daily Alta California* of Friday, December 29.

8. *Daily Alta California,* January 3, 1855.

9. Ibid., January 19, 1855.

10. Bigler 1855: 44–46.

11. *California Assembly Journal* 1855: 87.

12. Ibid., 114.

13. The resolution passed by this meeting is given in Sioli 1883: 119–20.

14. Ryland's report was printed as *Report of Committee on Internal Improvements on Assembly Bill* #16, document 27 in the Appendix to the *Assembly Journal,* 1855. Henderson's report appears as Exhibit A. Ryland received two other field reports that he appended along with Henderson's. These were Major Case's reconnaissance of the Carson route, and Atlas Fredonyer's rather comprehensive report on the geography of the northern Sierra, offered in support of a route around the north of Mount Lassen.

15. The debate is reported in the *California Assembly Journal* 1855: 601–3.

16. Text of the bill is in California *Statutes* 1855: 180–81.

17. Voting on the bill is reported in the *California Assembly Journal* 1855: 619–20.

18. Unruh (1979: 88) quotes the *Herald* on this point.

19. Day 1855.

20. California *Senate Journal* 1855: 658–69.

21. Text of letter at Marlette 1856: 7.

22. Text of McConnell's letter to Marlette is at Marlette 1856: 7–8.

23. *Daily Alta California,* July 7, 1855, reprinted from the *Sacramento Daily Union.*

24. Hittell 1897, 4: 172.

25. Marlette 1856: 12–13.

26. Peabody 1989: 53–59 provides much information on Bradley and water supply projects in Pleasant Valley.

27. Marlette 1856: 11.

28. *Daily Alta California,* July 9, 1855, reprinted from the *Sacramento Daily Union.*

29. Day 1854.

30. Goddard 1856: 101.

31. Ibid., 104.

32. *Daily Alta California,* November 3, 1855. The *Alta* had reported favorably on the Emigrant Road Committee's activities in San Francisco but opposed the state's road legislation.

33. Ibid., December 30, 1855.

34. Ibid., January 11, 1856.

35. Wood 1968: 8.

36. Senate *Journal* Appendix 1856: 187–91.

37. Reprinted in the *Sacramento Daily Union,* August 20, 1856.

38. *Sacramento Daily Union,* October 9, 1856.

39. Day 1856: 82–83.

40. *Sacramento Daily Union,* May 8, 1860.

41. Sioli 1883: 121.

42. Unruh 1979: 88.

43. Marlette 1856: 191–92.

44. Mitchell 1955.

45. *Sacramento Daily Union,* August 25, 1856.

CHAPTER 6. THE DISTANT PROSPECT OF RAILROADS

1. *House of Representatives Report* no. 140, 31st Cong., 1st sess., Committee on Roads and Canals, pp. 2–3. This document reprinted Whitney's 1845, 1846, and 1848 memorials.

2. California *Statutes* 1850: 465.

3. Benton's speech and the language of his bill are in the *Congressional Globe,* 30th Cong., 2d sess., pp. 470–74

4. Benton's speech and the text of his 1850 bill are in the *Congressional Globe,* 31st Cong., 2d sess., pp. 56–58.

5. *Congressional Globe,* 31st Cong., 2d sess., p. 132.

6. "Memorial upon the subject of Constructing a Railroad from the Pacific to the Valley of the Mississippi," Document #58, *California Assembly Journal,* 4th sess., 1853. This document does not appear to have had any legislative import, but rather is something a sympathetic member of the assembly read into the record.

7. Gwin's speech and the resulting exchange are in the *Congressional Globe,* 32d Cong., 1st sess., pp. 2466–67.

8. The Douglas bill is discussed in Russel 1948: 95–96.

9. Gwin's speech is in the *Congressional Globe,* 32d Cong., 2d sess., pp. 280–84.

10. For more information on Kern, see Robert V. Hine's *Edward Kern and American Expansion.*

11. This January 17 session can be found in the *Congressional Globe,* 32d Cong., 2d sess., pp. 314–21. Kern's letter, supplemented with extracts from Lt. J. H. Simpson and Maj. E. Backus, is on pp. 320–21.

12. This January 19 debate can be found in the *Congressional Globe,* 32d Cong., 2d sess.

13. Bell's February 5, 1853, speech, with questions from other senators, appears in the *Appendix* to the *Congressional Globe*, 32d Cong., 2d sess., pp. 221–24.

14. Bell's February 17, 1853, speech is in the *Appendix* to the *Congressional Globe*, 32d Cong., 2d sess., pp. 224–29.

15. *Congressional Globe,* 32d Cong., 2d sess., p. 798.

16. Davis 1853: 20.

17. Beckwith's route and report are summarized in U.S. House of Representatives 1855, 1: 58–62.

18. Williamson 1854: 5.

19. Ibid., 16–17.

20. U.S. House of Representatives 1855, 6: 9.

21. Ibid., 6: 3.

22. A comprehensive discussion of the Pacific Railroad Surveys and their political context can be found in Goetzmann 1959: 262–304.

23. U.S. House of Representatives 1855, 1: 29.

24. Richardson 1900, 5: 221.

CHAPTER 7. THE FEDERAL GOVERNMENT
BUILDS WEST TO CALIFORNIA

1. *House of Representatives Report* no. 95, 31st Cong., 2d sess.

2. *Congressional Globe,* 34th Cong., 1st sess., p. 1297.

3. Ibid., 414

4. Bell 1927: 377–85 provides a dramatic first-person account of these events.

5. *Congressional Globe,* 34th Cong., 1st sess., p. 1298.

6. The June 26 debate is in the *Congressional Globe,* 34th Cong., 1st sess., p. 1485.

7. *Congressional Globe,* 34th Cong., 1st sess., p. 1597.

8. Ibid., 2187–88.

9. Porter and Johnson 1972: 28.

10. Russel 1948: 220, quoting the Sacramento *Democratic State Journal* of August 29, 1856.

11. Porter and Johnson 1972: 26.

12. *Congressional Globe,* 34th Cong., 3d sess., 610–13, 627.

13. Ibid., 688–89.

14. Ibid., 612.

15. *Sacramento Daily Union,* June 15, 1857.

16. *Report upon the Pacific Wagon Roads,* 1859, Senate Exec. Doc. 36, ser. 984, 35th Cong., 2d sess.

17. *Sacramento Daily Union,* November 23, 1859.

18. Surviving material on Lander, apparently rather sparse and scattered, was assembled for a biographical article by Branch (1929).

CHAPTER 8. MAIL CONTRACTS
AND STAGECOACH SERVICE

1. Provisions of the law and a list of the bids and bidders can be found in Brown 1858: 986–87.

2. Brown 1858: 993–1011.

3. Banning and Banning 1930: 79.

4. Hafen 1926: 105–8; Banning and Banning 1930: 107–31.

5. *Sacramento Daily Union*, June 25, 1858.

6. Hafen 1926: 109–10.

7. Ellison 1927: 159.

8. Hafen 1926: 109–15, 122–26; Banning 1928: 178–82. Chorpenning (1889: 29) claims to have come in first, period.

9. Hafen 1926: 113–14.

10. For a review of the debate about the post office as a civilizing influence versus the post office as a business, see Hafen 1926: 129–41.

11. *Congressional Globe*, 33d Cong., 2d sess., p. 1117.

12. Majors [1893] 1989: 164.

13. Settle and Settle 1949: 36.

14. Ibid., 35–39.

15. Hafen 1926: 148–49.

16. Settle and Settle 1955: 25.

17. Settle and Settle 1949: 48–56.

18. Majors [1893] 1989: 166.

19. Hafen 1926: 165.

20. Majors [1893] 1989: 182–83.

21. Settle and Settle 1949: 75.

22. Majors [1893] 1989: 183–84.

23. Hafen 1926: 169.

24. The text of this annulment is given at Chorpenning 1889: 33–34.

25. The bond scandal and its aftermath are covered in great detail in Settle and Settle 1949: 95–120.

26. The somewhat vexed subject of Wells Fargo control of the Overland Mail and the Pony Express has been reviewed in great detail in Jackson 1966.

27. Hafen 1926: 189.

28. Ibid., 223.

29. For a biography of Ben Holladay, see Frederick 1940.

CHAPTER 9. A REVIVAL OF INTEREST IN
ROAD CONSTRUCTION IN CALIFORNIA

1. *Sacramento Daily Union*, May 4, 1857.

2. California *Statutes*, 8th sess., p. 272.

3. *Sacramento Daily Union*, May 2, 1857.

4. Both the news story and the editorial are in the *Sacramento Daily Union*, May 1, 1857.

5. The newspaper report on the Mokelumne Hill meetings and Brewster's speech were carried by the *Sacramento Daily Union,* May 4, 1857.

6. *Sacramento Daily Union,* October 15, 1856.

7. Ibid., May 7, 1857.

8. Ibid., May 4, 1857.

9. Ibid., May 11, 1857; *Placer Herald,* May 9, 1857. The latter, a weekly published at Auburn, devoted a page to the proposed road, discussing the route in detail and putting the whole matter squarely in the context of how to connect with the national road to Honey Lake. The *Herald* actually included a map, albeit a highly generalized and schematic one.

10. *Sacramento Daily Union,* May 8, 1857.

11. Ibid., May 11, 1857.

12. Ibid., May 12 and 13, 1857.

13. Ibid., June 11, 1857.

14. Ibid., June 17, 18, and 19, 1857; *Daily Alta California,* June 17, 1857.

15. *Sacramento Daily Union,* June 17, 1857.

16. Mitchell 1950: 59.

17. Information on Kirk as superintendent of the Sacramento and Carson Valley Wagon Road is from Sioli 1883: 123.

18. These were William B. Carr for Sacramento and B. T. Hunt for El Dorado.

19. California *Statutes,* 9th sess. (1858), p. 50.

20. *Sacramento Daily Union,* May 31, 1858.

21. Ibid., June 29, 1858.

22. This information is from the board's final report, published in the December 13, 1858, edition of the *Sacramento Daily Union.*

23. *Daily Alta California,* July 28, 1858 (reprinted from the *Sacramento Daily Union*).

24. *Sacramento Daily Union,* December 4, 1858. The text of the contract was printed in the *Union* on November 30, 1858, in an editorial referring to a dispute regarding performance.

25. Mitchell 1950: 59. The Board of Wagon Road Commissioners' second report to the supervisors of Sacramento and El Dorado counties was published in the *Sacramento Daily Union* on December 13, 1858. They were disappointed that Plummer had not yet finished the bridge or the road approaches to it and that there were still rough spots around Slippery Ford, but they expressed confidence that he would finish soon.

26. *Sacramento Daily Union,* May 19, 1857. Also see Mitchell 1950: 59.

27. Mitchell 1950: 61. Hawley Grade remains largely intact today. Its uppermost portion is now buried under a steep embankment of rock fill left from the realignment of U.S. 50 in the 1940s. This eliminated access by motor vehicles and thus helped to preserve the old road. Now a National Historic Trail, reached at its downhill end via Upper Truckee Road about 5 miles south of U.S. 50, Hawley Grade offers hikers an unusual opportunity to see a relatively undisturbed, though somewhat eroded and overgrown, road from the stagecoach era.

28. Simpson [1876] 1983: 98.

29. Ibid., 95–103. Italics in original.

30. *A Peep at Washoe* and its sequel, *Washoe Revisited,* were originally published in serial form in *Harper's Monthly Magazine* in the early 1860s and reprinted in book form by Paisano Press, Balboa, California, in 1959. Browne describes the silver rush, and his travels (and travails) between Virginia City and San Francisco, with a verve and wit that put his book in a class with Mark Twain's better-known *Roughing It.* Curiously, considering his eye for geographic and social detail, Browne is rather vague on the dates of his trip.

31. Browne 1959: 24.

32. Ibid., 29–30.

33. Ibid., 35–36.

34. Ibid., 112.

35. Ibid., 117–18.

36. Ibid., 122.

37. *Sacramento Daily Union,* June 6, 1860.

38. Sioli 1883: 123.

39. Mitchell 1950: 62–63.

40. Ibid., 61.

41. Day 1856: 79.

42. Mitchell 1950: 63.

43. Again Browne's narrative is short on dates. But it is clear from his opening remarks in *Washoe Revisited* that he had just returned from an extended stay in Europe. According to his biographer Rock (1929), Browne and his family were back in California from Germany in the spring of 1864, and Browne's own narrative suggests that he returned to Washoe soon after.

44. Brown 1959: 156.

45. Ibid., 162.

46. Ibid., 171–72.

47. Ibid., 152–53.

48. Bancroft 1890: 230.

49. This was the new road constructed by the Central Pacific as a temporary stand-in for the railroad. It is considered in chapter 10.

50. Bowles [1869] 1990: 309–11.

51. Judah 1862a: 49–51.

52. Jackson 1967: 22.

53. *San Francisco Bulletin,* May 3, 1860.

54. *Sacramento Daily Union,* May 26, 1860.

55. This story by the *Marysville Appeal* was reprinted in the *Sacramento Daily Union,* July 7, 1860.

56. Jackson 1967: 26–27.

57. Ibid., 27.

58. Hafen 1926: 277.

59. *Mother Lode Magazine,* April 1955, p. 4.

60. Mitchell 1950: 64; McIntosh 1962.

CHAPTER 10. THE CENTRAL PACIFIC RAILROAD

1. Vance 1961.

2. Judah 1854: 15–17.
3. Ibid., 32.
4. Judah 1857: 5.
5. Ibid., 3–31.
6. Judah 1863: 5–10.
7. *Sacramento Daily Union,* April 5, 1861.
8. Ibid., June 5, 1862.
9. Ibid., October 6, 1862.
10. Ibid., August 6, 1863.
11. Ibid., September 25, 1863.
12. Ibid., October 4, 1864.

EPILOGUE: TRANS-SIERRA ROADS AFTER 1869

1. Mitchell 1950: 66.
2. Ibid.
3. Blow 1920: 103.
4. Ibid., 67.
5. Ibid., 113.
6. Mitchell 1950: 67–68.
7. *California Highways and Public Works,* February 1934, 16, 17.
8. Farquhar 1965: 102. William Brewer left a lively description of the Silver Mountain boom and mining fever in the summer of 1863 (1930: 431–34).
9. Creed 1950: 28–29.
10. Mitchell 1950: 64, 66.
11. A story in the *Sacramento Bee* on November 14, 1965 (p. B4), discussed the pros and cons of a proposal to keep Highway 88 open all winter. The story mentioned that the state was about to open bids on a 2.4-mile stretch of new road from Hope Valley to Carson Pass up the mountainside north of Red Lake. This shows how recent the present road around the north side of Red Lake really is. On August 19, 1972, the *Bee* announced that arrangements had been made to keep the road open, at a cost of $3.4 million, though this would happen only if the new Kirkwood ski area opened in November as planned.
12. Perkins 1929: 244–45.
13. Farquhar 1965: 200; Fletcher 1987: 67–70.

REFERENCES

Adler, Pat, and Walter Wheelock. 1965. *Walker's R.R. Routes—1853*. Glendale: La Siesta Press.

Bagley, Will, ed. 1991. *A Road from El Dorado: The 1848 Trail Journal of Ephraim Green*. Salt Lake City: Prairie Dog Press.

Bancroft, Hubert Howe. 1890. *Works*. Vol. XXV. *History of Nevada, Colorado and Wyoming, 1540–1888*. San Francisco: The History Co.

Banning, William, and George Hugh Banning. 1930. *Six Horses*. New York: Century.

Barnard, Helen M. [189?]. *The Chorpenning Claim*. N.p.: M'Intosh, printer. In Bancroft Library.

Beck, Warren A., and Ynez D. Haase. 1974. *Historical Atlas of California*. Norman: University of Oklahoma Press.

Beckwourth, James P. [1856] 1972. *The Life and Adventures of James P. Beckwourth, as Told to Thomas D. Bonner*. Introduced and with notes and an epilogue by Delmont R. Oswald. Lincoln: University of Nebraska Press.

Bell, Horace. 1927. *Reminiscences of a Ranger, or Early Times in Southern California*. Santa Barbara: Wallace Helberd.

Bell, James C. 1921. *Opening a Highway to the Pacific: 1838–1846*. New York: Columbia University Press.

Belloc, Hilaire. 1924. *The Road*. London: T. Fisher Unwin.

———. 1926. *The Highway and Its Vehicles*. London: The Studio.

Benton, Thomas Hart. 1850. *Highway to the Pacific . . .* Reprint of Senate speech of December 16. Contains an appendix, "North American Road to India," which was not in *Congressional Globe*. In Bancroft Library.

———. 1883. *Thirty Years View, or A History of the Working of the American Government for Thirty Years, from 1820 to 1850*. 2 vols. New York: Appleton.

Bidwell, John. 1890. "First Emigrant Train to California." *Century Magazine* (November).

————. 1964. *A Journey to California, 1841. The First Emigrant Party to California by Wagon Train, the Journal of John Bidwell*. Introduction by Francis P. Farquhar. Berkeley: Friends of the Bancroft Library.

Bigler, Henry W. n.d. *Memoirs and Journals*. Photocopy of typescript made in 1937 by Utah Historical Records Society, in Bancroft Library.

Bigler, John (Governor of California). 1855. Message to California Senate and Assembly, January 5. California Assembly *Journal,* 6th sess.

Blackstone, D. L. 1988. *Traveler's Guide to the Geology of Wyoming*. Bulletin 67. Laramie: Geological Survey of Wyoming.

Blow, Ben. 1920. *California Highways: A Descriptive Record of Road Development by the State and by Such Counties as Have Paved Highways*. San Francisco: H. S. Crocker.

Book Club of California. 1979. *Mountain Passes and Trails of California*. San Francisco: Book Club of California.

Bowles, Samuel. [1869] 1990. *Our New West: Records of Travel Between the Mississippi River and the Pacific Ocean*. Hartford: Hartford Pub. Co. Reprint Bowie, Md.: Heritage Books.

Branch, E. Douglas. 1929. "Frederick West Lander, Road-Builder." *Mississippi Valley Historical Review* 16(2): 172–87.

Brewer, William Henry. 1930. *Up and Down California in 1860–1864: The Journal of William H. Brewer*. New Haven: Yale University Press.

Brewster, John A. 1857. *Annual Report of the Surveyor-General*. In Appendix to Senate (also Assembly) *Journals,* 8th sess.

Brown, Aaron. 1858. *Report of the Postmaster General*. Senate Executive Documents, 35th Cong., 1st sess. U.S. Serials Set vol. 921.

Browne, J. Ross. 1959. *A Peep at Washoe* and *Washoe Revisited*. Balboa Island, Calif.: Paisano Press.

Bruff, J. Goldsborough. 1944. *Gold Rush: The Journals, Drawings, and Other Papers of J. Goldsborough Bruff*. Edited by Georgia Willis Read and Ruth Gaines. New York: Columbia University Press.

Bryant, Edwin. [1848] 1985. *What I Saw in California*. Facsimile reprint. Lincoln: Bison Books, University of Nebraska Press.

California Legislature. 1855. *The Statues of California Passed at the 6th Session of the Legislature*. Sacramento.

California Supreme Court. 1858. *Report of Cases Argued and Determined in the Supreme Court of the State of California in the Year 1856*. Sacramento.

Carson, Kit. 1935. *Autobiography*. Edited by Milo Milton Quaife. Chicago: Lakeside Press.

Caruthers, J. Wade. 1973. *American Pacific Ocean Trade: Its Impact on Foreign Policy and Continental Expansion, 1784–1860*. New York: Exposition Press.

Chapman, Arthur. 1932. *The Pony Express: The Record of a Romantic Adventure in Business*. G. P. Putnam's Sons.

Chiles, Joseph B. 1970. *A Visit to California in 1841, as recorded for Hubert Howe Bancroft in an interview with Joseph B. Chiles*. Berkeley: Friends of the Bancroft Library.

Chorpenning, George. 1889. *Statement and Appendix of the Claim of George Chorpenning against the United States*. In Bancroft Library.

Clark, John Hawkins. 1852. *Daily Journal of John Hawkins Clark During an Expedition from Cincinnati, O. to Sacramento, Cal. in 1852 Together with Recollections of the Route from Saint Joe to the Humboldt River and Reminiscences of Life in California 1852–1857*. Original and typescript in Bancroft Library.

Cleland, Robert Glass. 1914. "Asiatic Trade and American Occupation of the Pacific Coast." *Annual Report,* American History Association, vol. 1.

Cline, Gloria Griffen. 1963. *Exploring the Great Basin*. Norman: University of Oklahoma Press.

Clyman, James. 1960. *James Clyman, Frontiersman: The Adventures of a Trapper and Covered-Wagon Emigrant as Told in His Own Reminiscences and Diaries*. Edited by Charles L. Camp. Portland, Oreg.: Champoeg Press.

Conkling, Roscoe P., and Margaret G. Conkling. 1947. *The Butterfield Overland Mail, 1857–1869, Its Organization and Operation over the Southern Route to 1861; Subsequently over the Central Route to 1866; and under Wells, Fargo and Company in 1869*. Glendale: Arthur H. Clark.

Covington, William M., et al., Sierra Chapter, Sons of Utah Pioneers. 1974. *Mormon-Emigrant Trail: A Brief History of Its Origin and Development*. Placerville: El Dorado County Museum.

Creed, J. H. 1950. "Access to Alpine." *California Highways and Public Works* 29: 11–12.

Curran, Harold. 1982. *Fearful Crossing: The Central Overland Trail through Nevada*. Las Vegas: University of Nevada Press.

Dale, Harrison Clifford. 1941. *The Ashley-Smith Explorations and the Discovery of a Central Route to the Pacific, 1822–29*. Glendale: Arthur H. Clark.

Davis, James T. [1961] 1974. *Trade Routes and Economic Exchange Among the Indians of California*. Ramona, Calif.: Ballena Press. Reprint. University of California Archaeological Survey Report no. 54.

Davis, Jefferson. 1853. *Report of the Secretary of War*. Senate Executive Document #1, 33d Cong., 1st sess., U.S. Serials Set vol. 691.

Day, Sherman. Various years. Letters to and from his father, Jeremiah Day. In Bancroft Library.

———. 1854. Manuscript diary for 1854, plus various letters. In Palmer-Day-Stringham-Bacon family papers, Bancroft Library.

———. 1855. *Report of the Committee on Internal Improvement with Reference to a Road Across the Sierra Nevada, submitted April 10, 1855*. Document 22, Appendix to California Senate *Journal,* 6th session. Sacramento.

———. 1856. *Report on the Immigrant Wagon Road Explorations*. In Seneca Hunt Marlette, *Annual Report of the Surveyor-General of the State of California*. Appendix to Senate *Journal,* 7th sess, doc. 5.

Dellenbaugh, Frederick S. 1914. *Frémont and '49: The Story of a Remarkable Career and Its Relation to the Exploration and Development of Our Western Territory, Especially of California*. New York: G. P. Putnam's Sons.

Denevan, William M. 1992. "The Pristine Myth: The Landscape of the Americas in 1492." *Annals of the Association of American Geographers* 82(3): 369–85.

De Quille, Dan. [1886] 1954. *Snow-Shoe Thompson.* Reprinted from *Overland Monthly,* October 1886. In Bancroft Library.

DeVoto, Bernard. 1943. *The Year of Decision, 1846.* Boston: Little, Brown.

————. 1944. "Geopolitics with the Dew on It." *Harper's Magazine,* March 1944, 313–23.

Dornin, May. 1922. "Emigrant Trails into California." M.A. thesis, University of California, Berkeley. In Bancroft Library.

Durrell, Cordell. 1987. *Geologic History of the Feather River Country, California.* Berkeley: University of California Press.

Eaton, Herbert. 1974. *The Overland Trail to California in 1852.* New York: G. P. Putnam's Sons.

Eddy, William M. 1853. *Annual Report of Surveyor-General of the State of California.* Appendix to Senate *Journal,* 4th sess.

Ellison, Joseph. 1927. *California and the Nation, 1850–1869: A Study of the Relations of a Frontier Community with the Federal Government.* Berkeley: University of California Press.

Farquhar, Francis P. 1930. "Frémont in the Sierra Nevada." *Sierra Club Bulletin* 15(N): 74–95.

————. 1943. "Jedediah Smith and the First Crossing of the Sierra Nevada." *Sierra Club Bulletin* 28(3): 36–53.

————. 1965. *History of the Sierra Nevada.* Berkeley: University of California Press.

Fletcher, F. N. 1924. "Eastbound Route of Jedediah S. Smith, 1827." *Quarterly of the California Historical Society* 2(4): 344–49.

Fletcher, Thomas C. 1987. *Paiute, Prospector, Pioneer: The Bodie–Mono Lake Area in the Nineteenth Century.* Lee Vining, Calif.: Artemisia Press.

Frederick, J. V. 1940. *Ben Holladay the Stagecoach King: A Chapter in the Development of Transcontinental Transport.* Glendale: A. H. Clark.

Frémont, John C. [1845] 1988. *Report of the Exploring Expedition to the Rocky Mountains in the Year 1842, and to Oregon and North California in the Years 1843–'44.* Reprint Washington, D.C.: Smithsonian Institution.

————. 1887. *Memoirs . . . including in the Narrative Five Journeys of Western Exploration, during the Years 1842, 1843–4, 1845–6–7, 1848–9, 1853–4.* Chicago: Belford, Clarke.

Geiger, Vincent. 1945. *Trail to California: The Overland Journal of Vincent Geiger and Wakeman Bryarly.* New Haven: Yale University Press.

George, Henry. 1868. "What the Railroad Will Bring Us." *Overland Monthly* 1 (4) (October): 297–306.

Gianella, Vincent P. 1959. "Where Frémont Crossed the Sierra Nevada in 1844." *Sierra Club Bulletin* 44(7): 54–63.

Giffen, Helen S. 1969. *Trail-Blazing Pioneer—Colonel Joseph Ballinger Chiles.* San Francisco: J. Howell.

Gilbert, Bil. 1983. *Westering Man: The Life of Joseph Walker.* New York: Atheneum.

Goddard, George H. 1855. Letter to Seneca Hunt Marlette from San Francisco, November 22, 1854. In Seneca Hunt Marlette, *Annual Report to the*

Surveyor-General of the State of California. Appendix to Senate *Journal,* 6th sess., doc. 5.

———. 1856. *Report of a Survey of a Portion of the Eastern Boundary of California and of a Reconnaissance of the Old Carson and Johnson Immigrant Roads Over the Sierra Nevada.* In Seneca Hunt Marlette, *Annual Report of the Surveyor-General of the State of California.* Appendix to Senate *Journal,* 7th sess., doc. 5.

Goetzmann, William H. 1986. *New Lands, New Men: America and the Second Great Age of Discovery.* New York: Viking.

———. 1991. *Army Exploration in the American West, 1803–1863.* Austin: Texas State Historical Society.

Graebner, Norman A. 1983. *Empire on the Pacific: A Study in American Continental Expansion.* Santa Barbara: ABC-Clio.

Graupner, A. E. 1906. "Storied Turnpike from Placerville to Tallac." *Sunset* 35: 668–74.

Graydon, Charles K. 1986. *Trail of the First Wagons Over the Sierra Nevada.* St. Louis: Patrice Press.

Gregory, J. W. 1932. *The Story of the Road: From the Beginning down to* A.D. *1931.* New York: Macmillan.

Gudde, Erwin G. 1962. *Bigler's Chronicle of the West: The Conquest of California, Discovery of Gold, and Mormon Settlement as Reflected in Henry William Bigler's Diaries.* Berkeley: University of California Press.

———. 1969. *California Place Names: The Origin and Etymology of Current Geographical Names.* Berkeley: University of California Press.

Hafen, LeRoy R. 1926. *The Overland Mail, 1849–1869: Promoter of Settlement, Precursor of Railroads.* Glendale: Arthur H. Clark.

Hart, George. 1987. *A Companion to California.* Berkeley: University of California Press.

Heap, Gwin Harris. 1957. *Central Route to the Pacific, with related material on railroad explorations and Indian affairs by Edwin F. Beale, Thomas H. Benton, Kit Carson, and Col. E. A. Hitchcock, and in other documents, 1853–54.* Edited by LeRoy Hafen and Ann W. Hafen. Glendale: Arthur H. Clark.

Hill, Mary. 1975. *Geology of the Sierra Nevada.* Vol. 37 of California Natural History Guides. Berkeley: University of California Press.

Hine, Robert V. 1962. *Edward Kern and American Expansion.* New Haven: Yale University Press.

Hittell, Theodore H. 1897. *History of California.* 4 vols. San Francisco: N. J. Stone.

Hopkins, Sarah Winnemucca. [1883] 1969. *Life Among the Piutes: Their Wrongs and Claims.* Edited by Mrs. Horace Mann. Bishop, Calif.: Chalfant Press.

Hopper, Charles. 1981. *Charles Hopper and the Pilgrims of the Pacific: A 1841 California Pioneer, His Narrative and Other Documents.* Edited by Franklin Beard. La Grange, Calif.: Southern Mines Press.

Hulbert, Archer B. 1921. *The Paths of Inland Commerce: A Chronicle of Trail, Road and Waterway.* New Haven: Yale University Press.

Hunt, Thomas H. 1974. *Ghost Trails to California: A Pictorial Journey from the Rockies to the Gold Country.* Palo Alto: American West.

Irving, Washington. 1961. *The Adventures of Captain Bonneville, U.S.A., in the Rocky Mountains and the Far West, Digested from His Journal by Washington Irving.* Edited by Edgeley W. Todd. Norman: University of Oklahoma Press.

Jackson, W. Turrentine. 1952. *Wagon Roads West: A Study of Federal Road Surveys and Construction in the Trans-Mississippi West.* Berkeley: University of California Press.

———. 1966. "A New Look at Wells Fargo, Stagecoaches and the Pony Express." *California Historical Society Quarterly* 45(4): 291–324.

———. 1967. *Historical Survey of the Stampede Reservoir Area in the Little Truckee River Drainage District.* Typed report for Historical Section of National Park Service, San Francisco, F 593 J3 Bancroft. Later published in four parts by the *Journal of the Sierra County Historical Society,* 3–4, 1971–72.

———. 1970. "Wells Fargo Staging over the Sierra." *California Historical Society Quarterly* 49(2): 99–134.

Jones, Helen Hinckley. 1969. *Rails from the West: A Biography of Theodore Dehone Judah.* San Marino: Golden West Books.

Judah, Theodore D. 1854. *Report of the Chief Engineer on the Preliminary Surveys, and Future Business of the Sacramento Valley Railroad.* Sacramento: Democratic State Journal Press.

———. 1856. *Report of the Chief Engineer upon the Preliminary Survey, Revenue and Cost of Construction, of the San Francisco and Sacramento Railroad.* San Fancisco: Whitten, Towne.

———. 1857. *Practical Plan for Building the Pacific Railroad.* Washington, D.C.: Henry Polkinghorn, Printer.

———. 1862a. *Report of the Chief Engineer on the Preliminary Survey, Cost of Construction, and Estimated Revenue of the Central Pacific Railroad of California, Across the Sierra Nevada Mountains from Sacramento to the Eastern Boundary of California.* October 22. Sacramento: H. S. Crocker. Bound in *Pamphlets on California's Railroads,* Bancroft Library.

———. 1862b. *Report of the Chief Engineer of the Central Pacific Railroad Company of California on his Operations in the Atlantic States.* Sacramento: H. S. Crocker. Bound in *Pamphlets on California's Railroads,* Bancroft Library.

———. 1863. *Report of the Chief Engineer upon Recent Surveys, Progress of Construction, and an Approximate Estimate of Cost of the First Division of Fifty Miles of the Central Pacific Railroad of Cal.* July 1. Sacramento: James Anthony.

Kelly, Charles, and Dale Morgan. 1965. Rev. ed. *Old Greenwood, the Story of Caleb Greenwood: Trapper, Pathfinder and Early Pioneer.* Georgetown, Calif.: Talisman Press.

Kemble, John Haskell. 1943. *The Panama Route, 1848–1869.* Berkeley: University of California Press.

Kirk, John. 1858–59. *Survey Report from Honey Lake East.* House Exec. Doc. 108, 35th Cong., 2d sess., pp. 36–45.

Kyle, Douglas. 1990. *Historic Spots in California*. Stanford: Stanford University Press.

Lass, William E. 1972. *From the Missouri to the Great Salt Lake, an Account of Overland Freighting*. Lincoln: Nebraska State Historical Society.

Lekisch, Barbara. 1988. *Tahoe Place Names: The Origin and History of Names in the Lake Tahoe Basin*. Lafayette, Calif.: Great West Books.

Leonard, Zenas. [1839] 1959. *Adventures of Zenas Leonard, Fur Trader*. Edited by John C. Ewers. Norman: University of Oklahoma Press.

Lienhard, Heinrich. 1961. *From St. Louis to Sutter's Fort, 1846*. Translated and edited by Erwin G. Gudde and Elisabeth K. Gudde. Norman: University of Oklahoma Press.

Lillard, Richard G. 1966. *Eden in Jeopardy: Man's Prodigal Meddling with His Environment: The Southern California Experience*. New York: Knopf.

Loomis, Nelson H. 1938. *Asa Whitney: Father of Pacific Railroads*. Proceedings of Mississippi Valley Historical Association 6.

Loomis, Noel M. 1968. *Wells Fargo*. New York: Clarkson N. Potter.

McAfee, Ward. 1973. *California's Railroad Era, 1850–1911*. San Marino: Golden West Books.

McIntosh, Clarence F. 1962. "The Chico and Red Bluff Route: Stage Lines from Southern Idaho to the Sacramento Valley 1865–1867." *Idaho Yesterday* 6(3).

Majors, Alexander. [1893] 1989. *Seventy Years of the Frontier, Alexander Majors' Memoirs of a Lifetime on the Border*. Chicago: Rand McNally. Reprint Lincoln: University of Nebraska Press.

Marlette, Seneca Hunt. 1855. *Annual Report of Surveyor-General of the State of California*. Appendix to Senate *Journal*, 6th sess., 1855, doc. 5.

———. 1856. *Annual Report of the Surveyor-General of the State of California*. Appendix to Senate *Journal*, 7th sess., doc. 5. Appendix to Assembly *Journal* has identical text.

Maule, William M. 1938. *A Contribution to the Geographic and Economic History of the Carson, Walker and Mono Basins in Nevada and California*. Prepared for California Region, U.S. Forest Service. In Bancroft Library.

May, Richard M. [1848] 1991. *A Sketch of a Migrating Family to California in 1848*. Fairfield, Wash.: Ye Galleon Press.

Miller, David H. 1955. *Snow Cover and Climate in the Sierra Nevada, California*. Berkeley: University of California Publications in Geography, no. 11.

Mitchell, Stewart. 1950. "Crossing the Sierra." *California Highways and Public Works* 29(9): 49–68.

———. 1955. "A Forgotten Exploration: In Search of a Route across the Sierra Nevada for the Pacific Railroad." *California Historical Society Quarterly* 34(3): 209–28.

Montague, Samuel S. 1864. *Report of the Chief Engineer upon Recent Surveys, Progress of Construction, and an Approximate Estimate of Receipts of the Central Pacific Railroad of California*. October 8. In *Pamphlets on California's Railroads*, Bancroft Library.

———. 1865. *Report of the President and Chief Engineer. . . .* December. In *Pamphlets on California's Railroads*. Bancroft Library.

Moore, Augustus. 1878. *Pioneer Experiences*. Handwritten in hardbound note-book. In Bancroft Library.

Morgan, Dale L. [1943] 1985. *The Humboldt: Highroad of the West*. Lincoln: University of Nebraska Press.

———. 1953. *Jedediah Smith and the Opening of the West*. Indianapolis: Bobbs-Merrill.

Morgan, Dale, ed. 1963. *Overland in 1846: Diaries and Letters of the California-Oregon Trail*. Georgetown, Calif.: Talisman Press.

Nettels, Curtis. 1924. "The Overland Mail Issue during the Fifties." *Missouri Historical Review* 18(4): 521–34.

Nevada Emigrant Trail Marking Committee (of Nevada Historical Society). 1975. *The Overland Emigrant Trail to California: A Guide to Trail Markers Placed in Western Nevada and the Sierra Nevada Mountains in California*. Reno: The Committee.

Nevin, David. 1974. *The Expressmen*. New York: Time-Life Books.

Ormsby, Waterman L. 1942. *The Butterfield Overland Mail*. San Marino: Huntington Library.

Peabody, George W. 1988. *Historical Perspective Supplement for the Pleasant Valley, Oak Hill, Sly Park Area Plan and Environmental Impact Report*. Placerville: El Dorado County Community Development Department, Parks and Recreation Commission.

———. 1989. *How About That! An Anthology of Historical Stories About Pleasant Valley, Oak Hill, Newtown, and Sly Park*. Placerville: El Dorado County Historical Museum.

Perkins, J. R. 1929. *Trails, Rails, and War: The Life of General G. M. Dodge*. Indianapolis: Bobbs-Merrill.

Porter, Kirk H., and Douglas Bruce Johnson. 1972. *National Party Platforms, 1840–1968*. Urbana: University of Illinois Press.

Preuss, Charles. 1958. *Exploring with Fremont: The Private Diaries of Charles Preuss, Cartographer for John Charles Frémont on his First, Second, and Fourth Expeditions to the Far West*. Translated and edited by Erwin G. Gudde and Elisabeth K. Gudde. Norman: University of Oklahoma Press.

Pritchard, James A. [1849] 1959. *The Overland Diary of James A. Pritchard from Kentucky to California in 1849*. Edited by Dale L. Morgan. Denver: Old West.

Reading, Pierson Barton. 1930. "Journal." *Quarterly of the Society of California Pioneers* 7: 148–98.

Richardson, James D. 1900. *A Compilation of the Messages and Papers of the Presidents 1789–1987*. 10 vols. Washington, D.C.: Government Printing Office.

Ricketts, Norma B. 1982. *Mormons and the Discovery of Gold*. Placerville, Calif.: Pioneer Press.

Rock, Francis J. 1929. *J. Ross Browne, a Biography*. Washington, D.C.: Catholic University of America Press.

Root, Frank A., and William E. Connelly. [1901] 1971. *The Overland Stage to California: Personal Reminiscences and Authentic History of the Great Overland Stage Line and Pony Express from the Missouri River to the Pacific Ocean*. Glorieta, New Mex.: Rio Grande Press.

Royce, Sarah. 1932. *A Frontier Lady: Recollections of the Gold Rush and Early California*. Edited by Ralph Henry Gabriel. New Haven: Yale University Press.

Russel, Robert Royal. 1948. *Improvement of Communication with the Pacific Coast as an Issue in American Politics, 1783–1864*. Cedar Rapids, Iowa: Torch Press.

Ryan, John P. 1953. "Some Notes on Early Day Travel over the Sonora Trail." Manuscript. In Bancroft Library.

Schallenberger, Moses. 1953. *The Opening of the California Trail; the Story of the Stevens Party from the Reminiscences of Moses Schallenberger as Set Down for H. H. Bancroft About 1885, Edited and Expanded by Horace S. Foote in 1888, and Now Edited with Introduction, Notes, Maps, and Illustration by George R. Stewart*. Berkeley: University of Cali-fornia Press.

Schmidt, Earl F., ed. 1982. *Trail Guide for the Henness-Zumwalt Pass, T.R.A.S.H. Trek VIII, 1982, Celebrating the 50th Anniversary of E Clampus Vitus Redevivus*. California: T.R.A.S.H.

Semple, Sen. James. 1846. Chairman of the Committee on Post Offices and Post Roads. Report of April 20, 1846. 29th Cong., 1st sess., Senate doc. 306.

Settle, Raymond W., and Mary Lund Settle. 1949. *Empire on Wheels*. Stanford: Stanford University Press.

———. 1955. *Saddles and Spurs: Saga of the Pony Express*. Harrisburg, Penn.: Stackpole.

Shumate, Albert. 1969. *The Life of George Henry Goddard, Artist, Architect, Surveyor, and Map Maker*. Berkeley: Friends of the Bancroft Library.

———. 1986. *The Notorious I. C. Woods of the Adams Express*. Glendale: Arthur H. Clark.

Simpson, Capt. J. H. [1876] 1983. *Report of Explorations Across the Great Basin of the Territory of Utah for a Direct Wagon-Route from Camp Floyd to Genoa, in Carson Valley, in 1859*. Washington, D.C.: GPO. Reprint Reno: University of Nevada Press.

Sioli, Paolo. 1883. *Historical Souvenir of El Dorado County, California, with Illustrations and Biographical Sketches of Its Prominent Men and Pioneers*. Oakland: Paolo Sioli.

Smith, Alson J. 1965. *Men Against the Mountains: Jedediah Smith and the South West Expedition of 1826–1829*. New York: John Day.

Smith, Azariah. 1990. *The Gold Discovery Journal of Azariah Smith*. Edited by David L. Bigler. Salt Lake City: University of Utah Press.

Smith, Murphy D. 1980. *Sherman Day: Artist, Forty-Niner, Engineer*. Wilmington, Del.: Michael Glazier.

Stewart, George R. 1953. *The Opening of the California Trail: The Story of the Stevens Party from the Reminiscences of Moses Schallenberger*. Berkeley: University of California Press.

———. 1962. *The California Trail, an Epic with Many Heroes*. New York: McGraw-Hill.

Thompson, Margaret Alice. 1931. "Overland Travel and the Central Sierra Nevada 1827–1849." M.A. thesis, University of California, Berkeley. In Bancroft Library.

Thompson, Robert Luther. 1947. *Wiring a Continent: The History of the Telegraphic Industry in the United States 1832–1866*. Princeton: Princeton University Press.

Tyler, William. [1881] 1969. *A Concise History of the Mormon Battalion in the Mexican War*. Glorieta, New Mex.: Rio Grande Press.

United States. House of Representatives. 1855. *Reports of Explorations and Surveys to Ascertain the Most Practicable and Economical Route for a Railroad from the Mississippi River to the Pacific Ocean*. Washington, D.C.: A. O. P. Icholson, Printer.

Unruh, John D. 1979. *The Plains Across: The Overland Emigrants and the Trans-Mississippi West, 1840–1860*. Urbana: University of Illinois Press.

Vance, James E., Jr. 1961. "The Oregon Trail and Union Pacific Railroad: A Contrast in Purpose." *AAG Annals* 51 (4): 357–79.

Verdenal, John M. 1852. "Journal Across the Plains, 1852." Typescript. In Bancroft Library.

Vernon, Mildred Haven. 1923. "The Daily Overland Mail to the Pacific, 1861–1869." M.A. thesis, University of California, Berkeley. In Bancroft Library.

Wadsworth, W. 1858. *The National Wagon Road Guide*. San Francisco: Whitton, Towne.

Watson, Jeanne H. 1986. "The Carson Emigrant Road." *Overland Journal* (Quarterly Journal of the Oregon California Trails Association) (Summer 1986): 4–12.

———, ed. 1988. *To the Land of Gold and Wickedness: The 1848–1959 Diary of Lorena L. Hays*. St. Louis: Patrice Press.

Wheat, Carl I. 1925. "A Sketch of the Life of Theodore D. Judah." *California Historical Society Quarterly* 4(3): 219–72.

———. 1949. *Books of the California Gold Rush*. San Francisco: Colt Press.

White, Chester Lee. 1928. "Surmounting the Sierras: The Campaign for a Wagon Road." *California Historical Society Quarterly* 7(1): 3–19.

Whitney, Asa. 1849. *A Project for a Railroad to the Pacific*. New York: George F. Wood.

Williams, John Hoyt. 1988. *A Great and Shining Road: The Epic Story of the Transcontinental Railroad*. New York: Times Books.

Williamson, Robert Stockton. 1854. *Report of a Reconnaissance and Survey in California in Connexion with Explorations for a Practicable Railway Route from the Mississippi River to the Pacific Ocean in 1853*. Washington, D.C. Bound in *Pamphlets on California's Railroads*, Bancroft Library.

Wilson, Elinor. 1972. *Jim Beckwourth: Black Mountain Man and War Chief of the Crows*. Norman: University of Oklahoma Press.

Wilson, Neill C. 1936. *Treasure Express: Epic Days of the Wells Fargo*. New York: Macmillan.

Wiltsee, Ernest A. 1931. *The Pioneer Miner and the Pack Mule Express*. San Francisco: California Historical Society.

Winter, William H., and Overton Johnson. [1846] 1932. *Route Across the Rocky Mountains*. Princeton: Princeton University Press.

Winther, Oscar O. 1936. *Express and Stagecoach Days in California.* Stanford: Stanford University Press.

———. [1945] 1968. *Via Western Express & Stagecoach: California's Transportation Links with the Nation 1848–1869.* Lincoln: University of Nebraska Press.

———. 1964. *The Transportation Frontier, Trans-Mississippi West.* Albuquerque: University of New Mexico Press.

Wood, R. Coke. 1968. *Big Tree-Carson Valley Turnpike, Ebbetts Pass and Highway Four.* Murphys, Calif.: Old Timers Museum.

Wozencraft, Oliver M. 1856. *Address Delivered before the Mechanics' Institute on the Subject of the Atlantic and Pacific Rail-road, and the Policy of Our Government in Reference to Internal Improvements.* San Francisco: Agnew and Deffebach.

INDEX

Abbot, Henry L., 113
An Act to Construct a Wagon Road from the Sacramento Valley to the Eastern Boundary of the State, 83–84
An Act to Construct a Wagon Road over the Sierra Nevada Mountains. See State road bill
An Act to Provide for the Survey and Construction of a Wagon Road from the Sacramento Valley to the Eastern Boundary of the State, 81
Adams, Alvin, 60
Adams & Company, 60–62, 126
Amador and Nevada Wagon Road, 53, 178
Amador County, 142
American Express, 61, 126
American River: South Fork of, fig. 2, 32, 63, 86, 90, 145, 151
Apaches, 26
Applegate, Jesse, 72
Applegate Trail, 72
Army transport services, 129–30
Ashley, William, 15
Aspinwall, William, 57
Atlantic & Pacific Company: Ebbetts survey for, 67–69, 185n26
Aurora, 177

Baker, E. D., 77
Baltimore & Ohio railroad, 166
Bancroft, Hubert Howe, 25, 158
Bartleson, John, 180n2

Bartlett, Washington, 77
Bartlette, John R., 126
Bayard, William, 115–16
Bear River, 37–38
Beaver trapping. *See* Trapping business
Beckwith, E. G., 111–12, 121, 164
Beckwith, Jennings, 70
Beckwourth, James, 70–71, 178
Beckwourth Pass: Carson route *vs.*, 52; to Quincy, 70–71, 185n35; as railroad gateway, 71, 174, 178–79; as stage-coach route, 82, 126, 146
Bee, Frederick A., 151
Belden, Josiah, 25
Bell, John, 107, 109–10
Bell, Samuel, 86
Benton, Thomas Hart, 67, 77; on Buenaventura River, 31; Pacific railroad bill of, 101, 102–3; preferred railroad route of, 29, 32–33, 104, 111
Bidwell, John, 23, 24, 162
Bidwell party: abandoned wagon trains of, 1, 24–25; John Bartleson of, 180n2; and Chiles party's route, 26, 27; geographic misconceptions of, 23–24
Big Bend: Stevens party at, 36, 37
Bigler, Henry William, 41, 43–44, 45, 72, 182n9
Bigler, John, 80–81, 85, 86, 91, 101
Big Trees route, 67, 89; after 1859, 176–77; Sherman Day's bill on, 97; Mokelumne Hill Convention on,

Compositor: BookMasters, Inc.
Cartographer: Lisa Hamilton
Text: 10/13 Sabon
Display: Stymie and Copperplate
Printer and Binder: Malloy Lithographing, Inc.